GOD
IN CHRISTIAN EXPERIENCE

GOD
IN CHRISTIAN
EXPERIENCE

BY

W. R. MATTHEWS

M.A., D.D.

CHAPLAIN TO H.M. KING GEORGE V.;
DEAN OF KING'S COLLEGE, LONDON

HARPER & BROTHERS PUBLISHERS
NEW YORK AND LONDON

Printed in Great Britain at
The Mayflower Press, Plymouth. William Brendon & Son, Ltd.

TO
MY WIFE

GENERAL INTRODUCTION

THE Editors of this series are convinced that the Christian Church as a whole is confronted with a great though largely silent crisis, and also with an unparalleled opportunity. They have a common mind concerning the way in which this crisis and opportunity should be met. The time has gone by when "apologetics" could be of any great value. Something more is needed than a defence of propositions already accepted on authority, for the present spiritual crisis is essentially a questioning of authority if not a revolt against it. It may be predicted that the number of people who are content simply to rest their religion on the authority of the Bible or the Church is steadily diminishing, and with the growing effectiveness of popular education will continue to diminish. We shall not therefore meet the need, if we have rightly diagnosed it, by dissertations, however learned, on the interpretation of the Bible or the history of Christian doctrine. Nothing less is required than a candid, courageous and well-informed effort to think out anew, in the light of modern knowledge, the foundation affirmations of our common Christianity. This is the aim of every writer in this series.

A further agreement is, we hope, characteristic of the books which will be published in the series. The authors have a common mind not only with regard to the problem but also with regard to the starting-point of reconstruction. They desire to lay stress upon the value and validity of religious experience and to develop their theology on the basis of the religious consciousness. In so doing they claim to be in harmony with modern thought. The massive achievements of the nineteenth and twentieth centuries have been built up on the method of observation and experiment, on experience, not on abstract *a priori* reasoning. Our contention is that the moral and spiritual experience of mankind has the right to be considered, and demands to be understood.

Many distinguished thinkers might be quoted in support of the assertion that philosophers are now prepared in a greater measure than formerly to consider religious experience as among the most significant of their data. One of the greatest has said, " There is nothing more real than what comes in religion. To compare facts such as these with what is given to us in outward existence would be to trifle with the subject. The man who demands a reality more solid than that of the religious consciousness, seeks he does not know what." [1] Nor does this estimate of religious experience come only from idealist thinkers. A philosopher who writes from the standpoint of mathematics and natural science has expressed the same thought in even more forcible language. " The fact of religious vision, and its history of persistent expansion, is our one ground for optimism. Apart from it, human life is a flash of occasional enjoyments lighting up a

[1] F. H. Bradley, *Appearance and Reality*, p. 449.

mass of pain and misery, a bagatelle of transient experience." [1]

The conviction that religious experience is to be taken as the starting-point of theological reconstruction does not, of course, imply that we are absolved from the labour of thought. On the contrary, it should serve as the stimulus to thought. No experience can be taken at its face value ; it must be criticised and interpreted. Just as natural science could not exist without experience and the thought concerning experience, so theology cannot exist without the religious consciousness and reflection upon it. Nor do we mean by " experience " anything less than the whole experience of the human race, so far as it has shared in the Christian consciousness. As Mazzini finely said, "Tradition and conscience are the two wings given to the human soul to reach the truth."

It has been the aim of the writers and the Editors of the series to produce studies of the main aspects of Christianity which will be intelligible and interesting to the general reader and at the same time may be worthy of the attention of the specialist. After all, in religion we are dealing with a subject-matter which is open to all and the plan of the works does not require that they shall delve very deeply into questions of minute scholarship. We have had the ambition to produce volumes which might find a useful place on the shelves of the clergyman and minister, and no less on those of the intelligent layman. Perhaps we may have done something to bridge the gulf which too often separates the pulpit from the pew.

[1] A. N. Whitehead, *Science and the Modern World*, p. 275.

Naturally, the plan of our series has led us to give the utmost freedom to the authors of the books to work out their own lines of thought, and our part has been strictly confined to the invitation to contribute, and to suggestions concerning the mode of presentation. We hope that the series will contribute something useful to the great debate on religion which is proceeding in secret in the mind of our age, and we humbly pray that their endeavours and ours may be blessed by the Spirit of Truth for the building up of Christ's Universal Church.

PREFACE

THE subject of these chapters is not only of perennial interest but of great immediate importance. To a discerning eye it must be clear that the main question which is being decided in the world to-day is whether or not the majority of men shall continue to believe in God. The debate has invaded world-politics through the dogmatic atheism of the Bolsheviks, who appear to persecute impartially all Theists. I have tried to write always with the thought of the intellectual and spiritual crisis of the present generation before my mind.

This book, however, is neither a work of apologetics nor a treatise on dogmatic theology, though it has obvious relations with both these branches of study. It is an attempt to state the essential elements in the Christian experience of God, and to formulate a view of the divine Nature, and the relation of God with the world, which may be acceptable to the reason of modern men. Of course such an attempt can never be wholly successful, and it is a part of the thesis which I maintain that the Object of our religious apprehension must be beyond our full comprehension. I have avoided the suggestion, I hope, that I claim to present a complete and logical account of the God whom Christians worship. The reader will misunderstand my purpose if he supposes that there are no problems to which I have not an answer, or that I imagine we can eliminate all mystery from our most adequate thoughts of God.

I believe that this book is a statement and a defence of the Catholic faith about God ; but I must admit that it is, in some respects, a departure from what has come to be described as Catholic theology. In my opinion, it is a misfortune that many writers who have no need to defer to the authority of Rome seem to take for granted that the Catholic faith has some necessary connexion with the Scholastic theology. To have insisted on that alleged necessary connexion is one of the injuries which Papalism has done to Christendom.

Several important works have appeared since this book was, in the main, finished. I specially regret that I have been able to make no use of Dr. A. N. Whitehead's *Process and Reality*, and less use than I should have wished of Dr. Tennant's *Philosophical Theology*. The references in the text do not show the full debt which I owe to other writers. I am conscious that the works of Dr. Inge, Dr. Gore, Dr. A. Caldecott, Professor C. C. J. Webb, Professor A. E. Taylor, and the late Dr. Rashdall have influenced my thought to a degree which no footnotes could adequately represent.

The first five chapters and parts of some others are based upon lectures which I delivered in Harvard University on the Noble foundation in 1928, but I have greatly expanded the material and, on some points, modified my opinions, so that no part of the book remains precisely as it was in its original form. I regret that the revision has taken so long and sieze this opportunity of thanking the authorities at Harvard for their generosity and patience. But for the stimulus of their invitation the book would not have been produced.

I owe sincere thanks to members of my "seminar" at King's College for constructive criticism. One by whose comments I have often profited, the Rev. G. W. Sibley, M.A., A.K.C., Vicar of Old St. Pancras, has died in the full tide of life, while these pages were passing through the press. I am under especial obligation to my friend and former pupil, Miss M. E. Sandbach Marshall, M.A., B.D., who has read the whole book in MSS. and has helped in many ways to clarify its thought and expression.

W. R. M.

KING'S COLLEGE, LONDON,
July 30, 1930.

CONTENTS

xv

CHAPTER IV

CHAPTER V

CHAPTER XII

GOD

In Christian Thought and Experience

CHAPTER I

MAN'S EXPERIENCE OF GOD

THE older Theology was accustomed to approach the doctrine of God without reference to the religious conceptions of those races which had not the benefit of the Christian revelation or the dimmer illumination of the Hebrew dispensation. If the beliefs and practices of the heathen were dwelt upon at all, they were mentioned as examples of the fallibility of human conjectures upon divine things apart from the assistance of the inspired teaching of the Gospel and as a means of emphasizing the darkness of the religious world outside the radius of the Christian light. This method of classifying religions into the two categories of true and false has, it must be confessed, the weight of authority on its side. Though the Apostles seem to recognize a natural impulse in man to seek after God and indeed declare that the Divine is not without its witness even in the minds of the pagans, it would be difficult to find in their writings any admission that the creeds and rites of the Gentiles have any seeds of truth or virtue in them, or are anything else than the products of the perverted imagination of unregenerate

B   1

humanity. There have been students of the New Testament who have thought that St. Paul was deeply influenced by the mystery cults of the Hellenistic civilization and that his doctrine of the Eucharist, if not the Eucharist itself, should be traced to this source ; but these theories have to meet as the principal objection the fact that St. Paul never betrays even a sympathetic understanding of religion outside the pale of Judaism and Christianity and that his mind is plainly still imbued with the contempt of the Hebrew prophets for the " idols of the heathen ". There is little need to labour the point that the attitude of the early Fathers of the Church was not different. Though in general they did not venture to deny all reality to the objects of pagan worship, they considered them to be evil spirits and the worship in their temples part of the mystery of iniquity by which men were led more deeply into condemnation. Even those Fathers who held a liberal attitude towards the writings of the Philosophers and were prepared to accept Plato as an ally of the Gospel, had little that is good to say of the Greek religion.

This posture of antagonism and this emphatic assertion of the antithesis between the Christian faith in God and all others had no doubt an historical justification. It was a salutary and necessary state of mind for those who were called upon to present a higher conception of God and a purer standard of conduct, and not only so but to resist in themselves the tendencies which would have drawn them back into the modes of religious thought and feeling from which, at their conversion, they had emerged. Nor can we question that a permanent truth is contained in the intransigeance of the primitive Church. Though we may prefer to regard the Christian idea of God as the culmination of all the conceptions which men's minds have entertained and see in all religion the *præparatio evangelica* which earlier generations found only in the Hebrew, we cannot let go the ancient claim that the Christian God is the only true God, the Father of the Lord Jesus Christ the only true object of worship, and that every declension from this thought of the Divine Being is to be resisted and condemned as a falling back into superstition and error.

Modern thought, as we have already hinted, would encourage a different point of view from that which the Church has on the whole adopted. It would seek to place the Christian experience of God and the Christian ideas of God in the context of the general history of religion. One important school of modern Protestant theologians would demur and, though for somewhat different reasons, agree with the exclusiveness of the early Church. The Ritschlians would treat the universal history of religion as strictly irrelevant for Christian theology, and would hold that only in the words and work of the historical Jesus do we find material for a Christian doctrine of God. With the reservation which has been already made, I propose, however, to consider Christianity in relation to the whole development of the religious consciousness. Two reasons seem decisive in favour of this course. First, we are led to adopt this method by a survey of the phenomena themselves. Religion, in spite of its wide diversity of forms, possesses a recognizable character throughout. It appears to constitute one movement of the human spirit, and though it has proved difficult to define, it is not hard to recognize. Indeed, the student of comparative religions is often startled by resemblances between its highest and its lowest forms. Perhaps this self-identity of the religious consciousness all through its history is often obscured because the attention is concentrated chiefly upon the ideas of divinity, upon mythologies and theologies which are multifarious in their diversity, rather than upon the mental attitude of the worshipper. There is an identity in the experience though an unlimited diversity in the concepts and images of religion. One of the chief merits of Professor Heiler's book on Prayer[1] is that he has brought out by means of very numerous examples of the prayer life of the most diverse individuals and races the inherent unity of the religious consciousness.

The second reason for the adoption of the method of placing the Christian consciousness of God within the larger frame of religious history as a whole is concerned with the interests of Christian thought and apologetics. Only so can we hope to arrive at an effective defence of the Christian faith for the modern world. That world is dominated by the notions of evolution and continuity. It is perhaps a defect that the ideas of a sharp break and a fundamental antithesis are not easy for it to apply ; but we must go with the modern mind so far as we may, even though at the end we may discover that there is an element in the Christian view of the world and God which will not fit into a merely evolutionary scheme. It will, at any rate, be well for us to dwell first of all on the common elements and universal motives which run through all religion. If we are persuaded that the religious experience of mankind is not wholly illusion but can be taken as in some sort an experience of reality, and if further we can see reason to believe that it is a progressive experience of Reality, or rather that an upward development can be discerned in it, it may be possible to trace that line of development and to show that it issues in the Christian experience of God and the Christian conception of God.

---

[1] *Das Gebet*, by F. Heiler.

This chapter and the two following may suggest a train of thought leading to that conclusion.

The problem of the " definition " of religion has been a favourite topic of philosophers, and their labours have at least been fruitful in a large crop of formulas, if not perhaps in great illumination. It would be easy to draw up a list of a hundred definitions all different from one another. A review of these essays, which range from the cynical dictum of Salomon Reinach that " religion is a sum of scruples which impede the free use of our faculties " to the evasive phrase of Matthew Arnold about " morality touched with emotion ", discloses that most of them have some purpose in view which is not that of philosophy. They are contrived from the standpoint of psychology or anthropology or " sociology " and for that reason are one-sided and abstract. They do not answer the question which we really have in mind. We wish to know what Aristotle would have called the τέλος or φύσις of religion. We are concerned to know what drives man forward in his quest for God,—or what allures him,—what religion in its essential nature is ; and this inquiry is suggested to us apart from any view which we may have about the truth of any particular religion. Even though with Mr. Bertrand Russell we may be convinced that religion is based upon illusion, yet that illusion is so persistent, so much a permanent characteristic of human culture in all its phases, that we cannot attribute it to the surface of the psyche or to fortuitous circumstances, but must seek for its root in the nature of the human mind itself. Contemporary events reinforce and illustrate this contention. Bolshevik Russia has presented us with an example, the first in history, of a large social group explicitly founded on an anti-religious basis ; not only, however, has that society been unable to eradicate the older religion, but, as Mr. Keynes and other observers have pointed out, it has itself become the organ of a new religion whose bible is *das Kapital* and deity Lenin.

It is generally recognized that one of the most important contributions to the solution of our problem of the nature of the religious consciousness was made by Schleiermacher, who was among the first to concentrate attention on religious experience and to make it the foundation of theology. We will set out from his description of religion in the hope that reflection upon it will lead us deeper into the reality which we have to explore. In his first work, the *Addresses to the Cultured Despisers of Religion*, Schleiermacher defended the view that religion consisted in, or was concerned with, a mental activity more " primordial " than conscious knowing or conscious willing. Religion, he declared, was a kind of " feeling ". At this period of his development he amplified his thesis by saying that it was a " feeling for the infinite ". His later reflection led him to modify this formula and to move away from its implication of Pantheism. In his epoch-making work on the Christian Faith[1] he propounded the thesis that religion is " a feeling of absolute dependence ". His full view of religion is not, however, contained in this famous phrase. He added to it some ideas which profoundly modify his theory. He attempts to show that all self-consciousness is accompanied by God-consciousness and that there is no mind possessed of awareness of itself which does not also possess, in however dim a form, an awareness of God. There are no true atheists. He argues further that the progressive evolution of the God-consciousness is intimately connected with the individual's consciousness of his place both in the order of nature and

[1] *Der christliche Glaube.* Eng. trans. *The Christian Faith.*

in the human race. And finally he holds that the specifically Christian consciousness of God is mediated through the Redeemer and the Church.

This is not the occasion for a detailed exposition or criticism of Schleiermacher's theology. Its chief value, from our point of view, is that it attempts to treat the religious impulse as an inherent and necessary quality of human consciousness which normally develops along with the mind itself, and we may state at once that any view of religion which will do justice to the facts must be in general agreement with him in this matter. There are, however, defects in his conception of religion, three of which are of importance for our present purpose. First, his reaction against the presentation of religion as merely morality or merely dogma led him to lay an exclusive emphasis upon " feeling ". The meaning of this term, however, is ambiguous, and he does not appear to have definitely distinguished between " feeling " in the sense of pleasure and pain, in the sense of emotion, and in the sense of perception. In fact, though Schleiermacher discarded the term " intuition " which he had at first used, his theory is really only intelligible if we take " feeling " to include some kind of perception or awareness. In any case, however, we cannot absolve him altogether from the charge of neglecting the part of reason and conscience in religious development. Closely connected with this defect is the second—that he conceives the religious life too much as passive. The feeling of absolute dependence, taken by itself, seems to rule out the sense of co-operation with God which has been an element in some at least of the most highly evolved religious experience. By passing over this aspect of religion Schleiermacher has unduly simplified the problem and has kept in the background a

paradoxical character of religion which we must not allow
to escape our notice.   In religious experience as a whole
we find a combination of attitudes of mind which, at
least on a superficial view, are contradictory—the attitude
of dependence on the Divine as the source of all power and
good, and the attitude which may almost be described as
" protectiveness ", in which the Divine is thought of as
needing and demanding our help.   Dependence is balanced
by co-operation.

Professor Rudolph Otto may help us to observe the
third defect in Schleiermacher's conception of religion,
for his well-known book, *The Idea of the Holy*, starts
from a point of view which is admittedly akin to that of
the great " romantic " theologian.   He contends that the
root of the religious consciousness is to be found in the
feeling of the " numinous ", a quite distinctive emotion
which appears in its most rudimentary form as a shuddering sense of the uncanny and becomes at the higher
points of religious experience the apprehension of the
transcendently " Other " and mysterious, separated by a
gulf which no reason can bridge from all that is " crea-
turely ".   Though the details of Otto's theory are open
to question and we may entertain doubts even about the
real existence of this special and distinctive " numinous
feeling ", there is an obvious truth in his position.   The
expression " feeling of dependence " does not meet the
need of an adequate definition, for there are feelings
of dependence which have no religious tone.   There is
something in the religious feeling of dependence which
distinguishes it from all other kinds, and that element,
in the more developed religions, is awe and reverence for
That on which we depend.

The foundation of the theories of Schleiermacher and
Otto appears to be sound.   We are concerned with an

experience which begins with the most primitive state of consciousness and does not have to wait for the development of full moral personality and self-conscious reasoning. The first spring of religion is some immediate intuition or "feeling" which lies below our ordinary conscious mental processes. But I would suggest that both these authors have been too eager to delimit religion as a specific form of experience, and have distinguished it too sharply from other activities of spirit. It is significant that neither of them gives us a wholly satisfactory account of how moral values and intellectual judgments come to be so closely associated with a form of the spirit with which, on their hypothesis, they have no necessary connexion.

In truth the "feeling" or intuition which lies at the root of religion is not ultimately different from that which lies at the root of all the higher functions of mind. It is an intuition or perception of continuity, which may become a feeling of dependence. The self realizes itself as being continuous with a reality which is, at the same time, "other" than itself. This apprehension of continuity and "otherness," of course, takes different forms in the more highly developed mind than those which it has in the dim twilight of the beginning of self-consciousness ; but it is present throughout the whole range of mental life as known to us. But there is much more in this than the oft-repeated truth that the "subject-object relation" is fundamental. In the foundation intuition we know something about the "other". The mind in contact with a merely "other" would be helpless and sterile, for it would never be able to issue from its isolated self-hood. This reality then with which we are continuous must be affirmed, and is recognized in the primordial intuition, as being not a mere not-self, but in some sense

akin. If we are in search of a compendious phrase to
denote this "feeling" or intuition we shall scarcely
improve upon one which we owe to the late Professor
Boutroux, "the Beyond which is within"; or perhaps,
if we wish to avoid some possible implications of the
phrase, we might retain our former word and speak of
"the Beyond which is akin".

That this sense of continuity with a Beyond which is
not completely "other" than the human spirit is a
permanent characteristic of religion might be shown by
illustrations from all stages of religious evolution. To
elaborate this at any length would be wearisome. Let
us, then, take religion at its most childlike expression and
at its most mature, and see if in both we shall be able to
hear the same undertone. The animist and polytheist
assuredly find their divinities outside themselves, the
spirits or gods are objects of which practical account has
to be taken ; but nevertheless it is an essential part of
this primitive creed, or rather of the mental attitude which
underlies it, that the divine beings are in some way akin
to the worshippers, with comprehensible motives and
"all too human" passions. At the other end of the
scale stands, perhaps we may allow, the mystical theist,
a Plotinus or an Augustine. What is his consuming ambition ? To rise, in an experience which transcends discursive thought, to a Being who is indeed far other than
himself, and yet a Being in whom he knows that he will
find his completion and his home.

But this sense of continuity is not by itself sufficient to
differentiate religion from the other aspects of man's
spiritual life. On the contrary, it is common to them
all and is in fact the germinal situation from which all
intellectual, æsthetic and moral activity springs. Throughout the whole of our life as spirit we are confronted with

an " other " which responds, or is believed to respond, to our efforts to come to terms with it in various ways. Religion is one of the ways in which we seek to come to terms with that other ; and in " coming to terms " we include " interpret ". Religion might be defined as one of the ways of " coming to terms " with the Other by means of a special mode of interpretation.

The truth of the unity of the life of the spirit, of its underlying identity in its various forms, is of the highest moment. It is a truth upon which we wish to insist, for it will affect profoundly our conception of religion, of the nature of its development and of its relation with other " forms " of the spirit which may at times appear to be its rivals. At the outset of our inquiry we would protest against any view of religious experience which would deny its intimate connexion with thought and conduct or which, in the endeavour to safeguard its specific nature and its independence, would cut it off from the general life of the mind. But here a particular consequence of the principles which we have been enunciating may be mentioned. It is often said that religion is essentially an " anthropomorphic " way of interpreting reality, and the statement is undoubtedly true ; but this is not a peculiarity of religion, for anthropomorphism is a characteristic which it shares with every other " form " of the spirit.

The possibility of any knowledge of " nature ", of any science, depends upon the assumption that the " other " responds to, is really interpretable by, the categories of our thought. It rests, in other words, upon the conviction that the " beyond " is in some way akin. There is no way of proving that this conviction is true. In its origin it is plainly not a " working hypothesis," and it seems most reasonable to hold that this ineradicable conviction is the expression of a fundamental intuition. It needs no argument at the present time to show that the scientific interpretation of reality is thoroughly anthropomorphic in the sense that it makes use of human modes of experience and thought.[1] The great authority of Professor Whitehead might be cited in support of this thesis[2]; but it needs no authority, for it is sufficiently evident that he who seeks to employ categories or ideas which are not human must first cease to be a man; and in fact every concept of science derives from an experience and is an abstraction or generalization from experience. This is true of " cause ", " substance ", even of " relation ".

An interesting illustration of the fundamentally " anthropic " character of scientific notions is furnished by the latest development of physics. The category of " thing " or " substance " seems to be vanishing from the stage on which for long it has played the central rôle and its place is being taken by more dynamic conceptions, among which that of " event " is specially important. The attempt is being made to envisage the natural order not as a collection of " things "-but as an inter-related system or series of " events ". An event, however, is just as much an " anthropic " idea as that of " cause " or " thing ". It arises from the fact that human attention is not absolutely continuous, but proceeds, as it were, in spasms, that it has a " time span " which forms a " specious now ". By " event " we mean, in the last resort, an experience which for some consciousness, possibly an ideal one, would constitute a

---

[1] The word " anthropic " has been coined by Dr. Tennant to denote the dependence of science on the human point of view while indicating a difference from the kind of " humanism " which is characteristic of religion. *Philosophical Theology*, Vol. I, p. 175.

[2] Specially his little book *Symbolism*.

" specious now ". The object of these remarks is not
in the least to depreciate the value of scientific knowledge ; on the contrary, the tendencies on the part of
some authorities on the new physics to philosophical
scepticism seems to the present writer deplorable. The
advance of scientific knowledge is indeed an advance in
our knowledge of the real world, and no one who reflects
upon the fact that science enables us in many cases to
predict events can doubt that it is, in a true sense, knowledge ; but this genuine acquaintance with and mastery
over " nature " is built upon one assumption, that we
are continuous with an " other " which is not merely
other, not simply alien, but responsive.

Science is one mode of interpretation of the object, and
we may state briefly its salient characteristics in order
that we may compare them with those of other modes
of interpretation. The scientific mode is essentially
analytical and proceeds by way of simplification and
abstraction. Its ideal is to reduce all its subject-matter
to the calculable : and, since only genuine units can be
counted, to see the world as a system of measurable
relations between countable x's.

The point which I have perhaps been unduly labouring
is illustrated, however, equally by the most elementary
form of knowledge—that perception from which all
science begins. In perception we meet with the same
basic condition of experience. We perceive the room in
which we are : it is an " other ", an object ; if it were
not an other there would be no knowledge of it, for there
would be nothing to know ; but equally in the act of
perception it has ceased to be wholly other and has come
within our consciousness—" a beyond which is within ".

But elementary perception and the intellectual construction which grows out of it—natural science—are

not the sole forms of the spirit, and we must now try to
indicate how those other "forms" exemplify the principle which we are setting forth as the basis of the whole
life of mind in general.   Every form of the spirit is,
regarded from one point of view, an interpretation of the
"other" in terms of the person or of some element
within the experience of persons; from another point
of view it is an essay towards eliciting a response from the
"beyond the self". Æsthetic experience is an aspect of
spiritual life no less fundamental than that of perception
and science. We may ask what conditions make æsthetic
experience possible. We shall be justified in rejecting
at once the paradoxical view of Croce that art comes
before nature and that we find beauty in nature because
we have first found it in art.[1] If that were true, it would
be difficult to understand how art could ever begin.
The precise opposite is the truth; we find beauty in
art because we have first found it in nature, and the
effort of the artist is to perpetuate a momentary revelation. This experience of natural beauty is surely best
described as that of a suddenly disclosed kinship with
ourselves.   We feel that we, at that instant, have understood that "other"; but it is an understanding of the
emotions and, as such, can never be expressed in concepts, it is a felt fellowship rather than a rationalized
relation. But "nature" in that experience is not melted
into mere "subjectivity": it does not become simply
a part of us. The consoling rapture of the æsthetic
experience would lose most of its power if we became
convinced that it had no objective source but was illusion
or dream. Why is that ? Because in that case it would
have lost its character of a revelation of real kinship.

---

[1] "As regards natural beauty man is like Narcissus at the fountain."
Croce, *Æsthetic*, E.T., p. 162.

Nature in the highest and most ecstatic experience of beauty or sublimity remains a " beyond ", an " other " than ourselves, yet it is now felt as in some way continuous with and akin to ourselves—" a beyond that is within ".

The world is, however, for us not merely a series of percepts or an object of æsthetic enjoyment but also a " realm of ends ", a sphere in which purposes are to be fulfilled and ideals or " values " realized. The practical life is also a " form " of the spirit. It is possible to regard this aspect of the activity of mind as the most fundamental of all, and Kant to some extent and Fichte with much greater thoroughness have taken this view. The " objective " world, according to the latter philosopher, exists as the condition of moral effort, being posited by the Ego as requisite for the development of ethical will.

We must confess that the moral consciousness appears, at first sight, to be peculiarly difficult to fit into our general scheme, since it has a characteristic note which is not obviously equivalent to continuity, indeed is almost the opposite. For in the experience of moral endeavour we seem to postulate of the " beyond " that it is not akin or congruous with the self. The moral life has meaning precisely because the objective world, the " given ", does not conform to our ideals. Morality lives in the contrast between " ideal " and " actual ", and if this vanishes it vanishes too. This undeniable fact has been taken by F. H. Bradley and many other thinkers as an indication that a merely ethical interpretation of reality is not finally true, that the moral consciousness belongs to the realm of " appearance ". We need not commit ourselves to the contrast between " appearance " and " reality " in the sense of the absolute idealists, but we must agree that the moral interpretation of the world is not the complete truth. It demands a supplement, or rather a crown, and that is to be found in religion. Morality is a form of the spirit with a distinctive nature of its own; it is not, as such, a kind of æsthetic feeling, nor is it religion, though it has affinities with both. It is not the whole life of the spirit.

Yet we need not abandon the formula which we have suggested as the general outline of the life of spirit. Though morality depends upon contrast, it does not depend on that alone. The ethical consciousness cannot regard the not-self as merely alien, simply impervious to ethical ends. The primary aspect of the not-self in ethical experience is that of opposition; but this aspect is itself, in some sense, a response to the moral self, since it is precisely that opposition which the moral will needs in order to be moral will. But further, in spite of Kant, the moral consciousness could not subsist in the face of a " nature " which was so " step-motherly " as to refuse all response to its ideals. If it could be shown that the " other " were essentially and as such the merely opposite, the totally recalcitrant to ideal aims, moral effort would cease. " Who can dwell with everlasting burnings ? " Still further, the moral consciousness seems to convey another implication, or rather perhaps there is an affirmation which the ethically developed person is impelled to make, namely, that its ideals and judgments of value are more than subjective, of greater validity than personal or racial preferences, that, on the contrary, they are founded in reality as a whole and " stand fast like the strong mountains ". At this point many moral philosophers would part company with us, and we will agree that when we make this claim for moral values we have already passed beyond the borders of the ethical consciousness into the sphere of religion. As we have already contended, it is not easy to separate these two forms of the spirit from one another ; here more plainly than else-where religion completes the dialectic of the spirit.

It is time to attempt the delineation of the religious consciousness in its determinate nature. As we have seen, it issues, like all other forms of the spiritual life, from a primal intuition of the continuity of the self with an " other " which is more than a mere opposite, an other which responds. It comes into being in an interpretation of that " other ", and here again it does not differ in principle from the remaining forms of the life of spirit. It differs from them, however, in this respect, that in religion the affirmation of continuity and the intuition that there is response in the Object to the needs of the self are much more thoroughgoing ; and hence the religious interpretation of the world is essentially different from the interpretations which are natural to the scientific, the æsthetic and the moral consciousness. We owe to Dr. Tennant a convenient distinction between " an-thropic " and " anthropomorphic ", the former being used to denote an interpretation which is based upon some aspect or element of human personality and its experience, the latter denoting an interpretation which is made in terms of human personality as a whole.[1] If we adopt this distinction, we may describe science, ethics and æsthetic experience as being " anthropic " interpretations affirm-ing, or if we please, " projecting ", one side of the whole self-consciousness, perception, emotion, will, while religion is in its inmost nature anthropomorphic, projecting or affirming the whole personality and interpreting the " other " in terms of the most concrete experience, that of the self before it has been dissected by analysis.

A great deal of discussion has been devoted to the question of the particular needs which impel human beings

[1] See note, p. 12, above.

C

to elaborate religious interpretations of the world. A popular suggestion, which is favoured by Mr. Bertrand Russell,[1] is that religion arises because men seek comfort in a world which, dispassionately considered, is a terrifying wilderness. It seems remarkable, if this is the sufficient explanation, that man has invented such a formidable array of deities, many of whom, one would think, can scarcely have afforded comfort to any human being. If the race has been seeking reassurance from its religion it has been singularly unfortunate in some of its imaginative flights. Such generalizations are worthless, because they select a superficial and partial character of some religion and attempt to stretch it into a universal cause. We must look for some deep and permanent needs of the human spirit if we would explain man's religiousness from the most degraded to the highest peak which it has touched.

Two salient and ineradicable needs of the spirit seek satisfaction through religion : the need for unity and the need for the substantiation of value. Let us first briefly consider the need for unity. We may admit that there is an element of truth in the view of the nature of religion which we may call " intellectualist ". According to this, religion is a crude and childlike speculation, of which the motive is curiosity and the purpose explanation. This opinion has been defended by Tylor, Sir James Frazer, and other anthropologists, and a similar theory is held by Croce, who regards religion as essentially mythology. We must, however, look deeper than conscious intellectual curiosity. The motive force of religion is not a need simply to seek out the causes of things nor are its first beliefs a clever hypothesis. It springs indeed from an impulse which is within the intellect, but one which is

[1] *Why I am not a Christian.*

also within the life of will, emotion, and imagination—
the impulse to unify, to bring into coherence inner and outer
experience.

It may seem a strange paradox to describe the thirst
for unity as a fundamental spring of religious experience.
The impression made upon our minds by such forms of
religion as animism, polytheism, and polydæmonism is one
of incoherence and diversity ; when we contemplate
them we are confronted with a world falling apart. But
this impression arises from the fact that we view the
religion of uncivilized man from our own standpoint.
Doubtless for us a return to polytheism would be a
regression towards chaos. But if we try to place ourselves at the standpoint of the primitive believer, we can
see that for him his belief in spirits or dæmons is a
relative unification. The world as interpreted by polytheism is a more coherent thing than the world not
interpreted at all. There is truth in the saying of
Professor Hocking, " All polytheism is imperfect monotheism ". To dwell upon this aspect of the religious
consciousness in its higher development is needless, for
there it is generally admitted. Baron von Hügel in his
Mystical Element of Religion has abundantly illustrated
the desire of the mystic and of all religion, in so far as it
is genuine and first-hand, to rise " away from multiplicity to unity ", from incoherence to coherence. It is
true that there have been expressions of this desire which
have been one-sided and imperfect, which have implied
a mere flight from the world to a One who is beyond all
multiplicity. " Otherworldliness " in the bad sense has
been a pathological state of religion. But that has not
been the road taken by the complete and fully developed
religious consciousness. In that more excellent way to
know God is not to negate the world and its multiplicity

but to affirm it in its true being as an element within the
unity ; and if Augustine can say, " Deum et animam scire
cupio. Nihilne plus ? Nihil omnino ",[1] it is because, like
Malebranche, he " sees all things in God ".

The second need which is met in the religious experience is that for the substantiation of values. The human
mind seeks for an objective basis for its judgments of
good and right ; it has a need to be assured that they are
not mere passing preferences but grounded in reality.
Here again what is in fact a truism is apt to appear to be
a paradox. We are often invited to observe that religion
and ethics have no necessary connexion and indeed that
very much of religion is opposed to any decent standard
of conduct. The contention is true in the sense that our
moral consciousness would condemn a great deal of
religion ; but the question is not whether religion always
substantiates our values but whether it substantiates any
values, and here there can be little doubt. Notoriously
the divine beings of uncivilized mankind are the guardians
of tribal custom and later of the accepted law, guardians
also of the social structure in which these customs and
laws are expressed. The monotheistic faiths have held
that God is the substance of values, Himself the supreme
Value. It makes no difference to our argument here that
the values themselves have changed and that the content
of the God-idea has correspondingly varied. That is
precisely what we should expect if our conception of the
nature of spiritual life is correct. The mind begins with an
intuition of its continuity with an " other " which is not
merely other, with a " beyond " which is akin, which is also
responsive to it. It follows, therefore, that man knows
God in proportion as he knows himself : but the con-
verse is also true, since man is not anything at all apart

[1] *Soliloq.*, 1. 7.

from the " other " with which he is in rapport ; he knows
himself in proportion as he knows God.

The religious attitude of mind has a peculiarity which
is not easy to define but which has been indicated by
most writers upon the religious consciousness in language
coloured by their own particular theories. Schleiermacher
touches upon it in his " feeling of absolute dependence ",
Otto in his " sense of the numinous ", and Professor J. B.
Pratt when he designates God as " the determiner of
destiny ". Religious states of mind contrast with those
which are scientific or simply practical or moral in this
respect, that whereas the scientific and moral are attempts
at mastery over the not-self, to bring the objective
material within the categories of the understanding or
to bend it to the purpose of the will, in religion the self
seeks rather to be mastered, to bend itself to that " other "
with which it is continuous. This is because, for religion,
the " other " is the realization of its values. In this
respect the religious attitude is more closely akin to that
of æsthetic enjoyment, which wishes not to alter the
object but to remain in its presence. There is, however, an
important difference from the æsthetic attitude. The
religious attitude, though self-abnegating, is not passive,
for it includes the possibility of co-operation. This
difference, on which we must carefully insist, is connected
with a difference in the interpretation of the object. For
the religious state of mind the object is not passive but
active, not dead but alive.

Closely connected with this aspect of religion is the
redemptive element which is present in every kind of
religious life and system. No doubt the idea of salvation
is more explicit in some religions than others, and the
conceptions of what man is redeemed from and what
redeemed to vary enormously even in the highest

examples of spiritual consciousness. There is, for example, a profound and significant difference between the salvation of the Buddhist and the Christian. The former seeks release from suffering, the latter from sin. But the thought of redemption is present in some form throughout the whole range of religion and springs from its essential nature. In so far as he is religious man feels himself to be, in the end, impotent and miserable so long as he remains in his isolated selfhood. Within him there dwells no power to achieve by himself the good, whatever that may be, which will satisfy him. Only if he can find some living power in the "other" which will unite itself with him, becoming indeed the Beyond which is within, can he emerge from the state of unsatisfactoriness and worthlessness. In the conception of the redeeming God the intuition of the responsiveness of the "other" reaches its most complete expression.

We are not here directly concerned with the defence of the validity of religious experience ; but it is relevant to remark upon a very common objection against every kind of religious interpretation of existence. We are told that every conception of God, and every so-called experience of God, is a case of "projection" ; man, it is said, projects his desires, ideals, hopes—himself, upon the outer world, or upon the unknowable, or upon "something I know not what" (the designations of the "other" conceived as merely blank or merely opposite are confusing, since the conception itself is contradictory). We may reply summarily in a two-fold manner. First, we must refuse to accept the abstract and arbitrary idea of the self which this view implies. We do not admit the assumption that the self "has" anything simply in its own right and as a merely private creation, and therefore that it can project its independent imaginings. The self never is thus isolated. It has being and it develops only through its relation with that " other " with which it is continuous. If it has ideas or desires or hopes or is a self, it has and is these things only through its constant dynamic relation with the beyond-self. All psychological " explanations " of religion which propose to be also exposures of its illusory character are due to this fallacy, which arises from the legitimate procedure of the science of psychology, which, like all sciences, isolates its subject-matter. Psychology, no less than any other science, when it pronounces finally on philosophical problems becomes ridiculous. Secondly, we must insist that, if this utterly untenable and viciously abstract conception of the self be maintained, the full sceptical consequences shall be drawn. They are alarming. There is nothing whatever which will not then be a " mere projection ", no concepts of science, no idea of the reason, no judgment of value which has not a psychical origin, and, if to be a projection is to be condemned, we must resign ourselves to the conclusion that no mental or spiritual activity of ours has any objective validity.

The view of the general character of man's experience of God which has been presented in this chapter has a consequence which we cannot pass over in silence. If we have rightly described it, religion cannot be regarded as a specialized activity. It is certainly a distinct form of the spiritual life and is not to be resolved into morality or art or philosophy ; but it is not the product of a separate faculty in the individual nor is it the peculiar prerogative of a special type of human being. It is native to the developed human consciousness. The recent interest in the lives and writings of " mystics " and the cult of the " religious genius " have been wholly beneficial in that they have drawn attention to a type of human

faculty which had been misunderstood and have emphasized the power of the religious motive in minds of
exceptional character ; but there is a danger lest this
type of religious thought should tend to suggest that
religion itself depends upon the possession of a rare combination of qualities.   It may be, too, that to judge
religion by its specialists is likely to give us a distorted
conception of its nature.   Religion, in our view, is the
completion of the other forms of the life of the spirit, the
climax towards which they tend, so that each of them,
when intense and full, passes over into religion.   Hegel's
phrase " Das denken ist auch Gottesdienst " was not a
poor excuse for not going to church, for the most severe
and faithful thought, not only thought about so-called
" sacred " subjects, is rèligious.   The æsthetic experience
again cannot be divorced from that of religion, as indeed
we might learn from the poetry of Wordsworth and from
the sayings of Schleiermacher that music is most akin to
religion and of Mr. Aldous Huxley that for many modern
minds it is an almost adequate substitute.   The moral
consciousness, as we have seen, trembles always on the
brink of religion and finds its support in an affirmation
about the objective reality of its judgments of value and
its fulfilment in an experience which goes beyond the
merely moral situation.   In religion the life of the
spirit of man reaches unity, and the richest religious life
has not left the other activities of spirit behind but has
taken them up into itself.   The Reality which it seeks
and thinks that it has known is One in which the thirsts
of the soul for goodness, beauty, and truth are not
annulled but satisfied.

CHAPTER II

THE DEVELOPMENT OF THE CONCEPT OF GOD

THE account which we have given in the previous chapter of the nature of religion has not divested it of all difficulty. It is not claimed for that account that it provides us with an understanding of the religious experience of such a kind that we can regard it as simple and straightforward. On the contrary, it is a part of the theory there propounded that there is a paradox in religion from the outset. If we may recall the discussion of the last chapter, we argued that religion is the supreme instance and culminating point of the life of the spirit. In all its forms, however, the life of spirit depends upon an intuition or immediate and ultimate postulation of an " other " which is at the same time not simply other, of a beyond-the-self which is within the self and akin to it. A paradoxical character, therefore, attaches to every activity of mind and emerges with full force in religion, which is the highest and properly the most inclusive activity of the human spirit. We shall be mistaken if we suppose that the paradox and the difficulties to which it gives rise are peculiar to religion, for they exist in every level of spiritual experience. The theory of knowledge, the theory of ethical value and the theory of beauty, all have their fundamental problems which arise from the central situation—that of the self in contact with an object with which it can neither be wholly identical nor from which it can be wholly different. This paradox

25

manifests itself with peculiar intensity in the life of religion, precisely because religion is the most intense form of the spirit's being.

The paradox to which we have referred comes to the surface in a theoretical form in the crucial problem of religious thought—the debate between transcendence and immanence. A philosophy which will justify the religious attitude must maintain both that God is immanent and that He is transcendent. On the one hand, a purely immanent deity turns out, in the last resort, to be undistinguishable from ourselves, and hence to be no possible object of adoration and aspiration, while conversely, a purely transcendent Deity is one with whom communion would be impossible. Either conception, in the long run, must deprive worship of its justification and prayer of its reality. The same paradox is found in the central exercise of practical religion—the life of prayer. As we have seen, God must be recognized as the " other than me ", or I cannot pray, and yet it is of the essence of prayer in its nobler forms that we should recognize, at the same time, that only the inspiration of God makes prayer possible, and indeed, in the language of the greatest masters of devotion, that God prays in us. All the problems which have vexed theologians and puzzled the simply pious may in fact be traced to this fundamental paradox as their root. One further instance will be enough. Human freedom and divine grace are both needful affirmations for the religious man. If he abandons the former he becomes a mere puppet in the universe and, as such, incapable of the religious attitude ; if he abandons the latter he declines from religion to moralism, and has denied his need for God. Theology and faith have swung backwards and forwards between these two poles, but have never finally rested at either. Both sides of the apparent contradiction must be affirmed together, as they are without scruple by St. Paul : " Work out your own salvation with fear and trembling, for it is God who worketh in you both to will and to do ".[1]

That there is an apparent paradox in religion has been recognized by many thinkers. Two passages from writers of a very different standpoint may be quoted. In a remarkable passage of the *Opus Posthumum* Kant has expressed it in terms of his moralistic conception of religion : " There is a Being in me, distinguished from myself as the cause of an effect wrought upon me, which freely—that is without being dependent on laws of nature in space and time—judges me within, justifying or condemning me ; and I as man am myself this being, and it is no substance *external* to me, and—what is most surprising of all—its causality is no *natural* necessity, but a determination of me to a free act."[2] Of still wider range, though vaguer, is Professor A. N. Whitehead's statement of the apparent contradictions of the religious interpretation of the world. " Religion is the vision of something which stands beyond, behind, and within, the passing flux of immediate things ; something which is real, and yet waiting to be realized ; something which is a remote possibility, and yet the greatest of present facts ; something which gives meaning to all that passes, and yet eludes apprehension ; something whose possession is the final good, and yet is beyond all reach ; something which is the ultimate ideal, and the hopeless quest."[3]

Only a superficial view would infer from this paradox which religion presents that it is illusory or mistaken. The contradictions which it seems to offer to our intellect

[1] Phil. II. 12.

[2] *Op. Post :* Adiches, ed. 1920, p. 824, quoted Webb, Kant's *Phil. of Religion,* p. 198.

[3] *Science and the Modern World,* p. 238.

are not of the kind which allow us to dismiss the object as unreal.   We have seen that they are not absent from other aspects of man's spiritual life.   They indicate rather that we are dealing with an object which is beyond our full comprehension.   The antinomies arise from the necessary effort to formulate in terms of our finite thought and experience a Reality which transcends their capacity. Neither Kant nor Whitehead draws this sceptical conclusion.   To them the paradox which is presented by the highest experience is a mark of the fact that in it we are in contact with reality in its most concrete form.   Professor Whitehead, after the sentences just quoted, goes on to point out that religion is the one element in human experience which persistently shows an upward trend. To the fact of this upward trend we must now briefly turn our attention, with a view to discovering if there is any law or principle in religious progress and in the development of the conception of God.

The fact which Dr. Whitehead roundly asserts may possibly be questioned.   We are not concerned here with the exclusive claim for religion as alone progressive among the elements of human experience, which perhaps would be difficult to defend, but with the question whether religious insight does in fact show development.   It may be pointed out truly that religion over a great part of the world has for long periods been stagnant or even regressive, and moreover that it has been at times the source of general stagnation and regression in civilization as a whole.   It is indeed important to recognize this fact. Nothing could be more at variance with the evidence than to represent the history of man's experience of God as a steady progress all along the line, or to suppose that every change in religious belief is good.   Progress has not been steady ; it has taken place rather in spurts and has made

rapid advance in short creative epochs. This characteristic appears to become more pronounced as we rise
in the scale of value, the higher religions being more
definitely the creation of prophets, "religious geniuses",
and inspired persons, than those of the less civilized
races. Still less can it be maintained that progress has
been uniform. We are here confronted with a situation
analogous to that in biological evolution. The picture of
life as a whole pushing forward to new and more complex
types of organism is a romantic imagination. In fact the
line which leads from the amœba to man is both wavy
and thin. The forward movement of life is like a trickle
of current passing through stagnant waters. So it is with
the development of religion. We have to discern the
progressive tendency amid the vast mass of religious
humanity whose faith seems to contain no impulse to
transcend itself and whose worship is but the repetition
of the ceremonies and the words which their fathers have
told them. But this statement does not represent the
whole truth. Just as in biological evolution there are
degeneration and parasitism so in the religious sphere
the constant change which governs the thoughts of men
may be in the direction of mechanical performance of
sacred rites, of distorted conceptions of deity and, ultimately, towards magic. The fact of degeneration has
perhaps not always been adequately recognized in
studies of comparative religion.

The development of religion in the sense of progress
towards a higher type of experience is reflected most
plainly in the concepts of the divine. An interesting
theoretical discussion might be started here on the
question whether the ideas of God are predominantly
cause or effect. Is the thought of the Divine Being
determined by the ethical and spiritual experience of the

race or, on the contrary, is the experience determined by
the idea ? It will be readily admitted that the concepts
of deity are coloured by the experience of the worshipping
community, but it must also be conceded that the action
is reciprocal. The idea of deity in turn determines the
experience, moral and religious, of the worshippers. In
tracing the development of religion we are concerned
neither with a purely dialectical process which consists in
the logical explication of concepts, nor with a merely
emotional or pre-rational process which has no element
of ideality ; we are concerned with a vital process which
throughout contains all the elements of the life of the
spirit—will, emotion, thought. We must keep this carefully in mind while we are discussing the evolution of the
idea of God, lest our theory should be vitiated by the
fallacy of intellectualism. It is in any case important to
remember that the human race does not consist of
professors.

The idea of the divine, when we consider it historically, appears, at first sight, to offer us only a mass of
bewildering confusion. There is, it would seem, scarcely
any type of being or thing or aspect of the world which
man has not at some time worshipped. Dr. W. P.
Patterson, in his Gifford Lectures on the Nature of
Religion, has attempted an exhaustive division of concepts of the divine or supernatural and has been compelled
to arrange them into no less than eight main classes with
many sub-divisions. Men have found their " determiners
of destiny " in inanimate objects, animals, ghosts, and
gods. The vast mantle of religion covers Fetish-worship,
Magic, Zoolatry, Spiritism, as well as the higher cults of
great deities. Amid all this illusion and superstition we
must look for the line of upward development and among
the ferment of religious imagining seek the germ from

which the higher faiths were to spring. The clue to our problem is found when we observe that the one progressive line of religious evolution is connected with the application to the divine of the analogy of human life and experience. Anthropomorphism is the road along which the believing mind has travelled from superstition to noble creeds. The fact is not surprising. An anthropomorphic religion has at least taken the step of postulating that the power on which we depend is not lower than ourselves and has admitted at the same time the principle of progress. For man is the deepest mystery of the world. He alone has the potentiality of indefinite development. Inanimate objects remain as they are, the lower animals move within the strict boundaries which instinct and environment draw for them, but man is constantly moving towards an end which is not known to him and discovering possibilities which he had not suspected. "The foxes have holes, and the birds of the air have nests, but the Son of Man hath not where to lay his head."[1]

Nevertheless, the proposition that anthropomorphism is the principle on which progress depends is at first sight somewhat startling, for it has been one of the reproaches against religious persons that they have made their gods after their own likeness. Doubtless, as the ancient critic remarked, if the oxen had gods they would be like oxen.[2] We cannot, moreover, forget that the burden of the accusation by reformers of religion has often been the absurdity of the anthropomorphism of current faith. The Hebrew prophets not less than Plato have joined in the protest against thinking that God is "even such an one as ourselves".

[1] St. Matt. viii. 20. St. Luke ix. 58.
[2] Xenophanes of Kolophon : *Satires*, XV, quoted by J. Burnet. *Early Greek Philosophy*.

There are two motives at work in this protest in which prophets and philosophers concur. First is the obvious thought that the humanity which is taken as the analogue of the divine is not human nature at its highest. The gods are envisaged as all too human in their caprices and their short-sighted selfishness. We must not allow even inspired poets to persuade us that the gods are at war with one another or that they feel enmity and jealousy, nor dare we believe that they can be guilty of fraud and evil desires.[1] But the remedy for this malady of religion is not the desertion of the human analogy but the application of the noblest only of the attributes and activities of man to the Divine. " Let us not then deem God inferior to human workmen, who, in proportion to their skill, finish and perfect their works, small as well as great, by one and the same art ; or that God, the wisest of beings, who is both willing and able to care, is like a lazy good-for-nothing, or a coward, who turns his back upon labour and gives no thought to smaller and easier matters, but to the greater only."[2]

But there is another motive in the protest against anthropomorphism which is of profound importance. Dr. Otto has brought out in his analysis of the " numinous " the element of " creature feeling " which he rightly holds to be a constituent of all genuine and developed religion. It is the same element as that which Schleiermacher isolated in his formula of " absolute dependence ". When they contemplate the Divine the worshipper and the prophet know themselves to be in the presence of a Being which transcends the human categories even at their highest, in comparison with which all the thoughts and virtues of man are of no worth. The Other which is akin to man remains Other. Under the

[1] *Euthyphro*, 6. b. *Repub.*, Book II.   [2] *Laws*, X, 913.

overwhelming impression of the unlimited power and the impenetrable mystery of God, Job exclaims, " I have heard of thee by the hearing of the ear ; but now mine eye seeth thee, wherefore I abhor myself, and repent in dust and ashes ",[1] and Isaiah, confronted with the vision of the Lord arising " to shake mightily the earth ", feels the nothingness of the human race ! " Cease ye from man, whose breath is in his nostrils ; for wherein is he to be accounted of ? "[2]

This latter cause of protest against anthropomorphism, however, never becomes in the great religious minds a complete rejection of the whole anthropomorphic method. Indeed it could not do so without undermining the whole structure of religion ; for, it is clear, once we have come to regard the Divine as " wholly other," utterly alien and beyond our ken, God has been reduced to a mere unknown quantity, a mere mystery which can inspire neither aspiration nor hope. It is not accurate to say that the determination of the divine nature by the values revealed in human life must necessarily lead to a conception of God which has lost every trace of transcendence, "otherness ", and mystery. On the contrary, the transcendent is implicit in the values themselves, and it is only a meagre and unimaginative conception of them which finds them to be complete and perfect here and now. The kinship of the divine and human, thought of as the Platonists have taught us, establishes the divine transcendence on a basis firmer than fear. Mr. R. C. Lodge has summed up the situation for us in words which, if somewhat technical, are pregnant with meaning : " God and man are essentially identical in nature, and it is by living the life of idealistic endeavour that the divinity within us flowers into a resemblance of the Divinity in

[1] Job XLII. 5, 6.   [2] Isa. II. 22.

D

whom and through whom alone can all that is achieve meaning and value. Our value-sense thus penetrates beyond the accidental surroundings of human life, material, sensuous, emotional, and social-conventional, and comes to rest in the contemplation of an ideal experience, an experience which includes these elements, takes them up into itself and transmutes them into its own meaning and value, but in origin and destiny transcends the empirical content which it includes and transforms."[1]

Reflection on the nature of religious experience leads us to see that anthropomorphism must be for it not only legitimate but unavoidable. We have argued that religion arises out of an impulse and need of the human spirit which feels or intuits its continuity and kinship with a Reality beyond itself, and that this impulse seeks, as it would seem, two satisfactions in particular—for unity and substantiation of values, both in the face of divergent appearances. It follows, therefore, that the determination of the nature of this Other, the discovery of its character, or as religion itself would say, its revelation of itself, must proceed *pari passu* with man's discovery of his own nature. It is only as man comes to know himself that he is able to catch a glimpse of the nature of the Other with whom he continually dwells, and by contact with whom he acquires self-knowledge. The two fundamental maxims of Greek and Hebrew aspiration respectively "Know thyself" and "Know God", are not contradictory but complementary, for man knows God in so far as he truly knows himself and he knows himself through knowing God.

When we have recognized the necessity of anthropomorphism, and the fact that it affords the only line of advance for religious ideas, we must proceed to distinguish

[1] *Plato's Theory of Ethics*, p. 330.

between the lower and the higher types of anthropomorphism. It is against the lower anthropomorphism
that prophets protest. At the root of polytheism is the
thought of deity as a magnified and powerful, perhaps
immortal, man ; and the social order of the nation or
tribe is projected into the unseen world, so that the
pantheon is a reflection of the court of a Homeric king
or the palace of an oriental despot. This simple-minded
religious imagery persists even in religions which have,
in principle, left it far behind, and Christianity both in its
Protestant and Catholic forms can still show abundant
traces of this rudimentary theology. Yet even in polytheism man appears to be seeking for some perfection
in the beyond which is above the achievement of his
ordinary state. As Sir Henry Jones has said, "The religious history of man gives no ground for believing that he
consciously worships a recognized imperfect God. For
the moment even the god of the polytheist, whom at
any instance he may toss aside, stands for the perfection
he needs ".[1] The history of religion is crossed by a " great
divide ". On the further side are those which have never
emerged from the stage in which man in his empirical
reality is the analogue of the gods ; on this side are those
which have attained the conception that man is essentially
spirit and that God must Himself be the supreme Spirit,
to be worshipped in spirit and in truth.

"Not lehrt beten ", and in the prayers which are
offered we may discern most clearly the kinds of need of
which the worshipper is conscious and the kind of deity
to whom he prays. Petitions reveal more candidly than
anything else a man's thought of himself and his thought
of God. The prayers of the lower culture are well on the
further side of the " great divide " and belong to the

---

[1] *A Faith that Enquires*, p. 58.

cruder anthropomorphism. The Dschagyanegeo spits four times in the morning towards the sun and says, " O Ruwa, protect me and mine ". The Masai prays every morning, " God of my distress, give me food, give me milk, give me children, give me much cattle, give me meat, my father ".[1] The affecting confidence of these prayers goes no further than the claim of the natural needs, and the deity is the benevolent provider for them. " Create in me a new heart, O God, and renew a right spirit within me " is the petition of the Psalmist[2], for whom the deepest need is righteousness and " truth in the inward parts ". In his thought God and man have passed beyond the natural to the spiritual, and the Divine is primarily the source of moral judgment and of purification. " The gnostic," says Clement of Alexandria, " who has reached the summit will pray that contemplation may grow and abide, as the common man will pray for continual good health."[3] In this saying we hear a note which in varying resonance sounds through all the higher religions, but most clearly in Christianity. God is no longer simply the source of satisfactions, even those of ethical rightness, He is Himself the final satisfaction and that Other which completes the human spirit, so that the aspiring soul can cry, " Whom have I in heaven but thee and there is none upon earth that I desire in comparison of thee ", and the life of time is regarded as " quoddam suburbium cælestis regni ", in which the unearthly joy may be tasted beforehand.[4]

The passage from the lower to the higher anthropomorphism is closely associated with the attainment of

---

[1] Heiler, *das Gebet*, p. 44.   [2] Ps. LI. 10.   [3] *Stromateis* VII, 7.

[4] The reference is to St. Bonaventura, *Soliloquium* IV. 1. " Si hæc cælestia gaudia jugiter in mente teneres, de hoc exilio quoddam suburbium cælestis regni construeres, in quo illam æternam dulcidinem quotidie spiritualiter prælibando degustares." Quoted E. Gilson, *St. Bonaventura*, p. 459.

monotheistic faith. Doubtless in every historical instance
of the rise of belief in one God out of an earlier polytheism
influences of a relatively external and accidental character
can be alleged. Political developments, fusions of tribes,
conquests, even geographical conditions, have played
their part ; but these factors are never the mainspring
of the development. There is an inner logic or dialectic
which pushes the religious consciousness beyond the
polytheistic stage. But this logic is not to be understood
as a revolt against anthropomorphism in principle,
but rather as the fuller development of that principle. For
man comes to realize within himself the presence of needs
to which the deities of polytheism cannot minister ;
needs which go beyond long life, protection against
enemies, prosperity, children, and crops. Two needs in
particular he discovers—that for the unification of experience, the intellectual need, and that for the substantiation of universal values, the moral and the æsthetic
need. When once the human spirit has, however dimly,
come to recognize the more than natural necessities of
its life the knell of polytheism has sounded. The many
gods can give no ground for the apprehension of the world
as one intelligible system, while the many divine wills,
often in antagonism, of the best ordered pantheon can
furnish no adequate response to a moral outlook which
has apprehended the universal character of moral good.

Nevertheless, the natural reaction against lower conceptions of deity may really be, in some instances, a reaction
against anthropomorphism in general ; and this is more
likely to be the case when the myths of popular religion
have been very much below the insight of the best minds.
For thus the tendency arises to despair of the attempt to
revise the idea of deity, which seems irretrievably stained
with the heritage derived from the nature-religion, and

to push behind the conception of God to that of a principle which has been purged of all the attributes of personality —to pantheism or to the conception of fate or destiny. Dr. Gilbert Murray remarks of the " Olympian " religion of Greece : " It is curious how near to monotheism and to monotheism of a very profound and impersonal type the real religion of Greece came in the fifth and sixth centuries,"[1] and it is clear that, in his opinion, the profundity is closely connected with the impersonality. A similar development is even more evidently to be seen in the Indian religions, which on the whole have rested on a pantheistic theology. But the effort to go beyond anthropomorphism leads to the failure of the religious enterprise, which is illustrated by the historical fact that pantheistic theology has everywhere proved to be perfectly compatible with polytheistic worship. It is only those faiths which have clung to the personal conception of Deity which have had a " jealous God " who will tolerate no other gods beside Him. Perhaps the reason for this is not really obscure. The " values " which religion seeks to find fulfilled and sustained in the Beyond the Self are indeed recognized as no creations of the human spirit, they are universal in claim and they are objective, but they have no existence, nor can their existence be conceived apart from personal life. A thought of God, therefore, which has expunged all tincture of anthropomorphism must decline into a concept of a being for whom no human values are real, into an unknowable ground of the universe or an order of nature.

The consideration which we have given to the place of the anthropomorphic principle in the development of the conception of God is strictly relevant to the study of the Christian doctrine of God, for it is sufficiently obvious

[1] *Five Stages in Greek Religion*, p. 92.

that the Christian religion may be regarded as the most extreme and consistent expression of that principle. The eagerness of some Christian thinkers to disclaim the title for their religion is due to the mistaken notion that such a type of thought about God must be superstitious and childish. As we have seen, this accusation can lie only against the lower anthropomorphism. As we shall see in the next chapter, the religious consciousness of Jesus was fashioned after this mode ; and it is surely significant that the two pivotal dogmas of developed Christianity are that man is made in the image of God and that God is made manifest fully in the man Christ Jesus. Let us not be afraid of the plain implications of our faith. The Christian doctrine of God depends more than any other on the legitimacy of the anthropomorphic approach.

Christianity is, first of all, the completion of the Hebrew religious experience ; but the Old Testament is not the only influence whose effects may be traced in the Christian conception of God. Two great streams flow together into the sea of Christian thought about God—the Hebrew and the Greek. They represent the two main aspects of the higher anthropomorphism, and Christianity therefore inherits the features of both. The Hebrew development represents, in an almost pure form, the working out of that side of the experience of God for which He is primarily the Source and Sustainer of ethical values. The onward movement of the Hebrew religious consciousness is motived by this thought. Doubtless influences of a philosophical kind can be discovered in Hebrew literature, in Job and the Wisdom writings, but they are not in the main stream of the development, nor are they, as philosophy, of great moment. It is a curious fact that the canonical literature of the Hebrews, a race which was in later times to produce one at least of the greatest philosophers, should bear so little mark of the philosophical impulse. The Hebrew consciousness of God is a meditation upon righteousness. It pushes to the furthest point the conception of Deity as the Vindicator of moral values, and for that reason it has a deep interest in history, in events, finding in them the revelation of the righteous purpose of God.

The Greek development, on the other hand, is dominated by the specifically philosophical impulse. Little of permanent value for the world has come out of the popular religion of Hellenism. Philosophers were the real teachers of Greece—men who sought to understand, to find unity in experience. Like all generalizations about human affairs, this is open to qualification in detail and can claim to be no more than an approximation to truth. It would indeed be ridiculous to overlook the moral interest which inspires the life of Socrates or Plato and to forget that Stoicism in its later phase was a moral teaching and very little a metaphysic. But the emphasis is upon reason throughout, reason often in isolation from the other aspects and faculties of human nature. The good life is the life according to reason : the reason is the divine element in man, and the most characteristic and consistent product of Greek thought on God is Aristotle's eternal Thinker who abides beyond good and evil.

We may claim for Christianity as one of its glories that it has at least tried to hold together these two elements in the higher anthropomorphic conceptions of God. It has found in the doctrine of God the satisfaction of the intellect's thirst for unity and coherence ; but it has found in Him even more the Source and Sustainer of all values, the Supreme Value who is also personal, entering into personal relations with us in worship and prayer. The

Hebrew prophet, in the last resort, would have chosen to rely upon his direct experience of Jahweh, the righteous God, and would have affirmed the reality of the voice which spoke in his conscience, even though that inward revelation seemed to have no relevance to any merely intellectual problem, even though it seemed to contradict the deliverances of man's " wisdom ". We know from Plato's own words the place which he would have given to " inspiration " compared with the conclusions of rational thought. The " inspired " utterances of poets and prophets are, at the best, symbolical adumbrations of truth and, at the worst, the source of degrading super-stitions.[1] Christianity has never abandoned the belief that the two impulses were reconcilable, that the Personal Righteousness is the explanation of the world. We might illustrate the fact of the synthesis between the specifically " philosophical " and the specifically " religious " motives which Christianity has attempted by a fantastic imagination. Some writer of imaginary conversations should attempt one between Plato and Jeremiah, the greatest man of the Old Testament. The dialogue would be difficult to manage, for it is not easy to see how the two interlocutors could get on to a common ground. They belong to different worlds of thought and experience. A second-rate person like Clement of Alexandria has perhaps no very deep understanding of either Plato or Jeremiah, but they both mean something to him. They both have something to say to him about God. The two worlds of experience and thought have flowed together.

The attempt at synthesis which is a glory of Christianity and one of the marks of its position as the supreme and absolute religion, has been, at the same time, the source

---

[1] *Repub.* 378 B.C. *Timaeus* 28 a.

of its internal tension and unrest.   The two elements
within its experience of God have never been completely
harmonized ; the personal, " psychological ", living God
of Hebrew tradition and piety has never been successfully
identified with the God of metaphysics whose ancestry
derives from Greece.   Christian thought has never
achieved a concept of God which fully satisfied the two
needs of its heart.   The labours of theologians have always
been a little remote from the religion of the saint and of
the common man, and the experience of the worshipping
community has often created forms of devotion which
theology has found hard to rationalize.   This inner
tension of Christian thought is a significant feature various
aspects of which will engage our attention in later chapters.
Here I will simply remark that it affords a justification
of our present enquiry.   The Christian conception of
God is not fixed and complete, not a doctrine fully thought
out and settled, so that a reopening of the question would
be a mere impertinence.   The identity of the personal God
of holiness with the Ground and Unifier of Reality which
Christian faith affirms presents us with a task for thought
as well as a resting place for the refreshment of our souls.
Every generation has the duty and opportunity of con-
tributing to the work of thinking out the Christian idea
of God in the light of its own special point of view.

CHAPTER III

THE CHRISTIAN EXPERIENCE OF GOD

WE argued in the last chapter that the two streams of Hebrew and Greek thought about God flowed together in Christianity, but we may take it as certain that the Hebrew influence is the predominant one in the New Testament. Recent criticism has pointed out some apparent connexion between St. Paul's thought and the mystery religions of the Hellenistic world, and it is probable that his vocabulary at least, if not his ideas, was affected by the terms current in the popular and living religion of the pagan Roman Empire. But the discovery of analogies has been made the basis of an unjustifiable exaggeration of St. Paul's debt to the non-Jewish circle of religious and mythological notions, and the trend of opinion is now back to the surely obvious conclusion that the Apostle of the Gentiles thought and felt always with the background of Hebrew monotheism. The Johannine writings, particularly in the prologue to the Gospel, bear traces of the impact of Greek philosophical ideas, and the prevailng view is still that the conception of the Logos is derived, perhaps indirectly, from the speculations of philosophers. Even here, however, the influence of Greek thought is questioned and it is held by some that the idea of the Word of God can be assigned a wholly Hebraic ancestry. The minute questions of scholarship which any discussion of these points would involve are outside our scope and we shall assume here that the New

Testament as a whole is the production of men for whom the Jewish idea of God was the unconscious premiss of all their thinking.

When we are concerned with the central element in the New Testament, the person and teaching of Jesus, the question is not really open to discussion. There can be no doubt that His thought and His experience of God emerge wholly from within the sphere of Palestinian Judaism. He was a Jew of the First Century if not perhaps, as Dr. McGiffert adds, " a devout and loyal Jew ". To understand the words of Jesus and the thought of God which He expressed we need know nothing of the philosophy of Hellenism or of the mystery religions, but we need to know much of the Law and the Prophets, and perhaps also of Eschatological writers.

There will be general agreement that, in some sense, the New Testament is the fountain head of the Christian experience of God and that it must remain normative for all later Christian generations. Though our conception of God may be enlarged and modified by the centuries of reflection which have elapsed and by the mass of new knowledge about the Universe which the last two hundred years have brought, any idea of God which can be called Christian must be in harmony with that which is presented to us in the New Testament as a whole and particularly in the records of the life and words of the Lord. It follows that we are not free to construct our conception of God in abstraction from history. We are not engaged upon original speculation. Our starting point is a creative experience which comes to us mediated through human testimony and documents of various historical reliability. Such a situation has seemed to many intolerable, and they have enlarged upon the unreasonableness of resting truth concerning God upon this foundation. Spinoza's

words are well-known : " The truth of an historical narrative, however assured, cannot give us a knowledge nor
consequently the love of God, for love of God springs
from knowledge of Him, and knowledge of Him should
be derived from general ideas in themselves certain, so
that the truth of an historical narrative is very far from
being a necessary requisite for our attaining our highest
good."[1] On this point Christianity is committed to an
opposite opinion, and depends to some extent upon an
historical narrative.

The Christian position in this matter may be defended
against Spinoza and others on more than one ground.
If our analysis of the religious consciousness is correct,
we are led to conclude that man's experience of God
does not originate in, nor does it consist of, the possession
of " general ideas ", however true those ideas may be.
It arises from a direct apprehension of a certain quality
or aspect of the world. Very much as the intellectual
construction of the order of nature is built up from
the immediate data of sense, the concept of Deity is
fashioned from the data of the religious experience.
That experience may indeed be " explained " or summed
up in general concepts of theology, but the concepts are
always inadequate, and are no more than the earthen
vessel in which, for a time, the experience of the Divine
Element in reality may be contained. The point of view
which Spinoza states in this quotation belongs to the
rationalist era which has passed away. The modern world
is not rationalist in the true meaning of that ambiguous
term : it does not rely on the deduction of consequences
from self-evident principles.   On the contrary, the
scientific method, which is the real distinguishing mark
of our present phase of culture, begins from the other end.

[1] *Tractatus Theologico-politicus*, cap. IV.

It sets out from the data of experience, and its general ideas are reached in the attempt to interpret what is given. The modern scientific temper, therefore, has no reason for objecting to a theology which starts from experience. Nor can it safely protest against reliance upon human testimony and records for acquaintance with the data to be interpreted, for science itself is in precisely the same situation. The phenomena with which it deals are known by observation, record and narration. The researcher must depend on human testimony. If he were confined to principles which are to him self-evident and experiences which he himself has had he could make no progress towards a science of nature. In the same way, the solitary thinker seeking unaided for the Divine with the support only of his own spiritual experience and power of reflection will get but a short distance on the road and reach but a meagre conception of God. The testimony which might have given richness to his belief and assurance to his faith has been omitted from his calculation, and he is in the position of a student of science who ignored the current textbooks and the observations of fellow enquirers. In the New Testament is to be sought, not a speculative doctrine of God, but the data which such a doctrine must take into account.[1]

To grasp the New Testament experience of God in any full sense is clearly impossible, for it is always beyond our power to enter completely into a creative moment of life. We are constrained to admit, therefore, at the outset that our enterprise is bound to be in some degree a failure ; but it will be an absolute and unrelieved failure if, at the conclusion of our study, we have nothing more than a collection of ideas about God, material for a work on New

---

[1] Cf. A. N. Whitehead, *Science and the Modern World*, Chapter I.

Testament theology. We must aim at recapturing something of that new energy of soul of which the New Testament is the creation, allowing, in Croce's phrase, the thoughts and imagination and emotions of that still living past to vibrate again in our own spirits. But we must here draw a distinction. Some writers, while justly asserting that the essential element in Christianity is a typical experience of God manifested in history, deduce from this that particular historical facts and even particular historical persons are of quite secondary importance. So Dr. Bosanquet writes : " The study of Christianity is the study of a great world-experience ; the assignment to individuals of shares in its development is a problem for scholars, whose conclusions, though of considerable human interest, can never be of supreme importance."[1] Opinions not dissimilar have been defended by Josiah Royce[2] and by the more extreme Roman Catholic Modernists.[3] Our approach to the subject is quite different. So far from attempting to minimize the dependence of Christianity upon historical events, we begin with the conviction that our religion rests upon an experience of God which was enjoyed by historical persons and, in a supreme degree, by one historical Person ; but at the same time we would add that the Christian religion can only remain pure and powerful in so far as that history is not mere historical data but becomes real for us by living again in our souls through the creative imagination, becoming thus for us present fact.

Our first and fundamental task is to grasp, so far as we can, the consciousness of God possessed by Jesus. If we are to carry out our line of thought we cannot avoid

---

[1] *Principle of Individuality and Value*, p. 79.
[2] Cf. his *Problem of Christianity*.
[3] Cf. Loisy, *l'Evangile et l'Eglise*.

this enquiry, for we have agreed that the truly Christian conception of God must be based upon that consciousness. The difficulties and objections to any such investigation are obvious. To some minds it will appear presumptuous and irreverent. We shrink naturally from reflection upon the inner life of One towards whom our proper and normal attitude is adoration, for we feel that reflection can hardly be separated from criticism. We must sympathize with this repugnance, which is more than justified by the excesses of some psychologists who find in the Son of Man an example of those " complexes " which seem to form the main article of faith in some circles. But the objection does not lie against an effort reverently to understand the thoughts of Jesus concerning His Father. Nor need we fear that knowledge so obtained will lower our reverence for Him. On the contrary, it will place that reverence upon a firmer basis.

Another more serious objection, however, arises. On any view which cares to keep in touch with the main stream of Christian belief, we should have to admit that the mind of Jesus is beyond our comprehension, and that we cannot hope to penetrate its secret places, because the analogous experience is lacking in ourselves. While confessing the truth of this, we must still maintain that the mind of Christ cannot be wholly closed to us. Even though a dog may penetrate but a small way into the thoughts of his master yet he penetrates some way, and by that penetration he lives. It would be a strange paradox if One who called Himself the Son of Man were entirely beyond man's understanding. There are, however, scholars, who are not careful to keep on terms with orthodoxy, who yet maintain, on other grounds, the incomprehensibility of the inner experience of Jesus. Professor Rudolph Bultmann may serve as a notable instance.

In his remarkable book, *Jesus*, he contends that a reconstruction of the Lord's experience is impossible because the evangelical records have left us no material for it. They do not interest themselves in this matter, and their evidence, such as it is, is vitiated by the mixture of legendary matter. This disability, however, Bultmann argues, need cause us no regret, for the experience of Jesus is not important for us. His significance for the world lies not in what He experienced but in " what He willed ", not in His thought but in His work. In this respect, it is added, He resembles all creative minds, for their distinguishing mark is that they have been interested not at all in themselves, in those " personalities " of which we make so much, but in what they set themselves to do. We too should be interested in " what they willed "—not so much in what they achieved, or in the sum of effects which they produced, but in what they intended.

We have, of course, to allow for the modifications of Jesus' words which Christian piety and theology have caused. There is little doubt that the sayings about the End have been sharpened in the tradition under the influence of the eschatological hopes which prevailed in some sections of the Apostolic church, and a comparison of Matthew with Mark shows perhaps that motives of reverence have been at work to prune away expressions which were distasteful to the Christian feeling of veneration for Jesus.[1] The Johannine gospel again is so plainly narrative coloured by theology that we can use it only with caution for the knowledge of the historical Jesus, though it is a document of the highest importance for our knowledge of the outcome of Christ's life and teaching. When we have made these admissions, however, we are

[1] This may be disputed, cf. H. J. White in *Church Quarterly Review*, 1915.

E

far from the conclusion that Jesus' thought and experience of God must be for us a closed book. Even Professor Bultmann holds that we have ample material for a knowledge of what Jesus willed. The theory that we can know this yet be wholly in the dark concerning Jesus' consciousness of God rests upon a psychology which is surely one of the strangest. Obviously we cannot separate the will from the personality in this arbitrary manner. What a man wills is the best possible evidence of the nature of his personality and his experience, for the will is the self in action.

We will first ask what we know of the form of Jesus' experience of God. We need not labour the point that He passed through stages of development, growing " in wisdom and stature and in favour with God and man ". At the present day there is no disposition to question the genuinely human character of Christ's life. It must be confessed that we have no real evidence on which to found a detailed account of the spiritual growth of the Saviour prior to the commencement of the public ministry. Probability and His own utterances make it safe to assert that He was nourished on the Old Testament, growing up in a circle of simple traditional piety. We do not know whether His environment was one in which Messianic hopes were vivid or whether His youth was passed among those who were affected by eschatological ideas, but He was certainly greatly influenced by the Prophets and His life and teaching are a revival of the prophetic ministry.

The salient features of Christ's experience of God are its unbroken and triumphant character. Jesus comes before us as one who is unshakably sure of God, so sure that the question whether God exists would have no meaning for Him. There is no word of His which hints at the possibility of doubt. This assurance of God is immediate. It rests upon a direct apprehension and not upon any train of reasoning or conscious appeal to authority. This obvious truth has naturally led to the description of Jesus as the supreme mystic, and, if by mysticism we mean simply the direct apprehension of God by the soul, the title is just ; but if something more definite than this is intended the case is less clear. Attempts have been made to show that there is a regular outline of development in the spiritual life of the true mystic and that it passes through three or four definite phases. Miss Evelyn Underhill, in her beautiful and impressive book the *Mystic Way*, has tried to discriminate these phases in the life of Christ. In the opinion of the present writer the thesis of the book can only be substantiated by a *tour de force*, though the author has taught us much by the way. The spiritual experience of Jesus does not fall into any scheme of this kind, and we may specially observe that there is nothing really analogous to those periods of depression and dereliction which form a part of the personal history of " normal " mystics.

The unbroken and triumphant nature of Jesus' communion with God has often been represented in theology by the assertion of the Lord's " sinlessness ". The aspect of His life to which this word calls attention is of great importance. There is no hint in the recorded sayings of Christ that He was conscious of any moral failure or had any feeling of the need for personal repentance and forgiveness. We cannot too much reflect upon this striking fact, remembering, at the same time, that the suggestion of overweening self-confidence is one which could scarcely live in the mind of anyone who had read the Gospels. But it is perhaps unfortunate that so much stress should have been laid on this word. It is negative, and therefore suffers from two inherent defects : it is incapable of proof, and it cannot adequately convey the positive nature of Jesus' communion with God. No conceivable fullness of tradition would be sufficient to demonstrate absolute sinlessness, and it is logically absurd to hope to do so on the basis of the very imperfect records which we possess. Moreover, a word which suggests the refraining from wrong action falls grievously short of the mark when it is put forward as describing Jesus. Ideas such as sinlessness are included within the positive phrase " filial consciousness ". Christ is, in His own inner consciousness, from first to last the Son of God. The note of discord and disharmony with God is absent from the words of Jesus. The experience of alienation was never His. The words from the cross, " My God, my God, why hast thou forsaken me ? " have been taken as the exception to this statement.[1] It may be that they are the expression of the bitterness of the feeling of failure which was the supreme pang of the Saviour, but it seems equally possible to take them as indicating that He was repeating the great psalm of consolation in the moment of deepest trial, and through these words keeping His thought firmly concentrated upon the God who was " throned upon the praises of Israel ".

William James has classified religious persons into two groups—the " once-born " and the " twice-born ".[2] The former are those who have grown in communion with God by serene progress from grace to grace, the latter those who have attained spiritual and moral stability through violent conversion, from sin and impotence to peace and power. In James's opinion nearly all the original and creative minds in religion have belonged to the second

---

[1] St. Mark xv. 34, cf. Ps. XXII.
[2] *Varieties of Religious Experience*, p. 80.

category. Jesus, however, appears to stand outside these classes, or rather, in some respects, to come under both. While, as we have said, He did not pass through a stage in which right relations with God were attained out of a previous condition of lower and distracted life, there is abundant evidence that this unbroken fellowship with God was maintained in the face of almost overwhelming temptations.[1] The experience of Jesus included the knowledge of the mystery and the force of evil, though not participation in it.

One further remark may be made on the form of our Lord's experience of God. We have argued that Schleiermacher's formula to describe the essential nature of religion, " a feeling of absolute dependence ", is defective on the ground, among others, that it omits the feeling of co-operation which is equally fundamental. The religious life of Jesus plainly exhibits both these elements. Throughout the words of Christ there is the sense of a dependence which is unlimited. It is God who clothes the grass of the field. Just as the Hebrew poets saw in nature and human life the direct action of God, so Jesus traces all events and all the life of man to the Creative Will. The " little faith " of men is shown by their refusal to rely upon God for the natural no less than spiritual needs. But this feeling of utter dependence does not exclude the thought of co-operation ; the fellowship with God is a true fellowship of will, and the spiritual consciousness of Christ is certainly not independent of moral effort. The Fourth Gospel puts into the mouth of Jesus the words, " My meat is to do the will of Him that sent me."[2] They are spiritually true and an apt summary of the impression which the Synoptic Gospels produce on our

[1] See, for instance, St. Matt. IV. ; XVI. 21 f. ; XXVI. 39 ff. and parallel passages in St. Mark and St. Luke.   [2] St. John IV. 34.

minds. The whole inner life of the Lord was concentrated
upon preserving that conformity and free co-operation
with the Divine Will. Any conception of the Person of
Christ which obscures that central fact is untrue to the
historical data and gives us a Christ who, however much
He may be decorated with the trappings of theological
veneration, is definitely lower than the heroic figure
which stands out from the records. Jesus is never nearer
to us and, at the same time, never more clearly our Master
than in the Agony in the Garden,[1] when we are allowed
to see something of the intensity of effort by which this
active co-operation was sustained.

We now proceed to consider the content of Christ's
experience and thought of God. In this we shall be
compelled to recognize the presence of two main factors
—the prophetic and the eschatological. One of the most
important results of recent study of the New Testament
is the recognition of the influence of the apocalyptic
writings and circle of ideas on the Apostolic Church and,
to some extent, upon the thought of Jesus Himself. The
degree of this influence, and indeed the question whether
it had any place in the teaching of Jesus, are matters of
controversy. All would, however, confess that we must
take into consideration that type of piety and religious
imagination which elaborated the idea of the coming end
of the age and the supernatural rule of God. There is,
nevertheless, little difference between the doctrine of God
held by the apocalyptic writers and that which was the
outcome of the line of Hebrew Prophets. The thought
of God which Jesus accepted without question was the
Jewish thought, and it makes little difference whether
prophetic or apocalyptic forms were uppermost in His

[1] St. Matt. xxvi. 36 ff. ; St. Mark xiv. 32 ff. ; St. Luke xxv.
40 ff.

mind. The Jewish idea of God is quite different from the Greek. As we have seen, it arose through a contrasted process of development, and the marks of this contrast are plainly present in its final form. For Judaism God is not an object of intellectual knowledge, nor is His nature known through speculative wisdom. God for Judaism is creative Will. He is known through His revelation, in Law and Prophets and in the events of history and nature, which are the direct products of His Will. This creative Will is sovereign, beyond understanding. " Let all the earth fear the Lord, let all the inhabitants of the world stand in awe of him. For he spake and it was done ; he commanded and it stood fast." The world and all that it contains exist for the glory of God. " Thou sendest forth thy spirit, they are created ; and thou renewest the face of the ground. Let the glory of the Lord endure forever ; let the Lord rejoice in his works."[1]

The God of Hebrew religion is thus both living and remote. He stands in relation to men as Creator, sovereign Ruler, and Judge. In His holiness, which through the work of the Prophets becomes inseparable from righteousness, there remains the note of awefulness, which goes back in its origin to the shuddering dread of primitive worship. But the God of Judaism is also near ; working in history, showing His will in the Law, entering into covenant relations with His chosen people, " dwelling with him that is of a contrite and humble spirit ".[2]

Such was the conception of God which Jesus received from His environment and did not radically modify. It was a view common to the greater Prophets and the eschatological writers. The latter conceived God as the holy and sovereign Ruler of the whole earth, but in two

---

[1] Ps. XXXIII. 9 ; CIV. 30, 31 ; cf. Bultmann, *Jesus*, p. 123.
[2] Isa. LVII. 15.

respects perhaps their emphasis was changed. The remoteness of God from the present order was suggested by their pessimistic outlook upon the condition of the world. Incurably evil and disobedient, it would go from disaster to disaster until the catastrophe which should usher in the reign of God. The God of Apocalyptic was more definitely the determiner of all destiny than the God of the Prophets. Determinism was the presupposition of eschatology. The fore-ordained series of events known to the divine Providence was revealed to the seer who disclosed the secret to the elect. The exaggerations of the eschatological school of New Testament interpretation as expounded by Johannes Weiss and Albert Schweitzer may be rejected, but it is difficult to believe that the idea of the Kingdom of God, which was the centre of Jesus' public teaching, had not in the mind of the hearers and of the Teacher some eschatological colouring. Doubtless the cruder pictures of the end and the world to come have little place in the Gospels, and probably had no place in the authentic words of the Lord. It was a spiritual consummation to which He looked forward and not a revenge on the enemies of the nation. It was a vindication of the righteousness of God which had no vindictiveness. Nevertheless we are compelled to recognize that the elements of the eschatological idea were present in Jesus' thought, and they are sufficient to put His view of the relation of God to the world and to history in a very different mental context from our own. The Kingdom of God was the direct act of God ; it had nothing to do with humanism or progress towards an earthly Utopia brought about by the co-operation of men of good will. It would be misleading to overlook this difference or to fall into the vulgar error of patronizing our Lord as a good liberal or a precursor of sentimental socialism.

We must maintain, however, that the prophetic and not the eschatological element is the most profound in Jesus' doctrine of God. This is true of the teaching concerning the Kingdom. Though the Kingdom is certainly represented as a future gift of God, none the less it has already come in the hearts of those who respond to the proclamation of the good news. The thought of the New Covenant written in the heart and depending no more on external ordinances and instruction, which is the profoundest and most spiritual conception of the relation of God and man contained in the Old Testament, is constantly suggested.[1] Is it not Jeremiah's New Covenant of which Jesus speaks on the night before His passion ?[2] This is the Kingdom which comes not with observation,[3] which grows in secret, which is within. It is this thought of the Kingdom which explains the nature of the ethical teaching. Some modern eschatological critics have argued that the moral teaching of Christ had no important place in His own view of His mission, and that the rules of life which we find in the Sermon on the Mount are " *interims Ethik* ", stop-gap regulations hastily thrown out for the short space which will elapse before the end. Nothing could be further from the truth. The New Covenant is the inward covenant, and the righteousness required therefore was one of motive and spring of action —not merely conformity to an external rule.

The God of Jesus is, like the God of the Prophets and the Eschatologists, a Righteous and Holy God, and therefore a Judge who makes stern demands upon men. The common opinion that Jesus came preaching forgiveness of sins is not false, but by itself tends to a mistaken emphasis. He came, first of all, proclaiming the need for repentance,

---

[1] Jer. xxxi. 31–34.   [2] St. Luke xxii. 20.
[3] St. Luke xvii. 21,

the lamentable falling short of all sorts of people when compared with the requirements of God. Dr. McGiffert has spoken truly : " He demands more than was generally demanded rather than less, He set up a higher ethical standard and insisted upon a more perfect conformity to it. Like Amos, He emphasized life rather than ritual and required justice and mercy rather than sacrifice. He judged His generation severely and believed that it needed a thorough moral reformation ; with a view thereto He was concerned less to offer men pardon than to summon them to righteousness, less to comfort than to convict of sin."[1]

In the Old Testament, and specially in the later Isaiah, the righteousness of God, and His judgment, are connected with His salvation. So far from the justice of God being in opposition to His mercy it is because God is righteous that He saves. " There is no god else beside me : a just God and a saviour."[2] " I bring near my righteousness, it shall not be far off, and my salvation shall not tarry."[3]

We are thus led, in the sequence of the doctrines about God, to that which has often been claimed as the peculiar and even the only essential idea in our Lord's teaching—the Fatherhood of God. That belief in the Fatherhood of God was original and characteristic with Jesus cannot of course be held by anyone whose reading of the Old Testament has proceeded so far as Psalm ciii. It is, on the contrary, even asserted by Dr. McGiffert that Jesus did not go beyond the accepted teaching of Judaism in this part of His teaching about God, and it must be admitted that a great part of what Jesus has to say on this matter can be paralleled from

[1] *God of the Early Christians*, pp. 11, 12.
[2] Isa. XLV. 21.   [3] Isa. XLVI. 13.

Jewish sources. We owe to Dr. Montefiore a clear statement of the real departure which the Gospel made from the standpoint of the best Pharisees.[1] The injunction to seek out the sinful, to constrain them to come into the Kingdom, was a new note. But this new note of ethical adventure was based, as was everything in Christ's teaching, upon his thought of God. Here is the fresh and truly revolutionary interpretation of the Divine Fatherhood. God's love is active not passive, it goes out to seek and save those who are lost. It is as unwearied as the shepherd who looks for the lost sheep.[2] On this foundation rests the missionary and expansive impulse of the Christian Church. It is the root of the Pauline doctrine of redemption. " At the heart of the Christian doctrine of God's dealings with the world is the conviction, proclaimed as a gospel, that the costliest effort has been made by God Himself."[3] In this faith in the Fatherhood of God as including the outreaching love which pursues all men, is implicit the universality of the Christian message.

The New Testament as a whole contains a twofold idea of the Divine Fatherhood which is derived from the teaching of Jesus Himself. In the widest sense God is the Father of the whole creation ; His mercy is over all His works. This embraces even the lower orders of life, so that not a sparrow falls to the ground without the Father.[4] And the evil and the good alike share in the benefits of sun and rain which are bestowed with generous impartiality. But in a special sense God becomes Father to those who have responded to the love which seeks them and have become members of the Kingdom. In the Apostolic version of Christianity this second and more specific fatherhood and sonship arises out of the new status into

---

[1] *The Synoptic Gospels.* Vol. I, p. cxviii.
[2] St. Luke xv. 4–7.
[3] J. K. Mozley, *The Doctrine of God*, p. 90.
[4] St. Matt. x. 29.

which the individual enters by being joined with Christ
and sharing His life. The true fatherhood is not of nature
but by grace.[1] In Dr. Scott Lidgett's words, it is "not
merely genial, not vague and expansive, but is, so to speak,
concentrated in the highest spiritual and moral values."[2]
We have become sons of God from being children of
wrath by the spirit of adoption in which we cry Abba,
Father, says St. Paul.[3] We who once were part of the world
which lies in darkness and the power of the Evil One are
now children of God, says St. John, "and it doth not
yet appear what we shall be but . . . we shall be like
him."[4]

There is, as we have remarked, nothing in the words of
Jesus which resembles a philosophical argument, nor is
there any indication that He conceived the necessity or
possibility of finding rational grounds for His belief ; but
there is a suggestion of a process of thought which has
some resemblance with one which has played a great part
in speculative theology. The *via eminentiæ* has been the
chief method by which theistic philosophers have sought
to determine the divine attributes. As used by the
Scholastic theologians this argument consists in the
inference from qualities or " perfections " in the created
world to their existence " in a more eminent manner "
in God. Thus from the attribute of knowledge in finite
beings we may conclude the attribute of omniscience in
God, from will that of omnipotence. Some train of
reflection of this kind was present in our Lord's mind.
" If ye then, being evil, know how to give good gifts
unto your children, how much more shall your heavenly
Father."[5] But it is important to observe the different
application of this " how much more ". Whereas the

---

[1] St. John I. 12.   [2] *God, Christ and the Church*, pp. 1–31.
[3] Rom. VIII. 15.   [4] 1 John III. 2.   [5] St. Matt. VII. 11.

Scholastic argument starts from abstract qualities, considered apart from the personal life in which they appear, and then arrives at an abstract notion of God, Jesus sets out from the highest human personal life, from the concrete self and its relations, and takes them as being faint shadows of the perfect but not less concrete and personal life of God. This is in fact the continuation of that anthropomorphic theology which we have already insisted upon—from human personality to the divine.

Did Jesus' conception of the Fatherhood of God lead Him to the thought of a universal mission and a world-wide brotherhood in the Kingdom ? Were the privileges of sonship in the full sense open to all those who were children of the Father by reason of His creation ? There can be no doubt that the Apostolic Church came so to interpret Him, but the evidence for Christ's own explicit teaching on this subject is not so unequivocal as we might expect. We find Him saying that He was not sent to any but " the lost sheep of the House of Israel ",[1] and the struggle which took place in the primitive Church over the inclusion of the Gentiles may suggest that the tradition contained no clear indication of the Lord's will on this matter. It is difficult to believe that the earliest Christians would have hesitated in launching out into the deep of the world outside Judaism if they had in mind definite commands of Jesus. On the other hand, there are sayings about the Kingdom such as that about the " many who shall come from the East and from the West ",[2] parables such as that of the Good Samaritan,[3] and the incident of the Centurion's servant,[4] which would support the conclusion that Jesus interpreted the Fatherhood of God in a wider sense than was immediately

---

[1] St. Matt. xv. 24.   [2] St. Matt. viii. 11 ; St. Luke xiii. 29.
[3] St. Luke x. 30–37.   [4] St. Luke vii. 2–10.

comprehensible to His disciples. It is, however, clear that the thought of God which Jesus held and from which His whole teaching proceeded was quite inconsistent with any restricted view of the area of God's grace ; even though it may be possible that He did not explicitly draw the universalistic conclusion, it was there to be drawn by those who meditated upon the Lord's words and works. The attitude of Christ to the ceremonial law confirms this conclusion. The letter of the law is brushed aside when it stands in the way of mercy, humanity, or human well-being in general. The food restrictions and the idea of ceremonial pollution affected the daily life of every Jew throughout the world, and were the main root of that social exclusiveness which constituted the great defect of Jewish morality. St. Mark is not wrong in adding to the words of Jesus the comment, " This He said making all meats clean ".[1] In uttering those memorable words our Lord was practically cancelling the whole system of the Mosaic law and its ancient taboos as a matter of eternal moral obligation. He could not have been altogether unconscious of this tendency. The practical abrogation of the ceremonial law removed the bar upon the Gentiles. This inference from the moral teaching of Jesus confirms the impression made by the Parable of the Good Samaritan and the incident concerning the Centurion.[2] We may safely hold that our Lord's conception of the Divine Fatherhood was universal in its scope, even though He may not have explicty announced the unrestricted validity of His gospel.

Not even the most summary account of Christ's religious experience can be complete without some reference to the

[1] St. Mark vii. 19.
[2] St. Luke x. 30–37 ; St. Luke vii. 7 ; St. Matt. viii. 20.   Rashdall : *The Idea of Atonement*, pp. 16 ff.   See the whole of Rashdall's valuable discussion of this question.

figure of the Suffering Servant of God.[1] We have seen that His idea of God, though selecting the noblest aspects of Hebraic tradition, was not original in the sense that it had no roots in the past. To admit this is not to deny the towering originality of Jesus, but to agree that He came to fulfil the religious aspirations of His people, and to complete the ethical monotheism of the Prophets. One phase of His spiritual pilgrimage, however, is governed by a thought which is in the strictest sense original. The Messiah had never before been connected with the idea of suffering. That the Messianic Age would be preceded by woes had been hinted in the Prophets and became a commonplace of Eschatology. The unknown author of poems which are included in the latter part of the book of Isaiah had painted the immortal picture of the Servant of God who was innocent yet afflicted for the healing of his people. Jesus fused together the two figures of the Messiah and the Servant. The passages in which the Servant theme is developed were plainly constantly in the mind of Jesus. The voice heard at the Baptism recalled the prophetic apostrophe : " Behold my servant whom I uphold ; my chosen in whom my soul delighteth ; I have put my spirit upon him."[2] The first preaching at Nazareth is based upon the same portion of prophetic literature. The response to the question of the Baptist is full of reminiscences of the same passages. Doubtless this circle of ideas is behind the mysterious saying of the Lord that He had come to be a servant and " to give His life a ransom for many.[3] There can be little doubt that Jesus thought of Himself as both Messiah and Servant. In this fusion of religious figures we may read the reason for the

[1] Isa. LXII.　　　　[2] Isa. XLII. 1.
[3] St. Luke IV. 18 ; St. Matt. XI. 5 ; St. Luke VII. 22 ; St. Mark X. 45 ; Isa. LIII. 11.

Passion. Jesus could have avoided the clash with the authorities which led to His death. He voluntarily challenged them with the purpose of bringing in the Kingdom. Jesus Himself wills to bear the woes which were the necessary prelude of the Messianic Age.

The Christian doctrine of God is brought sooner or later to the mystery of the cross. This is inevitable, for the cross is essential for the understanding of Jesus' thought of God. The Father's will, as He believed, led Him there, and refused to allow that cup to pass away from Him.[1] The kind of God in whom Jesus believed was One who required His suffering. We shall not see the deep things of the Christian idea of God if we attempt to minimise this fact. One disastrous deduction which theology has often made from it we will avoid. Some doctrines of the Atonement have suggested that God demands some suffering to satisfy His justice before He will forgive sinners, and this suffering Christ bore. At first sight perhaps, it might seem as though this pernicious superstition had its germ in the mind of Christ in that He believed He must wring the Kingdom from the grudging hand of God by the supreme sacrifice. This belief would certainly have been at strange variance with the conception of Fatherhood, and we should be forced to suppose that the earlier trust in the loving Father was replaced at the end by a gloomier and lower faith. The key to the understanding of this mystery is surely to realize that it was the Messiah who was suffering. Jesus conceived Himself as the representative of God, as the centre of the Kingdom, the Son of Man who was to come in the clouds of Heaven with the holy angels. It was therefore fitting that the representative of God should show that generous love which is the nature of God and should Himself bear the brunt of

[1] St. Mark xiv. 36 and parallels.

the struggle with the power of evil. The cross is the culmination of Jesus' faith that God is love and that the expression of love is self-sacrifice.

There is one further question which is prompted by a meditation on the place of the cross in Jesus' experience of God. In some sense the cross was accepted by Him as inevitable, and it has been held that His conception of the Providence of God was so strict that He believed every event to be predetermined in the divine plan. We have already observed that He thought of all things as depending upon the will of God, and in expressing this truth He ignores secondary causes, passing straightway to the Creative Cause. The writers of eschatological literature again, as we have seen, on the whole take a determinist view of history, and in so far as the eschatological idea is present in our Lord's teaching it suggests that He accepted the same theory of the inviolable providential plan. We must add that the Fourth Gospel seems to represent Christ as advancing, through all the acts of a foreordained drama, to the cross which He foreknew as His appointed destiny. Some of the unquestionably authentic sayings of Jesus may suggest, at first sight, a belief in the absolute determination of all events by God's will, though it need hardly be said that the abstract problem of freedom and necessity is not before His mind. The sayings which suggest determination are, however, counterbalanced by others, and His thought in the main does not depart from the prophetic conviction that it is in the power of men " to hear or to forbear ". The ultimate dependence of all things upon God's creative will does not abrogate the freedom of men or the possibility of rebellion. Though indeed no sparrow falls to the ground without the heavenly Father,[1] it is not said that the fall

[1] St. Matt. x. 29.

F

is directly due to the will or predetermination of the Father. Clearly Jesus admitted the existence of evil spirits and attributed to them illness and disease which are contrary to the will of God. Speaking of an infirm woman He does not say " this woman whom God hath afflicted ", but " this woman whom Satan hath bound ".[1] The inevitable cross was not made necessary by an inexorable fate nor by a fixed and unalterable plan, but by the deeds of men which were not inevitable and the conditions which those deeds had brought into being. He who prayed in the Garden that the cup might pass could scarcely have believed that it had been preordained as in all circumstances necessary ; and indeed it would be a strange paradox to assert that in Jesus' belief all happenings are the direct consequence of God's will, since it is the burden of His preaching that the will of God is not done, and that men must repent in order that it may be done in them and pray and labour that it may be done in the world.

[1] St. Luke XIII. 16.

CHAPTER IV

THE CHRISTIAN EXPERIENCE OF GOD
(*continued*)

THE Christian experience of God must not be identified with the religious experience of Jesus. Though the consciousness of God which the Apostolic Church possessed springs from the Messianic mission of the Lord and the ideas of God which it promulgated have all their roots in His words, the New Tetament religion is not an attempt to reproduce quite simply the attitude of the historical Jesus to His Father in Heaven. Historical Christianity is not the religion of Jesus but the religion which centres upon the Person of Jesus. Those who seek for genuine Christianity in the supposed simple Theism of Christ and would exhort us to cut away all the beliefs which have grown round the Person of the Lord can find no support in the Apostolic writings. In fact the direct appeal to imitate the earthly life and to reproduce the piety of the man Jesus of Nazareth has little or no place in the earliest Christian literature and, we must assume, had little place in the life of the earliest Church. It may be that there were Christians who did not go beyond the thought of Jesus as the ideal rabbi, the exemplar of the true Judaism, and perhaps we possess a document of this circle of believers in the Epistle of St. James. But the creative line of development, that which has nourished the specifically Christian religiousness, is found in the Pauline and Johannine interpretations of the significance of Christ.

67

The motive of imitation is not indeed absent. To have
the mind of Christ is the mark of the genuine believer ;
but the meaning of this imitation is significant. " Have
this mind in you which was also in Christ Jesus : who being
in the form of God, counted it not a thing to be grasped
to be on an equality with God, but emptied himself,
taking the form of a servant, being made in the likeness
of men."[1]   The Christian must imitate the generosity of
Jesus : " For ye know the kindness of our Lord Jesus
Christ, that, though he was rich, yet for your sakes he
became poor, that ye through his poverty might become
rich."[2]   The point in these passages is not the imitation
of the human Jesus but the reproduction of the life of the
pre-existent Christ who undertook the humiliation of the
similitude of men and the death of the cross for us.
" We shall be like him,"[3] says the Johannine writer
as summing up the goal of Christian progress ; Christ
should live in us so that it is no longer ourselves but
Christ who thinks and acts ; but this Christ is the eternal
and living Christ who was manifested in the flesh but who
was always with God and now is alive forevermore. It
is the supernatural life of Christ which is to be not so
much imitated as reproduced in the believer. The cosmic
drama of the redemptive death and resurrection repeats
itself in the soul of the Christian. We were buried with
Him in baptism,[4] we have died to our old selves, we are
risen with Him and seek the things that are above, " where
Christ sitteth at the right hand of God ".[5] These passages
and many like them declare without possibility of question
that the new life, the new experience of God, which is
at the heart of the Christian gospel as it was preached to
the pagan world, is something quite different from a

---

[1] Phil. ii. 5, 6.   [2] 2 Cor. viii. 9.   [3] 1 John iii. 2.
[4] Rom. vi. 4 ; Col. ii. 12.   [5] Col. iii. 1-3.

following of a human example however perfect : it is the participation in a personal Life which continues and which is divine.

For this new life " in Christ " is also a communion with God. The Apostolic writers do not depart from the Hebrew conviction that the end of man and his blessedness consist in knowing God. Eternal life is to know God and Jesus Christ whom He has sent.[1] The amazing fact is undeniable that there was no contradiction in the mind of St. Paul and St. John between their attitude to Christ and their inherited strict Monotheism. The Apostolic experience of God is mediated through Jesus Christ. It is not simply that Jesus has disclosed new views of the nature of God, He does not appear to them in the guise of the last and greatest of the prophets, He is the manifestation of God, in Him dwelt the fullness of the Godhead, in a bodily manner,[2] so that no longer do they seek for the knowledge of God through the Law or even through the Prophets save only as these spoke of Him. They find God through Christ. God is the Father of our Lord Jesus Christ. This experience of God in Christ is the mainspring of what is called the Christology of the New Testament. It is a misleading word, for it suggests that the Apostolic writers were engaged in a scientific attempt to solve an intellectual problem. There is thought and even theology in the New Testament, there is an attempt to grapple with a problem, but it is not a problem posed in the dry, unimpassioned manner of the philosopher or the theologian, rather an emotional readjustment, a re-orientation of the religious personality to include within the inherited Jewish piety the fresh experience of God in Christ.

The Christian experience of God as we may apprehend it in the creative period of the Apostolic Church is always

---

[1] St. John XVII. 3.   [2] Col. II. 9.

experience within the community. We shall misinterpret the facts if we isolate them from their social reference. The doctrine of God cannot be treated apart from the Church. Too often it has been thought that certain beliefs of individuals about God and Christ created the community and that the Church is a secondary element in the circle of Christian doctrine. One of the merits of Josiah Royce's strange book, the *Problem of Christianity*, is that he has seized upon the fundamental importance of " the beloved community ". Though the religious life which finds expression in the New Testament is that of individuals, of St. Paul and St. John, it is conditioned by the faith of the Church, it could not exist apart from the Brotherhood. " The Church of the Living God, the pillar and ground of truth," is the presupposition of every Apostolic writing. This Church was created by the Resurrection, and it differs from all merely human organizations in that it is the fellowship in which Christ is present, through the Spirit, His instrument and body for producing effects in the world,[1] so that every individual can regard himself as a member of Christ's body having his appointed function in the redemptive work of God.[2] This is the background out of which the Apostolic doctrine of God emerges.

The phrase " Christ-mysticism " has been coined to describe the religion of St. Paul. No doubt it is specially appropriate when applied to him, since it indicates the peculiar intimacy of the personal contact with the exalted Christ which was the centre of his devotion, but in so far as it describes the type of religion which finds God in Christ it is equally applicable to the New Testament as a whole. The Johannine writings have a note of exclusiveness which

---

[1] Eph. i. 22, 23 ; iii. 10 ; iv. 11, 12.
[2] 1 Cor. xii. 4–11, 27–30.

is not so strongly marked in St. Paul. Christ has revealed
the unseen God in His true nature as Light, Life and
Love, but the author of the Fourth Gospel puts into the
mouth of Jesus words which seem to deny the validity
of every previous revelation. " All that came before me
were thieves and robbers."[1] This common faith, that
Christ reveals the nature of God unknown in its fullness
before, is the foundation of the Apostolic doctrine of God.
To develop it and to guard against its minimization the
various " Christological " conceptions are employed.
It is not sufficient to think of Jesus as prophet ; though
God has spoken in the past through the prophets, in these
last days, says the writer to the Hebrews, He has spoken
through His Son. It is not sufficient to think of Him
as one of the Angels or Powers of God.[2] He is perhaps
never explicitly spoken of by St. Paul as God, but His
relation with God is one of identity of function with
respect to men. He is the Son, He is the Word of God,
He is the image of God,[3] He is the Spirit,[4] He is the
heavenly Priest who opens the way to God.[5] All these
and other images are various modes in which the earliest
Christian experience strove to embody its common conviction that Christ is the supreme and final revelation of
God, that God is fully known, and His grace received only
through Jesus Christ.

We have already remarked that the new thought of God
and experience of Him was held along with the Jewish
conception of God. The idea of deity which lies behind
the New Testament as a whole is Hebraic rather than
Greek, and this is true even of those writers who, like
St. John and the author of Hebrews, have incorporated
Platonic modes of thought and phrase. Hellenistic

[1] St. John x. 8.   [2] Col. ii. 18.   [3] Col. i. 15 ; 2 Cor. iv. 4.
    [4] 2 Cor. iii. 17.   [5] Heb. x. 9.

influence there is in the Apostolic writings, some effect was produced by the mystery cults upon the language of St. Paul, but it is certain that the conception of God remained Hebraic. The God of St. John and of St. Paul is first of all the Creator. We might almost say without being untrue to the Apostolic thought that it is in virtue of His creativeness that God is God. " His invisible things since the creation of the world are clearly seen, being perceived through the things that are made, even his everlasting power and divinity."[1] The prologue of the Fourth Gospel, which states the theme of the divine Word to be illustrated in the narrative which follows, begins with a phrase which recalls the opening words of Genesis. The Word is divine because associated with creation. The same thought is constantly recurring in St. Paul.[2] That God is first of all the Creator is a Jewish and not a Greek thought. For the New Testament God is not primarily an object of intellectual contemplation but the living source of all things and of every new beginning. The idea of creation is not prominent in the Hellenistic conception of the Divine. It is well known that the philosophical tradition did not lay great stress upon this attribute of God. Plato doubts whether all things should be considered as created by God. Aristotle's Deity, if he can be called creative at all, is so, as it were, by inadvertence, giving rise to the world not by an act of will but in the process of his eternal self-contemplation. The Gnostic mythologies with which Christianity was in contact and in conflict, represent the world as a prison-house in which the soul is confined, and some at least held that it is not the creation of the Supreme God but of an inferior and perhaps evil Demiurge.

Connected with this Hebraic thought of God as creative

[1] Rom. i. 20.   [2] Col. i. 16; iii. 10; Eph. ii. 10; iii. 9.

Will is the rather remarkable absence of any Theodicy or even suggestion that the problem of evil exists except as a practical challenge. St. Paul is indeed concerned to " justify the ways of God " in history and to show the divine Wisdom, though " unsearchable ", as turning the defection of Israel to His ultimate glory.[1] The question of God's justice when we are confronted with the inequalities of human lot, the pains and struggles of the common life, constitute for modern men one of the gravest obstacles to belief in God. In rather a different form they did also constitute a problem for the Gentile world, and it would be true to say that Gnosticism is a sustained attempt to solve that problem in the terms of mythology. To St. Paul the problem had little or no meaning. There are two reasons for this. He believed with the Old Testament that evil was due to the sin of man and that God's love was fully vindicated by His saving act in Jesus Christ. But his ultimate answer is the inscrutable will of God. " Who art thou, O man, that repliest against God ? Shall the thing formed say to him that formed it, Why didst thou make me thus ? "[2] These words which have been the subject of controversy concerning the Christian doctrine of man and his freedom are of primary importance for St. Paul's idea of God. They reveal the persisting Hebraism of the Apostle of the Gentiles. God is sovereign, creative Will.

God in the New Testament has not lost that attribute of Holiness which is characteristic of the Old Testament belief in God throughout its development. In the earliest religion Holiness was akin to taboo, the feeling of the separateness of the Divine, of its danger and awefulness. The Prophetic reform of religion gave to the idea of holiness an ethical content, and taught at least the higher

[1] Rom. xi. 25, 26.   [2] Rom. ix. 19.

minds of Israel that Jahveh's separateness was essentially one of moral purity; God is " of purer eyes than to behold iniquity ".[1] But the Hebrew consciousness of God never became a mere moralism and was always far removed from the modern theory which has been suggested by Kant and Matthew Arnold in their various manners that religion is one way of taking moral experience, and God, it would seem, almost a device to get us to do our duty. Hebrew reflexion upon God is always religious, and consequently never leaves behind that feeling of the divine transcendence, which in primitive form appears as taboo, and in the higher reaches of religion as the sense of the Holiness of God. This combination of two elements in the thought of the Holiness of God is reproduced exactly by St. Paul, who stands here in complete harmony with the prophetic religion. God's holiness is manifested in His righteousness and in His reaction against sin, but He is no mere personification of the Moral Law, nor even its guardian. The law is holy and good because it is the law of God.

The Holiness of God is closely connected with the wrath of God. This conception, which is perhaps little in accordance with our modern habits of thought, is of primary importance for the Pauline experience of God. Nor can it be said to be peculiar to St. Paul. Though St. John tells us that " perfect love casteth out fear ", yet it is only those who are made perfect in love who escape from wrath. " He that obeyeth not the Son shall not see life, but the wrath of God abideth on him."[2] The same intuition of the holiness of God has the same consequences in the teaching concerning wrath in the Epistle to the Hebrews. For those who fall away after having received the knowledge of the truth there remains a fearful

---

[1] Hab. i. 13.   [2] John iii. 36,

expectation of Judgment. " It is a fearful thing to fall into the hands of the living God."[1] Modern theology has interpreted this phrase, the wrath of God, as the reaction of perfect goodness against every kind of evil, and that is without doubt an essential note in the New Testament thought ; but the interpretation is too intellectual and too impersonal to do justice to the vivid experience of the New Testament writers or, we may add, to their daring anthropomorphism. We have only to read the great passage in Romans to feel that there is more here than a " moral Governor of the Universe ". " For the wrath of God is revealed from heaven against all ungodliness and unrighteousness of men, who hold down the truth in unrighteousness ; because that which may be known of God is manifest in them, for God manifested it unto them . . . wherefore God gave them up in the lusts of their hearts unto uncleanness."[2] The most adequate comment on this passage is that of Professor Otto : " We recognize directly the jealous, passionate Jahweh of the Old Testament, here grown to a God of the Universe of fearful power, who pours out the blazing vials of His wrath over the whole world."[3]

Clearly the thought of the Holiness of God thus understood carries with it a dualism between God and that which is opposed to Him. The metaphysical doctrine of dualism is, of course, far from the thoughts of the New Testament writers who are not concerned with the problems of speculation, but there is a practical and religious dualism at the very centre of their experience of God. As we have seen, the human world is alienated from God, the object of His wrath ; though dependent upon God as the Creator, it has, through its sinfulness, become the realm

[1] Heb. x. 26–31. [2] Rom. i. 18–24.
[3] *Idea of the Holy*, E.T., p. 89.

hostile to Him. This opposition is by St. Paul and perhaps also by St. John conceived as extending beyond the sphere of human nature and includes the whole natural order. " The whole world lieth in the evil one."[1] Thus the natural man has no good thing within him. The " flesh " is opposed to the spirit, the mind of the flesh is enmity against God.[2] To mind the things of the flesh is to be immersed in the natural order which is opposed to God. And therefore the transition by which the Christian enters the Kingdom is no gradual process of coming to a fuller knowledge of the truth : it is an abrupt passage from the darkness to light, from death to life, from being a child of wrath to being an adopted son. This spiritual dualism is again one of the elements in the New Testament doctrine of God which are strange to our modern minds dominated as they are by the notion of evolution, and on any philosophical view is obviously difficult to reconcile with a monotheistic faith ; but we shall miss the driving force of the Christian experience of God if we pass it over. It is no relic of an unenlightened age which can be eliminated from the Christian doctrine without injury to its value. Because of this dualism the Christian consciousness of God separates itself off from all pantheistic religiousness and has little in common with the piety which finds in God first of all a rest and a refuge. " There remaineth a Sabbath rest for the people of God ",[3] but it is in the future. The Apostolic faith is one for a Church militant. The mystical character of the Johannine writings, with their emphasis on eternal life here and now, might be expected to abolish this note of contrast and conflict, and we must confess that the sound of the trumpet is not the prevailing tone of the Fourth Gospel ; but it is

[1] 1 John v. 19.   [2] Rom. VIII. 5–7.   [3] Heb. IV. 9.

precisely in these writings that the dualism of life and death, light and darkness, church and world, reaches the most absolute form. The Christian must keep himself free from all love of the world and the things within it.[1] God is Spirit, the very antithesis of flesh.[2] The language of militancy, of sustained effort, is the common strain in the Pauline epistles. We are to fight the good fight of faith, we are to run the race.

But this idea of conflict introduces us to another aspect of the New Testament dualism. The wrestling to which St. Paul refers is not, he tells us, against flesh and blood but against principalities and powers, against the world-rulers of this darkness.[3] The Ephesian Christians before their conversion had been dead in trespasses and sins, not simply as the natural consequence of their " fleshly " nature, but because they were under the influence of the Prince of the Power of the Air who now works in the sons of disobedience.[4] There can be no doubt that the dualism of the Apostolic world-view is something more than a contrast between the creation without God and the creation with Him. The sphere of Spirit is itself invaded by dualism. Belief in evil spirits and in Satan was a part of the common tradition of popular Judaism, and Jesus seems to have accepted the current opinion that disease was caused by their agency. In the mind of St. Paul popular demonology had a larger place, and probably his ideas on the subject were not unaffected by the luxuriant mythology of non-Jewish beliefs. Such titles as the Prince of the Power of the Air suggest that he shared the idea that the atmosphere was full of spirits, many of them malignant. Though it is true to say that the Gospel delivered men from fear of demons

[1] 1 John II. 15–17.
[2] Cf. Otto, *Idea of the Holy*, p. 96.
[3] Eph. VI. 12.
[4] Eph. II. 2.

and was a great emancipation from superstition, it is not true that the Gospel delivered men from the need to struggle with unseen powers of evil. It did not deny their existence, it intensified the sense of conflict; but it inspired a great conviction that the battle was already won. The demons could not prevail against the power of God. " All that opposition—here was the difference—all barriers, all distance, were annihilated by the love which, reaching down from the highest, held the redeemed man in an immediate grasp. ' I am persuaded that neither death, nor life, nor angels, nor principalities, nor things present,'nor things to come, nor height nor depth, nor any other creature, shall be able to separate us from the love of God which is in Christ Jesus our Lord '."[1]

The dualism which is thus so important in the Apostolic world-view must not, however, be taken as an absolute and final dualism. It is an attitude which is, as it were, forced upon the earnest seeker after God and righteousness in his pilgrimage and warfare. But though real it is not the complete truth, and it does not in the smallest degree detract from the foundation faith in God as the supreme Will and sovereign Creator. That the world alienated from Him should exist and that forces hostile to Him should have power over men are part of the mystery which lies hidden in the inscrutable wisdom of God. In one phase at least of his thought, St. Paul conceived this dualism as temporary, a part of the confused state of the creation prior to the great consummation of the purpose of God. At last the dualism shall be done away and even Christ, the Leader in the conflict and the Victor, shall be subject to " Him who did put all things under him, that God may be all in all."[2]   This

---

[1] Edwyn Bevan, *Hellenism and Christianity*, p. 88.
[2] 1 Cor. xv. 28.

overcoming of dualism is to be the result of two processes, on the one hand the extension of the reign of God through the triumph of the Church,[1] and on the other the annihilation of the evil who receive the wages of sin, which is, quite bluntly, death.[2] The essentially historical imagination of St. Paul pictured the end of dualism in dramatic form as the end of a process and a warfare. The Johannine writings are most different from St. Paul in that they have little historical sense and hence scarcely any suggestion of a development in time. Perhaps for this reason the dualism in the Johannine world-view is more profound and ineradicable than in St. Paul. The evil world remains over against the divine life and light, like its inseparable shadow. It may be that we can no more eliminate dualism from St. John than from Plato. But on the other hand, it is possible to hold that St. John had conceived a more profound overcoming of dualism—one not projected into the future but real now. Just as eschatology falls into the background and the coming Kingdom is translated into the present eternal life, so the conflict and the opposition are not ultimately to be done away in some future consummation, but are already abolished in that sphere of reality to which the faithful spirit rises when it turns away from the unreality and the darkness to the true life and light.[3]

The necessary emphasis upon the Holiness of God, upon the wrath of God and the dualism inherent in the Apostolic experience must not be allowed to confuse our apprehension of the fact that the central thought is the love of God. That is the heart of the Gospel.[4] Without it there would be no good news. But it is important to treat this in relation with the divine Holiness. The love of God is

[1] Eph. iv. 11, 12.
[2] Rom. vi. 23.
[3] 1 John v. 4, 5 ; 11, 12 ; 20.
[4] St. John iii. 16.

not in the least degree analogous with the easy-going complaisance which often passes for love in human beings. Though God is Love it remains true that without holiness no one shall see the Lord. The demands of the righteous God have not diminished. On the contrary, their scope and depth are now fully disclosed. The love of God is that of the Holy One who by His act of redemption lifts man out of the condition of sin and alienation to the condition in which he is forgiven and set upon the way of sanctification. Nothing could be further from the New Testament conception of God than that of the " good fellow " of Omar, or of the deity whose *métier* it is to forgive, of the dying Heine. It is only safe to approach the doctrine of the divine Love through the doctrine of the divine Holiness.

The fatherhood of God, which was part of the preaching of Jesus, is in the Apostolic writings generalized into the conception of the love of God. There is another and more important difference. For Jesus the divine Fatherhood rested upon an immediate intuition ; in speaking of it He seems to refer to a truth of which He was conscious in His inner life and one which needed no proof.[1] He does not argue in favour of it—He illustrates it.[2] For the earliest Christian experience the love of God is known through Jesus Christ. Only through Him are we able to be assured that this love is real. Apart from Him we are a prey to fear. But how does the fact of Christ reveal the love of God ? Much well-intentioned modern apologetic seems here to be very imperfectly in harmony with the New Testament. We are often told that the essential meaning of the Incarnation is that " God is like Jesus," and therefore the divine Being must be love. Doubtless

---

[1] St. Matt. xii. 25–27 ; St. Luke x. 21, 22.
[2] St. Luke xv. 11–23.

the New Testament does, in some sense, hold that God is like Jesus. In the Fourth Gospel the words, "He that hath seen me hath seen the Father"[1] certainly suggest this aspect of the truth that God was in Christ, and something of the same idea may be indicated in the saying of St. Paul concerning the "knowledge of the glory of God in the face of Jesus Christ."[2] But the primary foundation for the belief in the love of God is not the character of the human Jesus (though of course that is a necessary part of the revelation) but the act of God in Jesus. The passion of Christ is the revelation of the love of God, and this because it is the act of the Redeemer God who has thus made clear His compassion and His generous sacrifice. The wonder of God's love is dependent upon something more than a history of a personal life : it rests upon an act in the unseen. " He that spared not his own Son, but delivered him up for us all, how shall he not with him freely give us all things."[3] " God so loved the world that he gave his only begotten Son."[4] Vainly do we seek to purge the Apostolic faith in God of the element of theology or mythology or even dogma. The person of Christ Jesus brings to the Apostolic community the assurance of the love of God, but only because that person is interpreted in terms of a supernatural and divine act. Jesus of Nazareth dying on the cross has no message of the love of God to give : Jesus the Son of God in His passion is the assurance that God so loved the world.

As we saw in the last chapter, the Pauline and Johannine idea is not fundamentally different from that which governed the actions of Jesus Himself. For Him, too, the passion was not a human execution, it was the offering

[1] St. John xiv. 9. [2] 2 Cor. iv. 6.
[3] Rom. viii. 32. [4] St. John iii. 16.

G

of the needed tribulation, by one who represented God, for the sake of the Kingdom. The Pauline and Johannine theology of redemption is simply a more elaborate way of saying that Jesus was right. There are modern writers of the liberal school who deprecate the theological and dogmatic strain in the Gospels and still more in the Epistles. They would prefer to adopt St. Paul's belief that God is merciful and St. John's that He is love while leaving on one side the theories or series of pictures in which the Apostles expressed their belief that God was in Christ reconciling the world to Himself. Let us, they say, have the Apostolic religion without the Apostolic mythology. Perhaps the programme is possible. The conception that God is love appears, as a conjecture at least, in Plato ; but the difficulties suggested by the appearances of the world are so overwhelming that to most minds the conception must remain on this level, as no more than a conjecture. The ideas and images of the Apostolic Church lack, let us admit, the clearness and distinctness which we desire in metaphysical doctrines ; but after all metaphysics have not so far produced any conclusion about the universe which can be regarded as both certain and cheerful. If, driven by the impulse to identify the highest value with the supreme Reality, we would adhere to the faith that love is ultimate, we seem to be confronted with two alternatives. On the one hand, we might suppose that the world with its appearances of evil, failure, and cruelty is an illusion, the origin of which must be problematical : or on the other hand, if we are not willing to make this astonishing and really useless denial of reality to what seems most real, we may suppose that the world, clearly permeated by evil and in opposition to the expectations which we should form concerning a creation of love, is no illusion ; it really exists, created by God yet now alienated ; but we might add, the Living God by an act of sacrificial love has undertaken the salvation of this world. In contemplating this act we are assured that God is love, and reach a faith which in very truth overcomes the appearances of the world. Such was the position of the Apostolic Church. It is mythological and dogmatic, neither scientific nor philosophical ; whether it is less logical than that of those who would believe that God is love without believing that God is in Christ is open to question.

The Christian faith and the Christian experience of God are inextricably bound up with history. The supreme revelation of God has taken place in time : it began openly " in the fifteenth year of the reign of Tiberius Cæsar, Pontius Pilate being governor of Judæa, and Herod being tetrarch of Galilee, and his brother Philip tetrarch of the region of Ituræa and Trachonitis, and Lysanias tetrarch of Abilene, in the high priesthood of Annas and Caiaphas."[1] This elaborate dating of the opening of the ministry is one of the most significant things in the New Testament. The Christian revelation of God is not a system of truths which remain independent of the Person who enunciated them or the time in which they were first announced. The revelation is a Person who has His place in history and appears in the " fulness of time ". Thus there is implicit in the Christian experience of God a doctrine about the relation of God to history. It is not perhaps greatly different from that of the Prophets. Dr. Wildon Carr has claimed for St. Paul the distinction of being the father of the philosophy of history, and the claim is justified in that the Apostle has in the Epistle to the Romans worked out a theory of the significance of the fortunes of the Jewish race in the

[1] St. Luke iii. 1, 2.

providential plan. But the principle which St. Paul here applies to a particular problem is not new. In the vision of the Prophets events in the history of Israel manifested the judgment and the purpose of God, so that even the rise and policy of heathen nations were factors in the fulfilment of the divine purpose. Even more completely the Eschatological writings conceived the course of the world as determined by the divine Will. The relation of God to history does not seem to be, according to the New Testament, one of complete determination. Even though St. Paul uses language which can be interpreted as indicating absolute predetermination, he does not appear to think of the failure of Israel to respond to the offer of the Gospel as having been inevitable. His point is that, having occurred, it is overruled by the wisdom of God for His greater glory through the admission of the Gentiles.[1]

The relation of God to the historical process is not simply external. The realization of the divine purpose in the world is attained through the co-operation and inspiration of God. As Dr. J. K. Mozley has said : " The idea of immanence which is implied is one which derives its cogency from the belief that as God is the Creator and the Final Cause, so in the process which lies between the beginning and the consummation God is the Agent within the process, whereby its highest possibilities are made actual, and its explanation is seen to lie in the moral response to God and in the spiritual fellowship with Him which God Himself inspires. Not only ' of ' and ' to ' Him, but ' through ' Him are all things."[2] This immanence of God in the general historical course of events is one aspect of that immanence which is generally spoken of as the activity of the Spirit of God and of Christ. The Spirit who knows the things of God, bears witness with

---

[1] Rom. xi. 25–35.　　　　[2] *Doctrine of God*, pp. 91, 92.

our spirit, creates new faculties and powers, realizes in us
the higher possibilities.[1] Immanent in a supreme degree
in the believer, it is through the Spirit that the sinner
turns to the Redeemer, while at the summit it is through
Eternal Spirit[2] that the Redeemer offers His sacrifice.
The distinction which may be drawn between the in
dwelling of the Spirit and the presence of the Exalted
Christ is one which we need not dwell upon here. It may
be doubted whether St. Paul intended to make any
difference and does not use the two phrases indifferently.
The point on which we wish to insist here is clear enough.
The immanence of God is a part of the Christian experience of God. It is, however, if the phrase may be allowed,
an immanence which admits of degrees.[3] The divine
presence is within all creation, but in fullness and in
power with those who, responding to the divine initiative,
have become joined with Christ in affection and will.

To conclude a chapter on the Christian experience of
God without some reference to the doctrine of the Trinity
would be impossible, but only a few remarks can be made
here on a topic which, from another point of view, will
come before us later. The only matter with which we are
directly concerned here is the basis in the original experience and the teaching of the Church of the New Testament
for the later doctrine of the Trinity. It is sometimes said
that the trinitarian dogma is the characteristic feature
of the Christian doctrine of God. There is a sense in which
this is true. Those special features in the Christian
experience of God out of which the doctrine arose are
indeed peculiar to and form that element in Christianity
which marks it off from other religions. But of course the
doctrine itself is no part of the original gospel. The

---

[1] Rom. VIII. 16, 17.   [2] Heb. IX. 14.
[3] Cf. however p. 219 on this point.

Athanasian Creed and even the Nicene would have been strange in the ears of St. Paul and St. John. Nevertheless the experience, to preserve which the dogmas of the Incarnation and the Trinity were formulated, is plainly expressed in the New Testament, and is the spring of the propagandist energy as well as of the specific character of Christian Theism. The central point of that experience, as we have seen, is that of God in Christ reconciling the world to Himself.[1] Christ, in some way variously defined, represents and mediates the Divine life and the redemptive action of the Creator.[2] This conviction, growing out of the deepest spiritual life, is held within the framework of an uncompromising Jewish Monotheism. Moreover, through the experience of God in Christ there arose a vivid feeling of the immanence of the Divine power in human life and particularly in the fellowship of those who are called by Christ's name.[3] Thus the thought of the Spirit of God, deeply rooted in Old Testament religion, takes on an added definiteness, being now the Spirit of God and of Christ. The fullness of the Christian experience of God is summed up in the Apostolic benediction : " The grace of our Lord Jesus Christ and the love of God and the fellowship of the Holy Spirit " ;[4] it is through the favour of the Lord Jesus Christ that we know the love of God and are partakers, in full measure, in the fellowship of the Spirit.

No attempt will here be made to summarize the discussion of the Christian experience of God with which these two chapters have dealt, but we must refer in conclusion once more to the salient feature. The experience of God shown in the life and words of Jesus forms the apex of the prophetic consciousness of God. That

[1] 2 Cor. v. 19.   [2] Acts iv. 10–12 ; Rom. iii. 23–26.
[3] 2 Cor. i. 21, 22.   [4] 2 Cor. xiii. 14.

experience, as we have argued, was in its nature a development of the higher type of anthropomorphism almost exclusively in its aspect of the satisfaction of the need for a Sustainer of Values. Jesus' experience of the Heavenly Father expresses itself in the form of a concrete idealization of human personality. Abstract ideas are absent from His thought of God. But further, He thinks of Himself, under the titles of Messiah and Son of Man, as the means of the supreme intervention of God in the world. This anthropomorphism, if so it may be called, is carried further in the Apostolic religious life ; for that experience is built on the affirmation that God is the Father of the Lord Jesus Christ, and the Creator is revealed as love through the Person and work of the Redeemer. The doctrine of the Incarnation, or rather the religious attitude for which it stands, is the completion and crown of the anthropomorphic religion of the Prophets and the Messianic consciousness of Jesus.

The Christian experience of God may thus be regarded as the highest form, the logical outcome by a kind of spiritual dialectic, of that anthropomorphic tendency which we have described as the line of upward movement of the religious consciousness of the race. But this anthropomorphism in the doctrine of God is rounded off and counterbalanced by Theomorphism in the doctrine of man. " Let us make man in our image " ; the Son of Man the express image of the invisible God : upon these two conceptions turn the Christian doctrine and experience of God.

Obviously this complex of thoughts and pictures concerning the Unseen needs more than mere statement to be recognized as true. The task of fitting it into the framework of our modern world may seem to be beyond the power of the Christian thinker, and the possibility is suggested to us that a view which was tenable in the infancy of knowledge when the scientific revolution was still far off is patently absurd in the setting of the twentieth century. I am convinced that this is not the case. Doubtless details of exposition and illustrative images which were forcible in the Apostolic Age may be almost useless for our own. The faith of the New Testament may sometimes best be embodied for our age in language which is not that of the New Testament, but in essence there is no inherent incompatibility between the modern conception of the Universe and Christian experience. This thesis will be defended in subsequent chapters : but before we approach the constructive statement of the doctrine of God we must take a general view of the course which Theology has taken in grappling with the idea of God.

CHAPTER V

THE THEOLOGICAL CONCEPTION OF GOD

" WHEN ye pray say our Father : "[1] " There is joy in heaven over one sinner that repenteth " :[2] " The love of Christ constraineth us."[3] There is no need to give the source of these quotations : let us follow them with others which are not so familiar. " There is but one living and true God, everlasting, without body parts, or passions ; of infinite power, wisdom, and goodness ; the Maker and Preserver of all things both visible and invisible. And in unity of this Godhead there be three Persons, of one substance, power, and eternity." " The Holy Catholic Apostolic Roman Church believes and professes that there is one living and true God, Lord of heaven and earth, omnipotent, eternal, immense, incomprehensible, infinite in intellect and will in all perfection : who being One, Singular, Absolute, Simple, Unchangeable, Spiritual Substance is to be regarded as distinct really and in essence from the world." The first is from the Articles of Religion of the Church of England, the second from the Decrees of the Vatican Council. When we place these quotations from dogmatic formulas side by side with utterances like those with which we began this chapter we are conscious of a profound difference. It is not so much that the one class appears to contradict the other as that they belong to different mental worlds and presuppose quite different attitudes of mind. The contrast of which we are aware is, of course, that between

[1] St. Luke xi. 2.   [2] St. Luke xv. 7.   [3] 2 Cor. v. 14.

religion and theology.   All our quotations deal with the
same subject matter, they are all from documents of
authority in the Church : but there is a profound diverg-
ence in spirit.   The one group is the direct expression of
religious experience, the other an attempt to formulate
that experience in abstract terms.

We need not dwell on the obvious fact that there is a
real distinction between religion and theology, but just
as it is an error to overlook the distinction it is a mistake
to exaggerate it.   For example, we should be wrong if we
bluntly declared that whereas theology is concerned with
the reason and aims at intellectual clearness, religion, as
such, has not this concern.   We have already seen grounds
for believing that an intellectual element enters into all
religious experience.   It cannot rightly be described as
mere feeling, as Schleiermacher sometimes tended to do,
nor the satisfaction of a moral need, inducing, in Spinoza's
phrase, " obedience rather than knowledge."   All religion,
as Croce has powerfully argued, has implicit within it a
view of the world and cannot therefore be radically
distinct from philosophy.   Still less can we maintain that
there is an absolute distinction between religion and
theology.

The main purpose of the present chapter is to call
attention to some defects and difficulties in the traditional
Christian theology in its dealing with the doctrine of God.
The discussion will of necessity be somewhat general, since
we are not engaged in a historical survey, and will be
confined to those points which are specially interesting
for our purpose of the construction of a doctrine of God
in harmony with modern ways of thought.   I would,
however, expressly state that I have no sympathy with
the ignorant contempt for the queen of the sciences
which is so common at the present time.   The intelligent

man does not interpret criticism of some of the accepted theories in any other branch of knowledge as an attack upon the study itself, and it should be no reproach to theology that some of its conclusions are open to revision. And it is indeed a melancholy fact that the despisers of theology should find allies within the household of faith itself. I have even heard the opinion expressed that candidates for ordination should be encouraged to give the greater part of their time to other subjects such as modern history or even biology and should acquire some smattering of divinity at the end of their course. Perhaps those who hold this view think of the study of theology as the " getting up " of the outline of the Catholic Faith or the Protestant Religion from textbooks. That indeed is no liberal education ; but theology nobly conceived and studied is the most far-reaching of intellectual efforts, for man's thought of God concentrates in itself the history of human culture. We need at the present day not less but more and better theology. As Father Tyrrell has said : " False political and economic theories have led the way to truth at the cost of much evil that instinct and common sense would have avoided ; bad theologies have checked the spontaneous growth of religion, but the theological attempt must fail and do harm before it can succeed and do good."[1] It may be that the way is now open for a theology more fully in touch with the religious life of Christendom than was possible in previous generations.

The main function of theology is to act as an intermediary between philosophy and religion. The direct impact of science upon religion is not great, though indirectly the advance of science must produce profound effects upon statements of the faith. In general, however,

[1] *Christianity at the Cross Roads*, p. 251.

the changes of scientific theory produce their first reaction in philosophy and hence ultimately upon religious thought. For example, the idea of evolution so long as it remains a biological hypothesis comes into contact only with the less fundamental elements in the Christian system ; it raises the question of the authority and interpretation of Genesis. But when evolution is adopted as a philosophical conception and a general theory of Reality is based upon it we are confronted with problems which go to the root of our belief in God and His relation with the world. The theologian is not engaged upon precisely the same problems as the philosopher nor does he follow the same method. He starts with some data and is concerned primarily with their interpretation. He begins with a " revelation ", an experience of God which he accepts as giving the law to his thinking. But like all data and all experience it needs to be understood, to be thought out and brought into some harmonious relation with the rest of accepted truth. Knowledge, experience or data which are unconnected with the general body of our thinking are bound, in the long run, to be ineffective and transitory ; and the work of theology is not, therefore, an unnecessary exercise but a permanent need of religion itself. Without it a religion can scarcely survive. Just as a " purely spiritual " religion, in the sense of an unorganized religion, cannot hope to maintain itself as a considerable social force but must take to itself organization in order to adapt itself to its social environment, so a religious experience completely unformulated and unrationalized cannot survive as an element in human culture.

It is of course *a priori* possible that the thought of any age should be inadequate to the task of formulating the spiritual reality—the revelation—with which theology is

concerned. We. may go further and add that, if by
revelation we mean the self-disclosure of God, this
inadequacy is not only possible but certain. Nevertheless
theology has to work with the materials which are at
hand ; it must be affected by the current system of ideas
and must use them for its purpose. The main thesis of
this chapter may be stated quite simply. We are perhaps
almost too familiar with the cry that there is a need for
the restatement or the transformation of Christian
theology, and in particular that our doctrine of God needs
to be enlarged and deepened. It is usually added that the
restatement is called for by our new outlook upon the
physical universe which has arisen from the unexampled
progress of natural science. No one would be so foolish as
to question the truth in this ; but Christians appear
frequently to regard it as a regrettable necessity that our
theology should be revised. It is supposed that we should
be better off if we could remain securely fortified in the old
dogmatic fastness. I wish to suggest that this is not really
true. The theological construction has always been
inadequate, and its imperfection has been due not simply
to contradictions which may have been discovered between
it and modern knowledge, but to some more general cause.
It has never in fact succeeded in doing justice to the data
which it had to interpret.

Christian thought as a whole presents a curious
spectacle, which, so far as I know, has no parallel else-
where. It is infected by a kind of creative restlessness
which is due to a tension within itself. The cause of this
tension is the incommensurability between the religious
affirmations on the one hand—the experience which is the
centre of the Gospel—and theological statements on the
other. The New Testament itself is at once the foundation and the solvent of Christian doctrine ; the source

from which it springs and the source also of its continual refashioning.

Three elements have contributed to the structure of Christian theology. First, the element with which we have already dealt—Christian experience, loyalty and devotion to Christ and the felt assurance of the love of God through Him. This is the " given " of Christian theology, and it is being constantly renewed from generation to generation as human spirits thrill again, through the medium of the Scripture, with the creative emotion of the first days of the Christian faith. Secondly, the written word of Scripture entered into the structure of Christian doctrine as a distinct element. The Church inherited from Judaism a dogma of the verbal inspiration of the Bible which was extended to the canon of the New Testament and played in many respects a disastrous part in Christian history, nowhere more deplorable than in its influence upon the idea of God. Though to some extent the theory of a "mystical" meaning of Scripture, allowing an allegorical interpretation of passages which were difficult to reconcile with the teaching of the New Testament, mitigated the evil, it was at the expense of suggesting a mechanical and almost magical conception of revelation which even now has not wholly vanished from the Church. We must never forget that the authors of the traditional doctrine of God were, for the most part, under the dominion of the dogma of an infallible book and were therefore compelled to accommodate within their theological construction the acts and commands of the tribal deity of Israel.[1]

The third element, in which we are here chiefly interested, is the philosophical—the intellectual presuppositions

[1] See, however, a surprising statement of Agobard, quoted by R. L. Poole : *Illustrations of Mediæval Thought*, p. 46.

and concepts which have, to a considerable degree, determined the form of the theological system.

We are frequently told by such writers as Dr. Inge that Platonism is the loving nurse of Christianity, and if we mean by Christianity Christian theology, the statement is historically true. Even though we may be inclined to think that the time has now arrived when the services of the nurse can be dispensed with, not without due expressions of gratitude, we cannot deny that Platonism furnished the general conception of the universe into which the Christian message was fitted and to which it was early adapted. The attempt to enlist Plato in the service of revealed religion had already been made by Philo, who thought that he had found in the Platonic system a philosophical basis for Judaism. Within the New Testament itself there are clear traces of a mode of thought which, if not precisely Platonic, is under the influence of the same circle of ideas. The Epistle to the Hebrews, for example, is a strange mixture of Old Testament imagery interpreted in a Platonic manner. The Apologists, among early Christian writers, were naturally the foremost in claiming support for their faith from the recognized philosophical teachers of Greece, and of those there was none who in authority and profoundly religious outlook could compare with Plato. Clement of Alexandria and Origen were the teachers who pursued this line of thought in the most systematic manner. To them Christianity in its highest form was a kind of γνῶσις, or rather the γνῶσις to which all others were approximations, and in their hands the idea of God was, when properly understood, that of a *Deus philosophorum*.

The alliance of Christian thought with the more spiritual tradition in Greek philosophy was doubtless inevitable and had consequences of the greatest value. Without this

alliance the Gospel could never have commended itself
to the educated classes.   But its consequences in the
doctrine of God were perhaps not wholly admirable, and
were at least a source of confusion.   The parts of the
Platonic teaching which had entered into the current
philosophy and were adopted by the Christian Platonizers
were not those in which the philosopher speaks as an
ordinary Theist, as in the *Laws*, but those parts in which
he develops his transcendent metaphysic of the ideal
world and of the supreme idea of the Good which is
ἐπέκεινα τῆς οὐσίας.

In Neo-Platonism these aspects of Plato's thought were
partly amalgamated with Aristotle's equally transcendent metaphysic ; and in Plotinus there comes into the
world a closely compacted system of philosophy in which
the divine Source of all existence is the eternal and ineff-
able One from which there proceeds by emanation every
grade of being.   This system did not wholly originate with
Plotinus.   Its main tenets were already commonplaces
in Platonic circles when Plotinus produced his mystical
philosophy, according to which the supreme Being, the
One, is beyond knowledge so that no affirmation can be
made about it ; only in ecstasy can the human spirit
unite with it.   A conception of the nature of God which
in essentials differs hardly at all from this can be found
even in Clement of Alexandria.   For him no less than
for Plotinus God is the infinite and unnameable One,
the unthinkable who is beyond even abstract unity.
It is of course true that Clement and Origen, since they
are Christians, hold that the unknowable God has been
revealed through the Word of God and in the Person of
Jesus ; but the Christian tradition and living experience
and the philosophical concept of deity are never fused
together.   They run side by side in the thought of the

Christian Platonists like sundered streams or are mixed like oil and water never forming a real whole. If they are asked what God really is they must reply in terms of Platonic transcendence not of Christian personalism. In the words of a distinguished American writer, " God is not for Clement really the Jehovah He is represented to be in the Law and the Prophets, capable of love and sympathy and indignation, not really the Father as He was known to Jesus . . . these feelings are only attributed to him by a kind of economy in condescension to human weakness, while in fact He is eternally and absolutely *atreptos*, without motion or emotion of any sort."[1]

It is a fact of supreme moment in the history of Christian thought, that from its first appearance as a system of belief which could be accepted by reasonable and educated men, it necessarily adopted from the intellectual environment a conception of the essential nature of the Divine which is derived from a very important but still special type of philosophy, and has no direct connexion with the Hebrew and Christian experience of God. The personal or, in Dr. Schwartz's words, the " psychological " idea of God which comes from the Hebrew Bible is accompanied by the *Deus philosophorum*, the abstract concept of Deity. It is a presupposition of this philosophical conception that Deity can be defined in and for itself. The characteristic qualities of Deity are the opposite of human qualities. The Divine is the eternal in contrast with the temporal, the self-sufficient in contrast with the dependent and incomplete. God is the transcendent, self-sufficient, eternal Unity. The consequences of this transcendent conception of God, with its implication that the Divine is primarily

[1] P. E. More : *Christ the Word*, p. 72 ; cp. H. Schwartz : *der Gottesgedanke*. Teil I, pp. 153 ff.

H

that which is other than the human and temporal, are most plainly seen in the controversies concerning the Person of Christ. Beyond question the religious interest in these disputes was the supreme issue. Nothing less was at stake than the preservation of the foundation of Christian life and worship—God in Christ and redemption through the cross. We need not question that, given the problem as it was stated in the terms which were then available, the answers of the Catholic Church were right and did in fact preserve the substance of the Gospel. The problem was to find some statement of the Church's belief about Christ which would be in harmony with Monotheism. Even the most conservative historians of dogma, however, admit that the value of the decisions of the great Councils is chiefly negative.[1] They rule out solutions of the problem which would have stultified the central Christian faith and in the end would have destroyed the characteristic Christian experience, but they do not succeed in producing a really coherent doctrine of the nature of the Incarnate Word ; they state more clearly the conditions of the problem, but they do not solve it. The cause of this failure is obvious. The problem, as it presented itself to the minds of the first Christian centuries, was inherently insoluble ; for if we begin with a conception of the Divine which regards God as, in His own nature, utterly distinct, disparate from and even contradictory of humanity, no subtlety of dialectic can fuse the Divine and human together into the unity of a personal life.[2]

In the strange and powerful mind of Augustine the two streams, the Gospel of the Love of God and the Platonic conception of ultimate Reality, flowed together and

---

[1] Cp. C. Gore : *Belief in Christ*. See Chap. VII.

[2] Cp. my essay on " The Doctrine of Christ " in the *Future of Christianity*.

mingled in a manner which was to be of decisive importance for the Christian thought of the West. " Augustine," writes Mr. Hanson, " in a supreme spiritual
experience fused Platonism and Paulinism, identified as
the ground of his own spiritual being the Ultimate
Being of the Platonic-Aristotelian tradition with the God
and Father of our Lord Jesus Christ."[1] The " fusion ",
however, of which Mr. Hanson speaks was one achieved
in religious experience and by no means successfully
carried through in the region of thought. Augustine
came to Christianity from Manichæism *via* Neo-Platonism,
and his respect for Plotinus remained after he had completed the journey ; so much did he rely on the essentially
Christian nature of the new Platonism that he believed
Plotinus and his friends, had they lived a little later,
would have " changed a few words and phrases " and
become Christians.[2] Few who have read the section
of the *Enneads* which deals with " Gnosticism " will share
Augustine's belief ; and in his own system the two elements
were less harmoniously combined than he supposed.
The conception of God as creative activity which Augustine took from the Christian tradition and experience
consorted uncomfortably with the Platonic-Aristotelian
concepts. The great treatise on the Trinity shows us
the man of Christian experience and the Platonic philosopher as it were living in the same book side by side.
As the one Augustine thinks of God in terms of personality
and must conceive the Divine Life under the analogy of
self-consciousness, as the other he thinks of the Divine
as the absolutely " simple ", unmoved, and unchanging
One. When we consider Augustine as dogmatic theologian
we are constrained to agree with the dictum of Dr.

---

[1] " Mediæval Scholasticism " by R. Hanson in *Dogma in History
and Thought* (Nisbet), p. 107.   [2] W. R. Inge : *Plotinus.* Vol. I, p. 21.

Schwartz, " in Augustine all the disharmonies of the inherited idea of God resound again ". The Augustinian doctrine of God left for subsequent thinkers not a solution but a problem.[1]

The Christian doctrine of God based on the Platonic-Aristotelian philosophy reached its most systematic expression in the Scholastic theology of the thirteenth century. The movement of thought of which Bonaventura and Thomas Aquinas are the greatest representatives is one of the most considerable achievements of the human mind. Thomism, with its dual foundation of Aristotelian logic and Biblical revelation, presents us with a magnificent synthesis of material unified by a coherent metaphysical theory. It is, moreover, a system of thought which is still living and effective in the modern world, for the Roman Church has installed St. Thomas as the greatest *Doctor Ecclesiæ*, and a vigorous school of writers is engaged in defending, elaborating, and adapting his thought. Great claims are made for it as both *philosophia perennis* and the only Christian philosophy. Even the sectarian narrowness of professional philosophers has in some measure been vanquished by the weight and enthusiasm and learning of neo-Scholastic scholars such as M. Gilson and M. Maritain, and they have begun to admit that Thomism is a system which must be taken into account. Certainly no part of the Christian Church has any speculative doctrine of the divine nature which can be compared with the massive structure which Aquinas built on Aristotle and the Bible.

To criticize this body of teaching as it deserves would demand a treatise as large as the *Summa* itself. If we proceed to make some critical remarks on it and point

---

[1] H. Schwartz : *der Gottesgedanke in der Geschichte der Philosophie.* Teil I, pp. 229 ff.

out some respects in which its conception of God seems
grievously defective we must in justice make mention
of its merits. It is in intention and inspiration profoundly
Christian. It adheres to the Biblical revelation with
perhaps undiscriminating loyalty, but it does not question
the supreme authority of the life and words of Christ.
The corporate experience of the Church has entered
into its structure—perhaps again sometimes in question-
able form, since it accepts the dogmatic decisions of the
Councils without criticism. But with whatever imperfections this theology has grown up in an atmosphere
of worship, and, at least in the case of its greatest minds,
has been thought out by men whose inner life was directed
towards God as the goal of all their endeavour. It is at
the same time splendidly rationalist. In the form which
has had the imprimatur of the Roman Church, it asserts
that the existence and the fundamental attributes of God
can be demonstrated by the reason unassisted by revelation. It is magnificently insistent upon the divine transcendence. In definite antagonism to any theory that the
Divine is the order of the world, or the immanent reason,
or the qualities of value or sublimity which the world
displays, it affirms that God is " distinct really and in
essence from the world ", its Source and Creator.

The defect of this noble construction, worthy to stand
beside the cathedral of Chartres, lies still in the imperfect
coalescence of the philosophical concepts with the religious
content. The philosophy, which is in theory the preparation
for theology, in effect threatens to neutralize the doctrines
of which it should be the support. There is still the presupposition that the nature of Deity is given to us, in
principle, through the analysis of concepts which are in
the end abstractions. God is in essence the infinite First
Cause, the Pure Activity of Aristotelian metaphysics.

It is, of course, quite consistent with this standpoint that the being of God should be treated in this system before the doctrine of the Trinity and the so-called " metaphysical " attributes before the " moral ". Revelation is not for this theology an indispensable pre-requisite for the knowledge of God. On the contrary, Revelation comes to complete the knowledge which reason had by itself acquired. Doubtless Revelation is necessary that man may know the truths which concern his salvation, but not to impart the thought and disclose the reality of God. We must confess that the Scholastic doctrine of God is not in intention abstract. On the contrary, the thought of God as *Actus Purus*, the conception that in Him all " perfections " or values are realized without limit, is concrete. But the determining ideas are those of infinity, unity, simplicity, perfection—the " metaphysical attributes " which are defined as " the perfections of God considered in Himself independent of all relation with the world ".[1] Sublime audacity which elevates the created mind to assume a knowledge of God " in Himself " !

But this sublime audacity has its nemesis. The metaphysical attributes which are taken as fundamental, as giving us the nature of God " in Himself ", threaten when they are rigorously considered, to bring to nothing those qualities and acts of God which form the burden of the Christian Gospel. Unity, infinity, and perfection are the attributes of God " in Himself," and these qualities are conceived in an abstract manner so that it is assumed that we have a logically accurate notion of what in principle they mean. The two concepts of infinity and perfection are of special importance. It seems to follow from the abstract idea of infinity that all the concrete qualities of God must be different from

[1] E.g. Gaston Sortais : *Traite de Philosophie*. Tome II, p. 577.

those which we know in finite being in so great a measure that we can form no idea of them except of a negative kind. The divine Knowledge and the divine Will, being those of an unlimited Being, must be quite different from knowledge and will as they occur in our experience. But the will of God which the Prophets announced and which Jesus fulfilled was not a will unrelated with time ; it was a will concerned with events, like a human will, only holy and wise. But it is the closely related conception of " perfection " which, by its abstractly logical interpretation, has produced the strangest consequences. It seemed evident to the Scholastic writers that the meaning of perfection is capable of being accurately defined. It means, or it implies, the self-sufficient. A perfect being would be one who finds the completion of his nature in himself, whose satisfaction can neither be increased nor diminished. Closely connected with this is the idea that change must be completely foreign to the perfect Being. That which is perfect cannot change.

But a very remarkable conclusion follows from all this. We are told in the Scriptures, that God is angry with sin, that He loves the world and desires the salvation of sinners, that He spared not His own Son. The appeal of the Gospel to our hearts depends upon the belief that these expressions denote something real. We can scarcely attach any significance to them at all which does not imply that there is a need in the divine Experience, a going forth on the part of God to the creatures, a desire that they should become in full reality His children. But on the Scholastic view of the meaning of the divine Perfection nothing of this kind can be really true. There is no need in the heart of God, for His utter self-sufficiency precludes that He should require the love or the repentance of any creature to satisfy His desire.

This consequence is particularly important in connexion with the two central Christian doctrines of creation
and redemption.   The logical deduction is explicitly drawn
that the creation of the world makes no difference to God :
it cannot add to the satisfaction of the divine Experience
nor could its degeneration or annihilation diminish the
fullness of the divine bliss. All the sources of God's
perfect Life are found within His own being. We are
here far indeed from the Biblical picture of the sons of
God shouting for joy and the Creator rejoicing over
all His works. It is surely a curious result of Christian
philosophy that it should lead to a doctrine of God which,
through anxiety to preserve His real divinity, excludes
from His experience any real care for the world which
He has created. In the same way, we are precluded by
this philosophical conception of the nature of Deity from
believing that the phrases in which religion expresses
its thought about the meaning of sin and the reality of
redemption have anything more than a merely metaphorical or " economic " truth. The eternal satisfaction
and self-sufficiency of God suffers no hurt through the
sin of man, nor can it be increased by the turning again
of the prodigal and his restoration to communion with his
Creator. We are far away in this circle of ideas from the
central Christian affirmation that " there is joy in heaven
over one sinner that repenteth ".

Mr. Hanson in his eloquent and witty defence of
Scholastic theology[1] suggests, perhaps half seriously,
that the revolt of modern men against this system of
thought is due in part to the self-conceit which makes it
intolerable to think that God can do without us. Doubtless the motive is not absent, but there is a deeper and
more respectable one. This *Deus philosophorum* is not

[1] Op. cit., p. 107.

the God and Father of our Lord Jesus Christ. Those who thought out the system, in spite of their profoundly Christian experience, did not succeed in fusing the Aristotelian metaphysic with the Christian Gospel. We cannot believe in the Deity who emerges from their logic, not because He is too high but because He does not really sustain the Christian values.

We might have expected that the Reformation theologies would have produced a drastic change in theological ideas, and this expectation is to some extent fulfilled in the sphere of the doctrines of redemption, man and the Church; but the effect of the Reformation on theology in the narrow sense, on the doctrine of God, was singularly small.[1] The Reformation movement was, it is true, partly the reassertion of the mystical experience of God which had pursued its course side by side with the rationalist theology and had indeed often found a home within it. Luther in particular marks a return in experience and teaching to the living, " anthropomorphic " and " psychological " God of the Old Testament and St. Paul. Vague and incoherent as Luther's theology was, it had the signs upon it of the depths of inner struggle from which it sprang. In his chapter on the Numinous in Luther, Professor Otto has collected some remarkable passages in which the Reformer embodies an idea of God as Life and Power which is profoundly different in spirit from that of the Scholastic. But on the whole the formal theology was content to remain in the old paths. " The philosophical element in the new Scholasticism," writes Dr. Franks, (namely the doctrines of God and the world) " was practically taken over bodily from Mediævalism, and in reality presents no new growth when compared with its

[1] R. S. Franks : "Dogma in Protestant Scholasticism" in *Dogma* (Nisbet), pp. 115 ff.

predecessor. The bold speculative outlook of the Middle Ages is lost. There is no longer the same independent interest in the philosophical problems of epistemology and metaphysics in their religious application. We have merely a statement of what may be called in modern phrase ' the approved results ' of the earlier scholastic investigations, and of these alone. All is calm and cautious and dull, as compared with the vigour and freedom of the Middle Ages."[1]

The only Reformation system of theology which can claim to approximate to the originality and systematic unity of Scholasticism is that of Calvinism. Calvin was, before all else, a Biblical theologian, and his conception of God is not a rationalist one in the same degree as that of Thomas ; but he, too, has in effect taken an abstraction and treated it as constituting the essence of Deity. Calvinism is built up round the idea of sovereignty considered as a logical notion. The God of Calvinism may perhaps be less remote than the God of the Aristotelians, but He is the presiding genius of a terrific tyranny. By abstracting the concept of sovereignty or power and making God practically equivalent to this idea, Calvin really destroyed the validity of moral distinctions. He is logically bound to deduce them from the arbitrary will of God and to hold that they depend solely on that will. The issue is a practical agnosticism which in the end is more devastating than the veiled agnosticism of the Mediæval Scholastic, for it implies that God Himself is beyond values. He is not the Sustainer of Values in any intelligible sense, for they have no ground in His nature. They are the arbitrary choice of a Being who is beyond comprehension. It follows that God in Calvinist theology

---

[1] R. S. Franks : "Dogma in Protestant Scholasticism " in *Dogma* (Nisbet), p. 115.

is even more remote from human experience than in the rival systems of mediæval philosophy. Two quotations taken from Dr. J. K. Mozley's book on the Impassibility of God may suffice to illustrate this statement. Commenting on Genesis VI. Calvin writes, " The repentance which is here ascribed to God does not properly belong to Him ; that repentance cannot take place in God easily appears from this single consideration that nothing happens which is by Him unexpected or unforeseen ; the same reasoning and remark applies to what follows, that God was afflicted with grief. Certainly God is not sorrowful or sad but remains for ever like Himself in His celestial and happy repose : and yet because it could not otherwise be known how great is God's hatred and detestation of sin, therefore the Spirit accommodated Himself to our capacity." And commenting on Isaiah LXIII. : " In order to move us more powerfully and to draw us to Himself the Lord accommodated Himself to the manner of men by attributing to Himself all the affection, love, and compassion which a father can have . . . not that He can in any way endure anguish, but by a very customary figure of speech He assumes and applies to Himself human passions."[1]

Professor Pringle Pattison has summed up the matter in a passage which puts clearly one side of the truth. " The traditional idea of God may be not unfairly described as a fusion of the primitive monarchical idea with Aristotle's conception of the eternal Thinker. The two conceptions thus fused are, of course, very different ; for power which is the main constituent of the former has in the ordinary sense no place at all in Aristotle's speculative ideal, but there is common to both the idea of a self-centred life and a consequent aloofness from the

[1] *Impassibility of God,* p. 120.

world."[1] We may make two reservations. The two ideas
of which Pringle Pattison speaks have never been
" fused " : they have existed side by side ; and his summary
statement does not remind us of the fact, which we should
never forget, that the traditional doctrine of God has
been accompanied by an overtone of mystical experience
and evangelical piety flowing from the New Testament,
which has softened the lines and neutralized, at least
partially, the mistakes of the theological systems. The
God of the simple Christian who loves Jesus has always
been greater than the theological God. The idea of deity
which we have been criticizing, says Mr. Paul Elmer
More, revives in a more subtle form an ancient heresy.
" This conception of God as seeming to have qualities
which He really has not is precisely an extension of the
docetic heresy which reduces the humanity of Christ to
mere appearance and the fact of His Incarnation to a
moral make-believe."[2]

It is worth while to point out that the Scholastic method
of approach and the Scholastic doctrine of God did
not close their career with the Reformation and Renais-
sance. We have been taught to date the beginning
of modern philosophy with Descartes ; but the writings
of Professor E. Gilson and his pupils have abundantly
shown that this division is arbitrary and misleading.
There is a continuity of thought from the Middle
Ages to Spinoza, and the system builders of the
seventeenth century were not the philosophical Mel-
chizedeks one would suppose from many textbooks of the
history of philosophy. Many of the leading ideas of the
mediæval theologians reappear in slightly modified form
as the central concepts of Descartes, Malebranche, and
Spinoza. We hear still of substance, first cause, infinity,

[1] *Idea of God*, p. 407.   [2] *Christ the Word*, p. 72.

perfection, simplicity. Why is it that the philosophical movement of the seventeenth century issued not in a transcendent idea of God but in the pantheistic system of Spinoza ? The answer to this question is both interesting in itself and significant of the real tendencies of the traditional theology. Philosophers who had shaken themselves free from ecclesiastical authority and revelation were gradually led to abandon the dogma of creation which had been already recognized by Augustine and Aquinas as singularly intractable by reason. The conception of creation, involving as it does a sphere of finite existence which is somehow outside of and distinct from the infinite Being, suggests obvious difficulties ; but it was solely this dogma of creation which maintained any ultimate distinction between God and the world. Once this has been given up the next step is to identify, as Spinoza does, God and the order of the universe, to think of the Eternal Substance as *natura naturans* and to speak of *Natura sive Deus*. It is no fancy that finds a new era of theological construction opening with Kant and taking the first great forward step with Schleiermacher. The metaphysical structure which Kant undermined in his attack on " rational theology " and " rational psychology " had seemed a necessary bulwark of the Christian life and faith, but in fact it was not so. Its *Deus philosophorum* was not the Christian God, though He had been robed in some of the majesty of Yahweh and the loving kindness of Christ. His removal from the apex of metaphysics left the way clear for a doctrine of God based upon the moral and religious consciousness.

I will try to sum up the contentions of this chapter. We have argued that the effort to form a speculative doctrine of God is necessary and that the demand for religion without theology is the cry of ignorance or despair.

The actual attempt which was made to meet this need, extending over all the Christian centuries, up to and including the seventeenth, is one of the most impressive monuments of the human intellect. No one who understands the problems which were under discussion or the human interests which were at stake could speak without reverence of this theological heritage. Yet it did not wholly succeed in its purpose. The construction which it was able to make with the material to its hand was inadequate to the Christian experience of God and even, in fact, issued in a contradiction of that experience. This partial failure cannot be attributed to lack of intellectual power on the part of those who contributed to the theological structure nor to their lack of personal acquaintance with actual religion. The fault lies rather with the intellectual tools which were available. Philosophy, as they were acquainted with it, was incapable of fulfilling the task which they imposed upon it. Created in a milieu which was not Christian, it remained in some measure alien to the Christian view of the world. From whatever causes, however, the imperfection may have arisen, it consisted in this—that the heart of the Christian Gospel was not taken up into it. It remains to ask with what hope of success we in the present age may address ourselves to the same task, and in view of changed philosophical presuppositions and enlarged knowledge approach from our standpoint the eternal problem of God.

CHAPTER VI

TRANSITION

NOTHING is more certain than that our presuppositions, outlook, everything which is included in the vague but expressive phrase " mental atmosphere ", are entirely different from those amid which the Christian belief in God grew up and reached its traditional formulation ; and we need not waste time in demonstrating an admitted fact. Yet though we are conscious that a change has occurred we do not find it easy to determine the main character of the contrast which we feel. There are no instruments of precision to gauge the variations of intellectual climate. But if we hope to present the Christian doctrine of God in a form which will appear reasonable to the " modern mind " we must arrive at some general view of the tendencies which are native to that mind. To study the modern mind and pay great attention to its questions, axioms, and convictions, is not, as is sometimes suggested, to attribute infallibility to it or even to imply that it is in every point superior to previous generations, but only to assume that it is a mind and happens to be the mind of the age in which we live. It is my own opinion that the present period of intellectual development will rank in history as one of the most important and that it will be found that even the confusions of the mind of the age contained the germs of a great advance in insight. In any case, the Christian idea of God is scarcely likely to be the creed of the future if its defenders feel obliged to ignore or minimize every acquisition of new knowledge.

In our previous chapter we distinguished three factors which have contributed to the traditional theological conception of God, the authority of Scripture, religious experience, and the philosophical theories which formed the intellectual background. It will be convenient to consider these three factors in our present inquiry, the first two very shortly and the third at somewhat greater length.

The persisting Christian experience may be described as the ultimate datum for the Christian thinker ; and this factor more than any other manifestly possesses the quality of self-identity through temporal change. In the experience of men God in Christ is " the same yesterday, to-day, and for ever ". The fundamental reactions of the Christian soul in redemption, loving trust, spiritual power, worship, are constantly renewed. They are essentially the same in all Christian generations, in St. Paul's converts, in the piety of the Middle Ages, in Wesley, in the believer of to-day. When we look only at the various and embattled theologies we may wonder whether Christianity is not just a name which covers a multitude of different faiths ; but when we look at the Christian life and devotion which is behind the theologies we realize the unity, the undeniable self-identity of our religion, and we perceive that it owes this unity to the living power of the words and story of the Man of Galilee which vibrate again in the souls of men from generation to generation.

Nevertheless, this self-identical experience is not static. We can observe changes in emphasis which reflect individual temperaments, social conditions, and the general state of culture. The spiritual life of Christians at the present time has not precisely the same proportion or orientation as that either of the primitive Church or of mediæval Catholicism. The identity of the persisting experience renews itself in difference : that is the sign of its life.

Two points of difference may specially be remarked upon. First, Christian piety has been deeply affected by the results of New Testament criticism which have led to a firmer grasp of the true humanity of Jesus. The Son of Man was never wholly obscured by the dogmas which had defined His godhead. His voice always penetrated through the system of doctrine. But now more perhaps than at any other time we are able to recover the Son of Man as an authentic being who moved and spoke in the streets of Nazareth and Jerusalem. As a result we have been able better to understand the heroism of Jesus. We see Him no longer as One who enacted a rôle known beforehand, with clear sight of the triumphant end, but as One who adventured to the utmost in faith in God and God's Kingdom. Secondly, the modern world has been affected by social idealism, and this moral change has reacted upon religion. Men find in the Gospel an inspiration in the efforts for social righteousness and think of God's Kingdom in terms of progress and brother-hood. There is undoubtedly a danger in this. We have not always avoided the blasphemy of seeming to harness God to our reforming chariot, treating Him as if He were a means to an end greater than Himself instead of the end towards which all things move. In spite of this, however, we must recognize the importance of this new social note in the religious experience of the nobler spirits of our day. It has brought with it an enlargement and adapta-tion of the idea of the Kingdom of God, it has caused the motive of individual salvation to fall more into the back-ground and the thought of God in Christ as the Redeemer of the human race to occupy the foreground of our minds.

I

We may dismiss very briefly the changes which have taken place in our attitude to Scripture, because the subject has been dealt with fully by several writers, notably by Professor Dodd in his book on the Authority of the Bible in the present series. It is difficult to overestimate the profound transformation which theology has undergone through the changed conception of the nature of Scripture. Even those who read the classics of theology, whether Patristic, Mediæval, or Reformation, with respect and admiration will confess that they find themselves in a different world. The dogma of the infallible book was a presupposition for the greatest minds in Christendom. An impassible gulf separates the modern theologian from the whole past of his science. He cannot argue as his most revered predecessors argued ; their presuppositions are not his. This change of attitude towards Scripture is not due solely to the historical and literary criticism of the Bible itself but perhaps equally to the rise of the comparative study of religions, in the light of which the Bible takes its place among the sacred writings of the world. What authority, then, for the modern theologian resides in the Scripture ? Not the authority of an infallible oracle but that which resides in religious experience itself. The Old and New Testaments can claim a place of supreme importance among the data of our thought just because they contain the record of a religious experience unique in its continuity and its sustained elevation.

We are here mainly concerned with the third factor, the intellectual background in accordance with which the work of theology has to be accomplished. The constructive period of Christian theology, as we have seen, found in existence a philosophical view and an array of conceptions which, up to a point, afforded the material for a Christian philosophy. Here we must record a total difference between the present situation and that of the third and thirteenth centuries. When the intellectual horizon is scanned at the present time the most optimistic observer can find small promise of the coming of any generally accepted philosophy. I suppose that never before was it so difficult to find any theory of Reality which could claim to be the characteristic and agreed " modern philosophy ". Even the basis of constructive thought is the subject of controversy and indeed, as Professor Dewey has remarked, there is disagreement not only about solutions but about the problems which have to be solved. Only the most self-confident dogmatist could assert that his particular philosophy was the modern metaphysic.

And yet, it will be said, there is a generally accepted body of knowledge which stands for the modern world as solid and unquestionable as the logic and metaphysic of Aristotle stood for the later Middle Ages. Natural Science answers to this description ; and we are well accustomed to the contrast which is drawn between scientific knowledge on the one hand and philosophy and theology on the other. The former, it is pointed out, furnishes us with a system of truth which is certain, constantly enlarging, never receding, while the latter gives us nothing but vague and fluctuating speculations which repeat themselves in somewhat modified forms but have within them no principle of progress.

It would, of course, be foolish to deny that the growth of physical science and, still more, the triumphs of scientific method are the distinguishing feature of our modern civilization and constitute, both practically and intellectually, its chief difference from all previous periods. This growing body of knowledge about the world really exists, and the successful application of the scientific method is a fact. More important than the results of scientific research is the influence of the scientific method and the changed view which it brings of the ideal of knowledge. It carries with it an alteration in the conception of the nature of truth as well as of the way to reach it. Writers of very different standpoints have pointed out that the so-called ages of faith were also, in the proper sense, ages of reason.[1] The conviction was then dominant that certainty was to be attained by a process of deductive reasoning from self-evident principles. The syllogism reigned supreme, and the method of research was essentially analytical. Scientific method, on the contrary, begins not with first principles but with observed fact. First principles are the end of the inquiry not the starting-place. There is an important change to be recorded, therefore, in our natural approach to the problems of religion. We have seen that the *a priori* method of the traditional theology cannot be credited with more than a magnificent failure. The modern mind, with its training in the method of science, is prepared for a new beginning in theology, and can have no reasonable objection to our procedure if we start from the facts of religious experience and attempt to understand them. The more philosophical men of science have readily confessed that religion as a phenomenon cannot be omitted from among the facts of the world and that it may serve as the starting-point of a theory of Reality. Professor J. S. Haldane, Professor Whitehead, Professor Eddington, and Mr. Julian Huxley among others have given expression to this view, and though we may think their conclusions inadequate we can but approve of their method.

At the same time, we must accept with caution the picture drawn by popular writers of the resistless march

[1] E.g. Mr. G. K. Chesterton and Professor A. N. Whitehead.

of science contrasted with the variable opinions of philosophy. A moment's reflection is sufficient to show that the image of the unwavering advance of a conquering army into the unknown is an undue simplification of the real position. The progress of science is not exactly like that. Professor Eddington has used the illustration of a jig-saw puzzle where we succeed in fitting more and more pieces into the pattern. Professor Eddington himself would be the first to admit that the analogy is imperfect. The puzzle is alive. Every great scientific advance produces a thorough modification in the whole body of existing knowledge. We may illustrate this by the case of the introduction of the concept of evolution. Applied at first within the sphere of biology, it has passed into other departments of investigation, so that there is no branch of natural or moral science which has not been radically modified by its influence. Doubtless the principle of relativity is destined to have similar far-reaching consequences. Thus it appears that the scientific view of the physical universe is a body of thought which grows in the proper sense of the word, not by accretion but like an organism, undergoing from time to time transformation as a whole.

A more penetrating glance at the intellectual conditions of the time will, however, disclose a fact which is probably more significant for the future than the obvious influence of scientific method. It is remarkable that the period which has seen some of the most astounding successes of science has seen also doubts about the ultimate validity of scientific truth, which have been raised within the circle of science itself. The limits of scientific method are beginning to be recognized, and we have the conclusion suggested that by its nature it can never lead us to anything but a symbolical interpretation. It is governed

by the ideal of precise description and reduction to
calculable terms and necessarily seeks to reduce reality
to those aspects which lend themselves to mathematical
treatment.   Thus it is impelled to conceive the universe
as expressible in equations, or to use Professor Eddington's
phrase, " a series of pointer readings ".   In so far as the
rigidly scientific method can be applied to mind, a scientific
psychology will necessarily find mechanism there too.
It follows, however, that science by itself can never
lead us to the Reality which we are most concerned
to know ; it can never reveal to us Reality in its concrete being, discover the Soul of the world or indicate
any animating principle within it which gives it meaning
and value.

Further, we must observe a growing scepticism concerning the objective validity of the categories which science
employs.   Can we even be sure that the uniformities
which we find in nature are really there and have not been
imposed upon it by our mind ?   This doubt, formerly
dismissed as the logomachy of useless metaphysicians,
now appears in writers whose sole aim is to consider
the foundations of science.   It would be easy to multiply
references.   Two may suffice.   Mr. Bertrand Russell in
his recent work, the *Analysis of Matter*, asserts that it is
even probable that the universal " reign of law " of which
we have heard so much is nothing but a fiction of the mind,
a convenient make-believe.[1]   Thus David Hume at last
takes his revenge.   A similar view has been more tenta-
tively stated by Professor Eddington.   " Mind exalts
the permanent and ignores the transitory, and it appears
from the mathematical study of relations that the only way
in which mind can achieve its object is by picking out
some particular quality as a permanent substance of the

---

[1] *Analysis of Matter*, pp. 236, 237.

perceptual world, partitioning a perceptual time and space for it to be permanent in, and as a necessary consequence of this ' Hobson's Choice ' the laws of gravitation and mechanics have to be obeyed. Is it too much to say that the mind's search for permanence has created the world of physics so that the world we perceive around us could scarcely have been other than it is ? "[1]

We may, I think, sum up the tendency of the modern mind by saying that it is being forced, even against its will, to take up again the old problems of philosophy in a new form and from a new angle. Though natural science has produced a permanent revolution in our thought, it is becoming plainly inadequate for any solution of ultimate problems or to provide a world-view. Theology must still seek for some philosophical ally, though it will be a philosophy which has absorbed the results of science.[2]

One direct effect of the progress of physical science may be admitted. We have learnt to take more seriously the boundlessness of the universe, and the vastness of the picture which is unrolled before our mental eye is said to have given the final blow to the comfortable anthropomorphism of Christian imagination. The observation is trite and only partly true. The doctrine of God as held in the most orthodox traditional theology is not affected in the smallest degree by our new apprehension of the extent and complexity of the natural order. The attributes of infinity and " immensity " have always been ascribed to God, and no enlargement of our idea of the physical universe can be logically inconsistent with what theology has asserted about the divine Nature. On the contrary, the majesty and mystery upon which the deepest

[1] *Space, Time, Gravitation*, p. 197.
[2] For the scientific need for philosophy, see J. S. Haldane : *Philosophy and the Sciences*, especially pp. 225 ff.

theology has always insisted are enhanced to our imagination by the conclusions of research.   The chief effects of the scientific revolution upon theology are to be found rather in the ideas which we form of God's relation with men. Christian teaching has certainly thought of the creation as anthropocentric ;   man has been for it not only the highest being in the visible order but also, in some sense, the being for the sake of whom that order exists.   Contemplation of the creation as we now know it may well seem to overthrow any such scheme of things.   It does appear almost an absurdity to believe that this human race is the central and most significant element in the world. We may admit that the Christian imagination has not yet adjusted itself to the new scale of the universe.

Nevertheless it is the imagination rather than the reason which needs adjustment, for reflection shows that we put the case in a misleading and one-sided way when we dwell solely upon the extension of the physical universe. What is it that anyone could be concerned to maintain about the centrality of man in the universe ?   The question has nothing to do with spatial considerations but with the position of man in some scale of value.   We may indeed find it hard to obey the admonition of the son of Sirach, " Say not, What is my soul in a boundless creation ? "[1] but the thought is not far behind that it is the human mind which has discovered the complexity of this creation.   If there is an infinity in the object there is a corresponding infinity in the subject, and the illimitable power of thought answers to the unbounded nature of the world.   To a considering man increase of knowledge of the universe is an added confirmation of the majesty of the mind which has to some extent grasped it. Here alone, so far as we know, in the visible universe are

[1] Ecclus. xvi. 17.

there understanding and valuation. In man the cosmos begins to know itself. If science is a revelation of the majesty of the world it is, at the same time, a revelation of the majesty of man.

The theory of relativity suggests that the physical universe is not, in fact, infinite and has destroyed the older presupposition of absolute space and time. The universe infinitely extended in space and time is probably, it would affirm, a mental construction made for practical purposes out of the space-time systems of experience. Dr. Wildon Carr has pointed out with, I think, irresistible cogency that the relativity theory issues in a dramatic reinstatement of the human mind at the centre. " The old material constitution is gone. The space-time framework is relative not absolute. What then is fundamental ? What is absolute ? What is the pivotal fact on which the whole conception revolves ? Clearly the central basic fact in the new conception, the fact on which everything depends and from which the whole scientific construction is reared, is the observer attached to his system of reference and for whom that system is at rest, not a disinterested observer contemplating an outside reality, but an observer who must co-ordinate the phenomena of nature for himself as the necessary condition of his active participation in reality. The principle of relativity and the new scientific concept of the universe starts from this and reverts to it."[1]

We have already passed the border of philosophy ; and we must now make some attempt to estimate the tendencies of metaphysics. The strange confusion of the prospect has already been noticed, and it is evident that in such a time of transition prophecy is a more than usually gratuitous form of error. For the theologian the

[1] *Unique Status of Man,* pp. 170, 171.

position is embarrassing, since he is confronted with a task of larger reach than his predecessors. He must find the straw for his bricks. He has to settle, at least provisionally, some of the hotly debated problems of logic and metaphysics. We may forgive him if he is sometimes impatient when it is demanded that he should produce a theology in accord with the thought of the modern world, for when he asks what is the thought of the modern world a noise as of the builders of Babel answers him.

The agnostic tradition has not succumbed to the criticism of James Ward and F. H. Bradley. Does any philosophical idea ever really succumb ? It has attained a new virtue in the hands of Mr. Russell in the guise of "Neutral Monism". We shall gain no help from this in our quest for a view of reality, for it is simply Herbert Spencer's Unknowable with new trimmings.

Human knowing, and indeed all human experience, implies and contains the distinction between subject and object, the experience and the experienced, the knower and the known. A duality is thus involved in every conscious act. This dualism which runs through the whole mental and spiritual life the philosopher aims at transcending, by showing it to be comprised within a unity. Neutral Monism supposes that it has overcome dualism by the hypothesis of a reality which is neither mind nor matter, neither subject nor object. I fear that this solution takes us into the region not only of the unknowable but of the unmeaning. Apart from those who have lost themselves in the illimitable inane of the unknowable, we may classify philosophical theories on the basis of this duality of subject and object. On the one hand, those who go under the general name of Idealism have chosen to regard mind in some sense as the " stuff " of which the world is made, as the real, and to resolve the object world into perceptions, ideas, creations of mind. On the other hand, thinkers who are ranged under the banner of Naturalism have sought to build their view of Reality starting from the standpoint of the objective world.

The cleavage between these two types of thought is fundamental. They are impelled by their respective presuppositions to attack different problems, or at least to see the same problems differently and to approach them in a different order. Thus, to take an important example, to the Naturalist philosopher the problem will present itself in the phrase which is the title of Dr. Broad's book, *The Mind and its Place in Nature*, the assumption being that "nature" is given and the inquiry therefore is how to account for this very remarkable entity, mind, as one of the objects of nature. To the Idealist, however, the problem as stated by Dr. Broad appears to be wrongly put. For him the question is rather, What is nature's place in mind? Given the reality of thought, which is beyond possibility of doubt, the need arises to determine what we mean by the objective order, by "nature" as it is taken for granted by common sense and science.

Diverse as these two traditions are, the conclusions which they tend to reach are not so widely separated as we might anticipate. Dr. Bosanquet was justified in the contention of one of his last writings that there is a "meeting of extremes" in contemporary philosophy. The *rapprochement* to which he drew attention is worth careful consideration by those who wish to construct a doctrine of God which shall be in touch with modern thought.

In trying to underline the converging thought of different schools I may begin by referring to one who can never be mentioned without honour. We all remember with what fervent zeal William James argued and fulminated against what he called the "block universe", by which he understood any theory of Reality which regarded all as given and fixed, and activity, freedom, and change as illusions. Such philosophy seemed to him to be subversive of spiritual values and moral heroism. His prophecy of the coming ruin of the "block universe" has in part been fulfilled. In both the great divisions of philosophical tradition there is a gathering trend towards the affirmation of real activity, real history, real newness and value and away from the doctrine of the completed whole of which it could be said *tout est donné.*

Though James directed his polemic chiefly against the "Absolute Idealists" represented by Mr. Bradley, there was another theory which deserved his reproaches— the system of mechanistic Naturalism, which assumed the title of the "scientific" philosophy. The general idea which underlay this philosophy in all its forms was that evolution consists in the growing complexity of the arrangement and combination of primordial units according to fixed laws, and is therefore a process in which the higher finds its explanation by the lower and the end is implicit in the beginning. We have already seen that the advance of science itself has gravely damaged this "scientific philosophy". The breaking up of the space-time framework in the theory of relativity and the astonishing results of research on the constitution of matter issuing in the quantum theory have left this mechanistic "block universe" in the air. "Radio-activity", says Professor Millikan, "not only revealed for the first time a world changing, transforming itself continually even in its chemical elements, but it began to show the futility of the mechanistic pictures upon which we had set such store in the nineteenth century."[1]

The Naturalist school in philosophy has not been dissolved ; but I think we may say that it has been transformed, very largely under the influence of new views in biology. The opinion so long and strenuously advocated by Professor J. S. Haldane that life has to be explained on principles which are different from those of physics has rapidly gained ground, and the consequences are felt in metaphysical speculation. Two English thinkers in particular stand out as representing this new Naturalism —Professor S. Alexander and Professor C. Lloyd Morgan. They are definitely realist in their outlook. They take their stand in the objective world and for them, no less than for Herbert Spencer and his followers, evolution is the key to the understanding of nature. But evolution is conceived after a different fashion and no longer on mechanistic lines. We have the new concept of "emergent evolution ". The precise interpretation of this idea of emergence differs with various authors, but the general conception is adopted by Dr. Whitehead, General Smuts, Dr. McDougall, Mr. Julian Huxley, as well as by the authorities to whom we have already referred. In the next chapter I shall offer some reflections on the limitations of the idea of emergent evolution, but here we are concerned to notice simply the change which has taken place in evolutionary philosophy. Emergence is a concept introduced to account for the appearance in time of new qualities and higher types of existence.

Certainly a world of which emergence holds is not a " block universe " nor one in which *tout est donné*. Some-

---

[1] *Evolution in Science and Religion.* Yale University Press, pp. 13, 14.

thing akin to creative activity has been admitted within nature. And the speculative theories which have been based upon this new idea of evolution enhance the impression that the background of philosophical thought has radically altered since the beginning of the present century. Professor Alexander traces the development of the universe from its beginning in the inconceivably simple " stuff " of space-time to the emergence of life, mind, and spirit. There is moreover, we are told, a " nisus " in space-time which has been the motive force of the evolution so far and may be depended upon to carry the world to yet higher levels of being. We are forbidden, it is true, to describe this " nisus " as a life-force, still less are we permitted to use the word " spirit ". Indeed we are at a loss to know wherewith to compare it ; but at least we may point out that the rigid frame-work of the older naturalist theory has dissolved. Some-thing within it has been discerned which has a strange resemblance to creative activity. There is no settled and completed whole.

The Idealist tradition was represented in England when James wrote chiefly by the very great thinker, F. H. Bradley, and Dr. Bosanquet ; in America the friend and critic of James, Josiah Royce, defended with singular power and literary skill a similar standpoint. The Absolute Idealism of the end of the nineteenth century might be described as Hegelianism interpreted in the sense of Spinoza. The general outlines of the theory are familiar to all students of philosophy, and it will be sufficient here to note that for Bradley and his colleagues Reality is spiritual, it is experience. This absolute experience constitutes a perfectly harmonious and co-herent whole, which alone is, in the full sense, real. The status in reality of those types of existence which common sense regards as most certainly real is determined by their measure of coherence, that is by the degree in which they approximate to the full systematic harmony of the Absolute. All are real in their degree, but none is fully real. The salient point in this philosophy which concerns us is that all change and activity, and hence evolution and history, belong to the world of appearance : they are aspects of the Absolute but not ultimately real or true. The Absolute, as Bradley says, has no seasons. We may observe in this system of thought the reappearance of the idea which we encountered in our last chapter—the perfect cannot change. In the Absolute we find both the contrast with and the promise of satisfaction for our haunting sense of incompleteness.

Let us not seek to deny the profound appeal of this type of thought. To me at least it is obvious that it contains an insight which no philosopher who cares to meet the deepest needs of the human spirit can neglect. It has one element which is of vital importance for the religious view of the world, for this sense of incompleteness and thirst for that Other without which we can find no rest is, as we have seen, at the root of all our spiritual quest.

> O searching hands and questing feet
> And love and longing still denied,
> There is not any hour complete
> Nor any season satisfied.
>
> The running winds of Springtime call
> For culmination and repose,
> And Autumn, letting roses fall,
> Sighs for the Spring that brings the rose.[1]

The Idealistic tradition has not remained without

[1] Gerald Gould.

modification in the present generation ; and it is important
to notice that it has been modified in a manner closely
analogous to that which has overtaken Naturalism. Here,
too, the ideas of the dynamic, of activity and history, have
reasserted themselves. The Italian philosophers Croce
and Gentile are the most important representatives of the
new Idealism. The differences between them, important
as they are, do not concern us here. Both have abandoned
the static conception of the Absolute and repudiated the
" block universe ". The new Idealism is idealism in the
most uncompromising form. All is mind or thought.
We dare not, says Gentile, admit any reality other than
or over against mind, for if we do so we shall be led, in
the end, to deny the reality of mind.[1] Mind is either the
sole reality or it is not real at all. But here we come upon
the essential difference between the old and the new
Idealism. Reality, in the conviction of the later idealists,
is not passive thought, *cogitatum*, thing thought, but
cogitatio, thinking. Mind is not substance but activity.
The ultimate and indeed the sole reality is the activity of
thought. It might appear that this philosophy was
committed to the absurdity of supposing that the world
is created by the thought of the individual ; but this is
avoided, at least by Gentile, through his doctrine of the
Transcendental Ego. That Transcendental Ego is the
true subject and the only real thinker. The " empirical
egos " of common experience and social intercourse are
not really subsistent subjects, but are themselves a part of
that objective world which the Transcendental Ego, in its
activity of thought which is its being, creates. The only
thinker is the Ego which can never become object, the
" person who knows no plural ".

An important consequence of this " activist " idealism

[1] *Theory of Mind as Pure Act*, pp. 18 ff.

is the attitude taken to the conception of " nature " and the Universe. The " nature " which science postulates as the sphere of its inquiries is not an independent order of being having a real existence independent of mind ; on the contrary, it is an abstraction made for practical ends from the concrete reality of history, it is in fact a creation of thought. In the same way, the idea of the Universe, understood as a whole of existence, a completed system, is illusory. There is no whole of physical being, no whole of any kind ; no system which includes within itself " thought " and " things ". The ultimate Reality is creative thinking, which in order to be active " posits " the objective world.

It is interesting to note that Gentile himself claims that his philosophy is the Christian philosophy and that in his metaphysic there has appeared, for the first time, a speculative doctrine which can support the essential Christian experience of God. There is some ground for this assertion ; and Gentile's thought must be recognized as coming close to that type of Christian mysticism which we find in its purest form in Eckhardt and of which Fichte gave some philosophical interpretation in his later writings.[1] But it can scarcely be admitted that his philosophy, as it stands, is adequate for the construction of a genuinely Christian doctrine of God. It seems to fail the Christian theologian precisely at the point where it departs most widely from common sense. The resolution of the finite self into some very shadowy reflection or projection of the Transcendental Ego, the swallowing up of the many thinkers in the one Thinking, is plainly contrary to our *prima facie* experience. To me at least it seems that one of the most certain facts about the world is that it is experienced at different centres of

[1] Otto : *West-oestliche Mystik*, pp. 303 ff. and 237 ff.

K

consciousness and acted upon from different centres of conation. And it is equally clear that the central Christian view of God and the world is opposed to such an absorption of the finite self. The Christian religion has consistently laid stress upon the enormous importance and value of the human self as the medium indeed for the revelation of God, but as having existence for itself and, within limits, power over itself. I suggest that the cause of this difference between Gentile and a fully Christian philosophy is the absence of any definite conception of creation from his theory. "Let us make man in our own image : "[1] no thought which does not give that its full significance, maintaining both the reality of the image and the finite self's otherness with respect to God, can be completely Christian.

In this chapter we have been taking a hasty bird's-eye view of the intellectual conditions of the time so far as they have relevance to our idea of God. We have seen that the tendency within natural science itself is towards a revival of philosophical reflection on the nature of Reality. No longer do we hear the confident assertion that science will solve all our problems. The type of Naturalism which formerly assumed the designation of the scientific philosophy has been irretrievably damaged by the latest scientific developments. The state of philosophical thought does not give us any generally accepted foundation on which theology can build. The confusion of the prospect is, however, somewhat relieved when we examine the tendencies of the conflicting systems. There is a real convergence. The evolving universe in which every event was theoretically predictable given a knowledge of the conditions has no longer much support. The problems of newness and value have

[1] Gen. I. 26.

forced themselves on the attention of naturalist philosophies and the view of the evolving world which is now
suggested is very different from that of the mechanistic
Naturalism. It is one in which we can find the presence
of a creative movement—perhaps of creative life.

The Idealist philosophy, again, has moved away from
the " block universe " conception and towards the conception of mind as activity rather than substance. In all
this we may observe one prevailing current. We are
passing from static modes of thought to dynamic. The
substitution of the electron and the proton for the atom
as the unit of matter is only one instance of a change
which is exemplified in every sphere of knowledge and
speculation. To this our thought of God has to be
adjusted, or perhaps it would be truer to say, this modern
movement challenges us to recover and rethink that
belief in the living God which has always been our
inheritance. But we must not disguise the fact that
the changed view leaves us with a new problem or rather
an old problem in a new form. The question arises :
given that the world contains, or perhaps is, life, change,
process, creation of values, does there still remain the
need for a transcendent God ? Is not the process itself
the sole reality ? Is not God just the " soul of the world
dreaming on things to come " ?

CHAPTER VII

TRANSCENDENCE

IN modern discussions of Christian Theism it has come to be a commonplace that the Christian idea of God must ascribe to Him both Immanence and Transcendence. This twofold relation between God and the world is often described as the characteristic feature of the Christian conception of God, and Theism is contrasted with Pantheism on the supposition that the latter is a doctrine of pure immanence which leaves no room for transcendence. I do not question the truth of what is intended by that phrase, but the expression is not without difficulties. The habit of describing theories which have a pantheistic tendency as theories of " pure immanence " is surely due to a confusion. Any pantheistic or absolutist theory must really repudiate the notion of immanence, for immanence implies the existence of something other than the Deity or Spirit who is said to be immanent, i.e. that in which He is immanent. Hence it appears that immanence and transcendence are correlative terms and any view which holds the divine immanence in the proper sense must also hold the divine transcendence.

The idea of immanence is, of course, connected with spatial images which it is not easy to discard completely even when we admit theoretically their purely symbolical character. Probably many who use the term cannot divest themselves of the idea that by transcendence they are committed to the picture of God seated in the heavens,

above, or at any rate outside, the world. When we make
a serious effort to define the meaning of transcendence
with no reference to space we become aware that the
significance of the term is by no means so obvious as we
had imagined. Clearly we cannot think of transcendence
without thinking of something which is transcended. The
obvious answer to the question, What does God transcend ? is that He transcends the universe. But it is
obvious that the word universe is highly ambiguous. By
it we mean sometimes the whole contents of space, the
natural order regarded as a system complete in itself.
But apart from the difficulty that the real existence of
such a system is open to grave doubt, we have to
consider the obvious fact that finite minds, on most views
of the nature of mind, transcend the physical universe.
When we speak of the divine transcendence we certainly
mean that God is more than " nature ", but we mean
much more. Again, we may mean by " the universe "
the whole of being, including God. In this sense of the
word we could not say that God transcends the universe.
Or we might mean that there is a whole of being apart
from God, and if there is, clearly, by definition, God must
transcend it. But here again the assertion that there is
any whole of being apart from God may be denied and,
I think, would be denied by any intelligent theist. Since
the word " universe " covers such confusion and should
never be used without a careful definition we may be well
advised to make no use of it in attempting to describe
what we mean by transcendence.

Plainly we can consider our experience at different
levels, and at each level it seems to suggest a relative
independence of all other levels. Thus we may take
experience at the level of sense-perception, and this, considered systematically, leads us to the conception of the

realm of " nature ". Or we may take our experience as
active beings, with purpose and values ; and if we consider this deeply we are led to the conception of history.
Each of these levels seems, while we are thinking and
acting within it, to be self-contained, though in fact it is
not so. Though the life of sense-perception and the concept of nature are apparently irrelevant when we are
concerned with history and moral effort, in fact the sense-
level and nature are presupposed ; and, in the same way,
we cannot wholly abstract ourselves from our historical
situation and become completely immersed in the world
of sense-perception and natural science, for both we and
our science are parts of an historical process. The fact
remains, however, that experience does fall into segments,
phases, or levels which have a relative, though not an
absolute, independence. The immanence of God means
then that no aspect or phase, even though fully completed according to its order, could fully manifest the
Being of God. Though nature were adequately known
we should not thereby adequately know God ; though
history were finally completed and its implications understood, we should not thereby have the whole nature of
God. And correlative with this affirmation of transcendence is the affirmation of God's immanence. There is no
level or grade of being which is without the presence of
God. He is within it, not simply in the sense that He acts
upon it, as we might metaphorically say that a man is
present wherever his influence extends, but the life of
God is in each grade of being. And further, it is this
immanent life of God which furnishes the signs and
indications of transcendence.

There are two aspects of transcendence which ought to
be kept distinct from one another. On the one hand,
there is the obvious transcendence of which we are aware

when we consider the different orders or types of being.
The merely material is the basis of the higher and different
order of being—life—which, at the same time, comes out
of the material and uses the material for an instrument.
Mind again is a different order of being from the merely
living, though mind is based upon life and emerges from
it, in its turn using the living organism as its instrument.
The higher order of being—spirit—which is mind illumin-
ated by the eternal values of goodness, beauty, and truth—
is rooted in mind and grows from it, making mind in turn
its servant.   Thus there is a transcendence in every level
of being, in the sense that it tends to become something
higher than itself.   And it would follow from this that no
complete account of any order of being, save the highest,
can be given solely from within that order.   If we wish
really to know what it is, we need to know what it tends
to become and what it subserves.

But secondly, beyond this tendency to actual self-
transcendence which arises from the existence of various
orders of being and their interpenetration, transcendence
presents itself in another form.   The study of any order
of existence with a view to its comprehension reveals the
need for postulating some principles or factors which are
not themselves given as part of that order, or perhaps
more accurately are not of the nature of that aspect of
experience with which we are dealing.   For example, out
of the perceptions of sense we build the conception of an
order of nature, but that order of nature, which is sense-
perception systematized and " understood ", is no longer
just sense-perception ; universals of various kinds have
entered in and, as we shall see, nature is not intelligible
apart from super-nature.   In the same way, when we
isolate the living from the inert and deal with the phenomena of life as relatively distinct and constituting a

separate sphere of being, we find that the full understanding of life requires us to make use of conceptions
which are not drawn from the biological order but from
one which transcends it. We shall return to these points
later in the present chapter and attempt to demonstrate
their truth. Here we are concerned simply to propound
the thesis that wherever we take experience, at whatever
level we begin our investigation, we come upon transcendence and that in a twofold manner, the temporal
and the timeless ; there is an actual tendency of one level
of being to pass into another ; but this is probably only
an aspect of that more profound transcendence, through
which one order of being, even regarded as a subsistent
whole, cannot be explained on principles drawn only
from that order.

The doctrine of the divine Transcendence is, of course,
more than this. It asserts more than the fact that
existence falls into orders or levels and that the meaning
of the lower depends upon the higher. The ladder of
being by which we ascend through the orders from
matter to spirit leads, in the conviction of religion, to the
supreme Being who is the Transcendent One, beyond all
orders of being, but at the same time the One whose
presence with every order and level gives them their
existence and constitutes them into orders, and into an
order. This absolute transcendence is safeguarded and
expressed in the doctrine of Creation. All existence is
interdependent, but all existence is, in the end, dependent
upon God. Here we have the article on which belief in a
Transcendent God ultimately rests. The Creator transcends all creatures, not as being one of many or one order
among others, but as the active Will in which they take
their origin. But the idea of transcendence is also closely
associated with another conception not less vital for

genuine religion—that of the *Deus absconditus*. The absolute transcendence of God means that He is in His nature incomprehensible by our minds, and this assertion, which is a commonplace in the utterances of religious spirits of every creed, is a necessary consequence of the idea of transcendence as we have tried to analyse it. If no order of being can be fully comprehended save from the standpoint of one which is higher and more concrete, it is clear that God cannot be understood. The mystery which religion has always held to be the ultimate goal of theological inquiry is not a device for burking awkward questions. On the contrary, any doctrine of God which does not leave Him in the end the *Deus absconditus* is necessarily false. This truth, which is trite enough, is nevertheless one which we must keep steadily in mind when we are confronted with the chief paradoxes of Theism. The fact of the profoundly mysterious being of the Transcendent God has sometimes been confused with the absurd suggestion of Herbert Spencer that the ground of the universe is unknowable and may be equated with God on this account. The incomprehensibility of God is not equivalent to His unknowability. A Deity who was unknowable in the proper meaning of the word would be as useless for the purpose of religion as he would be contradictory for thought. It would be impossible to worship a being of whom we could know nothing at all, and it is unmeaning to assert the existence of a " something I know not what ". The position in which we find ourselves with respect to a transcendent Deity is, to some extent, analogous with the relation of a dog to human beings. The mind of the human being is not absolutely opaque to the dog, because the dog can, in some measure, sympathize with and do the will of the man, but a full understanding of the man is beyond the animal's power.

The dog's experience goes some of the way with the human, but not all the way.

The incomprehensibility of God, then, must be distinguished from His unknowability. But a further consequence arises from the postulate of the divine transcendence. The real knowledge of God which we possess is necessarily of a symbolical character. The divine Life, Mind, or Experience is indeed really Life, Mind, and Experience, and therefore really to be understood in terms of our life, our mind, and our experience, but not wholly understood, for it is life, mind, and experience at the level of the transcendent.

We must now proceed to consider some of the reasons for affirming the transcendence of God. The purpose of this work is not primarily apologetic, and we are not therefore directly concerned with the defence of a religious view of the world. The presupposition with which we have approached the doctrine of God is that there is some content of truth and reality in the religious experience of the human race and that the Christian experience of God is religious experience in its purest and highest form. It is a corollary of the position here adopted that the fundamental ground for belief in God is the character of human experience. The so-called " proofs " of God's existence of various kinds are, in essence, simply attempts to articulate aspects of the general consciousness of God which is present wherever the human mind rises above the level of the brute and becomes capable of general ideas, of ideals, and of the recognition of value. It follows also from this position that the divine Nature is ultimately known by the same means. The being and attributes of God must be determined in our thought by that experience of God which is the sole reason for believing in His existence. That does not mean, of course, that every kind

of religious experience must be accepted at its face value
and that we need affirm the reality of the deities or devils
which the lower religions have imagined. Enough has
been said in previous chapters on the development of the
idea of God to make it clear that our view cannot be
accused of this absurdity. But if we find that there is a
character running through all the conceptions of deity
from the most primitive to the highest, we may safely
declare that this character corresponds to a necessary
element in the religious experience itself. Such a character we find in transcendence. It is of the essence of
any God who is really worshipped that He is transcendent.
If we may refer to our analysis of the religious consciousness, it will be remembered that we found religion to
consist in the intuition of, the faith in, a response to the
self which went beyond the responsiveness on which
knowledge, morality, and art depend. The God then with
whom religion is concerned is necessarily one who transcends every level of experience.

The traditional theology in its Scholastic form relied
upon two arguments in particular which were believed to
demonstrate the existence of God apart from any reference
to revelation or, we may add, to religious experience. It
is well known that these were the Cosmological and Teleological arguments. It would be out of place here to
discuss their logical value, and it will be sufficient to
remark that few philosophers at the present day would
be willing to allow their demonstrative force. It is
obvious that they do not really proceed in the rarified
atmosphere of pure logic. But for the existence of the
historical religions and of the religious consciousness they
would never have been put forward. They assume the
existence of the idea of God as understood by religion,
and St. Thomas Aquinas reveals the necessary back-

ground on which his reasoning proceeds by the phrase
" and this all men call God " with which he concludes his
demonstrations. The arguments though not demonstrative are not devoid of force. As we have said above,
they are formulations of aspects of that transcendent
suggestion which all experience contains. The Theist
holds that the existence of God is the most reasonable
hypothesis to account for this universal aspect of the
experienced world, and the " proofs " are one of the ways
in which this aspect may be presented—an abstract and
formal way.

Both the Cosmological and the Teleological arguments
in their traditional form " prove " the existence of a
transcendent God. In the Cosmological argument we
trace the series of finite causes back to its origin in the
First Cause, who is the Uncaused Cause and the source of
every secondary cause. So presented the argument
seems to issue in the idea of God who is transcendent but
not immanent. The series of causes implies the distinctness of every cause, and therefore of the First Cause, from
all the others. A God who is the first cause in this sense
would seem to be excluded from the series except in so
far as the result of His initial action persists in them. I
do not say that this has been the inference drawn from
the argument by the orthodox theologians who have
relied upon it, and certainly it would be far from the truth
to hold that St. Thomas has no doctrine of divine immanence, but the cosmological argument, presented in
its simplest form, has been the foundation of Deism, and
not without reason. The traditional form of the Teleological argument has had the same tendency. From the
evidences of design and purpose in the world it infers the
existence of a designer or a *Gubernator*. But when the
inference is made in this abstract manner, we have the

obvious suggestion that the Divine Ruler stands outside the material which He moulds, like the artisan or the potter with his wood or clay.

Every aspect of our experience, when we attempt to understand it, has a transcendent reference, we have suggested, and gives marks of its dependence upon that which is beyond itself. We must now briefly expand this assertion. Experienced reality may be considered from the three standpoints, nature, life, and history. We must consider each of these.

The philosophy of nature has not perhaps up to the present been a fruitful branch of speculation and has often consisted in the laying down by distinguished thinkers of what on *a priori* grounds nature, in their opinion, ought to be. Recent years, however, have seen a new type of philosophy of nature which promises better things. We have remarked that the development of physics has compelled scientists themselves to raise some of the problems of philosophy in the course of their researches, and it is from the ranks of mathematicians and physicists that the new philosophies of nature are drawn. No writer among them could be better worthy of attention than Dr. A. N. Whitehead. He has clearly before him the problems of modern physics and has made a strenuous and original attempt to grapple with the meaning of nature.

The nature which consisted of a number of things in motion has long been discarded, and it is clear that if we are to have units at all they must be of a more dynamic character. In Whitehead's terminology the natural world is a complex of " concrete occasions ", of events, that is, which are of " four dimensions ", having volume and duration. But these units, as we have said, form a complex, and are thus inter-related. They do so because it is one of their characteristics to be " prehensive ".

They are somehow adjusted to, almost aware of, other events and of the general pattern or organism of which they are members. But each event has an individuality of its own. Obviously it cannot consist in prehensiveness only, for in that case there would be nothing to prehend. The special peculiarity of an event arises from the manner in which it combines in a concrete occasion " universals ", which Whitehead calls " eternal objects ", such as shape and colour. But these universals alone would not be sufficient to account for and interpret nature. We have still to explain why these concrete events happen and form a unity or inter-related whole. We are thus led to the idea of an active Source of limitation and determination which is distinct from the whole system of concrete occasions.[1]

The details of this elaborate philosophy of nature, of which the foregoing paragraph is a very imperfect summary, are not here in discussion. The point of interest is that this attempt to think out the significance of a natural order issues in a view which admits two transcendent factors. The universals or " eternal objects " are, of course, closely analogous to Plato's ideal forms and the " intelligible world " of the later Platonism ; but apart from any historical affiliations, the universals which Whitehead requires have some kind of being which is certainly not entirely within the natural order. The idea of a Deity who transcends both the " eternal objects " and the " concrete occasions " of which nature consists is not introduced by this philosopher as a concession to the religious prejudices of the ordinary person. On the contrary, without the conception of the Determiner the account of nature cannot be completed. It may well be

---

[1] *Concept of Nature ; Science in the Modern World ; Religion in the Making ;* cf. also article by A. E. Taylor, *Dublin Review*, No. 362.

that the philosophy of nature which Whitehead has given us is open to criticism and revision, and it would be, in my opinion, a mistake to build Christian theology on the particular metaphysic which he has elaborated with such impressive power. We are referring to him here as the most important contemporary example of the truth for which we are contending, that any philosophical consideration of " nature " is compelled to postulate some principle or principles which go beyond nature. Nature, whatever we may mean by that ambiguous term, is not self-explanatory.

It is well known that biology is rent at the present time by a fundamental controversy between the defenders of the older mechanistic conception and those who hold that mechanical ideas are quite inadequate even for the limited aims of science. We observed in the preceding chapter that the theory of evolution appears to be entering on a new phase and that the problems of newness and value in the process of evolution have been shown to be insoluble on the principles of the older naturalism. Consequently we have a development of " vitalism " in various forms. The conception of an immanent " life-force " is not an easy one to make definite, and it would be impossible here to examine the very various forms of the theory which have been suggested. It will perhaps be sufficient to point out that the life-force is the idea of reality which is, in some sense, transcendent : it transcends the material world in which it finds some kind of home, and also the particular living things in which it finds some kind of expression. Thus we find an English exponent of Vitalism writing : " using the language of metaphor we may say that life enters into matter, animates it and gives form and shape to its material setting. Every separate vital unit constituted in this way is a living organism ; each is the objectivation of the force of life at a different level ".[1]

The theory of emergent evolution, however, intends to avoid the transcendence which lurks in the theory of vitalism. The invocation of any power, principle, or force from outside is utterly renounced, even though that principle be not God but an " entelechy " or *élan vital*. The emergent theory distinguishes between two types of events within the process of evolution, " resultant " events and " emergent " events or qualities. The latter kind of event, as the name indicates, cannot be explained as the composition of already existing conditions, and cannot therefore be predicted before it happens, though it is, no less than a " resultant ", a natural product. "Under what I call emergent evolution stress is laid on the incoming of the new ; salient examples are afforded in the advent of life, in the advent of mind, and in the advent of reflective thought."[2]

We are all familiar with the suggestions which have been made to base the interpretation of religious experience on the emergent or the vitalistic theories of evolution. It is held that the essential element, or the permanently valuable element, in religion can be justified without the postulate of transcendence. Professor Alexander and Mr. Julian Huxley, though it would appear with some important disagreement in detail, think that the direction or *nisus* in evolution will furnish us with grounds for religious reverence.[3] According to Professor Alexander's scheme, deity is that quality which is next to emerge, that towards which the *nisus* of evolution is

---

[1] *Matter, Life and Value*, by C. E. M. Joad, p. 139.

[2] C. Lloyd Morgan : *Emergent Evolution*, p. 1.

[3] J. Huxley : *Religion without Revelation*. But I find it difficult to say exactly what Mr. Huxley means. There are, I think, two inconsistent views of religion suggested in his book.

tending ; so that we can hold that deity is, in a way, an explanation of the world-movement, though not itself as yet existing. It would be easy to indulge in satirical remarks at the expense of this version of religion ; and it must be admitted that, in some of our less exalted moods, we might find a certain attractiveness in the thought of a deity who is always a little way ahead ; we can at least be certain that we shall never meet him face to face. But this evolutionary religion does in truth satisfy one of the most important aspects of Christian experience, that which aspires towards the Kingdom of God as a condition which is not yet in being but has the most undoubted right to be.

I confess that I find it difficult to understand precisely what the religion of evolution really proposes to us as the object of our reverence. Sometimes it seems to invite our worship and aspiration towards some unknown and problematic future development of life. In that case, we may note that it is a religion of transcendence ; its object is not found within the circle of existence. The deity who is not yet in time transcends the temporal order just as definitely as the Deity who is eternal. This form of evolutionary religion is a doctrine of temporal transcendence. But probably the really powerful form of this type of religion is one which concentrates attention on the life-force or the *nisus* in evolution (in this connexion there is no real difference between the two conceptions). This is the religion of which Mr. Wells and Mr. Shaw are the prophets, and it expresses itself in the favourite phrase of the former that the life-force is " making use of him ". Here if anywhere is the religious thrill. But, with the greatest respect for a genuine spiritual experience, we may ask, What does it really come to ? If we put it at the highest, the life-force is an unconscious

L

striving. "It begins unconsciously to struggle to overcome limitations." "Moved by an instinctive impulse it surges against matter." Such are the descriptive phrases which its defenders use.[1] When we meet with a crude theology we may be forgiven a crude rejoinder. This is nothing but the revival of zoolatry. We are not unacquainted with a type of life and sentiency which " unconsciously struggles " " moved by instinctive impulse ". It is the kind of existence we suppose to be possessed by the worm. It may be doubted whether the human race will find it consonant with its dignity to worship a worm, nor do I think it will take seriously the excuse that the worm is very large.

We must, however, attempt to estimate the value of the conception of emergence apart from the somewhat absurd theologies which have been deduced from it. I wish to maintain that emergence has a great use as a descriptive formula but is quite useless as a principle of explanation. The natural order has, in fact, this emergent quality, and we are indebted to the philosophers who have insisted upon it and invented a convenient phrase to indicate it ; but to put forward " emergence " as throwing any light upon our ultimate problems is surely to miss the point. After all we cannot be deprived of the right to ask why the emergent qualities emerge. One must feel respect for Professor Alexander's " natural piety " with which he exhorts us to accept newness as a fact. But we may feel some legitimate suspicion of a piety which forbids us to ask questions, and sets up a " no thoroughfare " notice for the mind.

The concept of " emergence " is really an attempt to find some middle way between teleology and mechanism. Purely mechanistic schemes of evolution are plainly

[1] C. E. M. Joad, *op. cit.*, p. 139.

bankrupt from a philosophical point of view. They can give no plausible account of the coming into existence of really new qualities, and they have nothing intelligible to say on the subject of value. The effort is therefore made to abandon a merely materialist hypothesis and, at the same time, to keep clear of the idea of teleology. But the middle term does not really exist. In vain we seek for a *vera causa* which is neither efficient nor final. And we may easily convince ourselves that the theories of emergent evolution are teleological in implication, if we consider the writings of those philosophers who have made use of the conception. Dr. Whitehead would not, I think, deny that purposiveness finds a place in his philosophy of the natural order, as indeed the summary which we have given above sufficiently indicates. Dr. Lloyd Morgan again, though insisting upon the right to interpret phenomena in the manner of his revised " naturalism ", that is, as a complex of efficient causes, maintains also that another point of view is equally legitimate and necessary, that of a Theism for which the natural process of evolution is the expression of the Mind and Will of God. He objects only, as many theologians have done, to the idea that the divine Will is manifested in interruptions of the natural order. Dr. Alexander will, it is true, have nothing to do with the conception of purpose or teleology. But though the word may be tabooed the thought will not remain outside. For we discover that his philosophical interpretation of religion and of value rests upon the assumption that there is a " *nisus* " in evolution which has pushed on towards higher types of existence and will continue to do so. It is not clear why Alexander believes that the *nisus* will constantly behave in this satisfactory way, and he probably relies here upon an act of faith ; but the point for us is that, the *nisus* in things is the significant fact of the world in his view, and that this tendency towards value is nothing but what we mean by immanent teleology.

But reflection seems to show that immanent teleology itself is only an imperfect and provisional idea. If we try to think it out we are compelled to supplement immanent teleology by transcendent teleology ; or in other words, every teleological process implies transcendence. Consider the nature of a teleological series of events. I imagine we should agree that a teleological series differs from a non-teleological in that all the members of the series, and the series as a whole, are to some extent determined by the final event of the series, and that consequently the series, and every member of the series, are not explicable apart from the final event. If a trivial illustration may be permitted, let us suppose that I walk across the room to turn on the electric light ; then all my movements are determined by the last event, the pressing of the switch, and no movement is capable of being fully understood apart from that. If on the other hand, inspired by *joie de vivre* or some less innocent spirit, I wave my limbs about in a random manner, the last movement throws no more light on the series than any other. In short, some kind of causal connexion exists in a teleological series between the final event and all the other events in it. It would seem, however, that what does not exist cannot act, but that a teleological series implies the action of the last term before it actually comes into existence.

It needs no great discernment to perceive that we have been brought back to an old argument in a new form, or rather in a new setting. The teleological argument reappears. For it is obvious that the only way known to us in which an event can exist before it happens is as a thought in a mind. Transcendent teleology can only be interpreted in some such way. Perhaps the reader will allow himself to be reminded that we are not here attempting to outline a teleological view of the world or to deal with the numerous problems which it suggests. We are not even contending here that the events which constitute what we call the order of nature are through and through purposive. We are simply concerned to demonstrate that any satisfactory theory of nature will imply a transcendent reference. We have seen that evolution cannot even be adequately described without some concept like emergence. We have seen that emergence cannot be distinguished from immanent teleology. And we have seen that immanent teleology is itself unintelligible unless we conceive it against the background of a transcendent teleology.

We must now turn to consider briefly the aspect or level of experience which is summed up under the term history, with the same purpose as we had in view when we were discussing the philosophy of nature—to show that its interpretation involves a transcendent reference. The existence of a modern philosophical theory which explicitly denies the thesis which we are maintaining will perhaps help us to keep the debate within reasonable limits. As is well known, Signor Croce holds that history is reality and that there is no need or justification for the assertion of any Reality, spiritual or material, beyond history. If it can be shown that his view does not meet the demands of history itself we shall have a striking indication of the presence of transcendent elements within the historical process. The historical idealism of the Italian school is derived from Hegel, but it has carried the immanence of Spirit, which was a part of his doctrine, to the extreme limit. Hegel conceived the whole development of the actual universe, and particularly the course of human history, as the manifestation of Spirit through a dialectical process. But there seems no doubt that it is an essential part of his theory that the process of development is not itself the Reality. Behind and within the process is the universal Idea or Mind which realizes itself in time but does not itself have a temporal existence. "The principles of the minds of peoples in a necessary sequence of stages are themselves only moments of the one universal Mind, which elevates and completes itself in history through them into a self-comprehending totality ".[1]

The New Idealism has endeavoured to get rid of the last vestiges of the scandal of transcendence which remains in Hegel under the form of the universal Mind, and has formulated a doctrine of complete immanence. For it the historical process is the progressive life of the Spirit, and Spirit has no being beyond the process. Nor indeed is there any reality outside history, for the common view that human history takes place within a framework of " nature " which exists independently of history, is, in their opinion, an illusion no less than the belief that there is a transcendent Mind. It would be out of place here to enter into the intricate refinements of Croce's thought, but we must observe that the idealism and the opposition to transcendence of this school are both uncompromising. There is no reality which is not mind, or perhaps rather, active thinking. The idea, then, that the past exists in some manner independently of mind is untenable, and we are led to the conclusion that the past exists only as an element in the present thinking, which is the sole reality. That the past exists somehow

[1] *Philosophy of History : Werke*, 1845, IX, p. 97, quoted Reyburn : *Hegel's Ethical Theory*, p. 262.

in the present is not an unfamiliar doctrine, but so long as we hold that it has some other existence or reality as well we have still a trace of transcendence, for the past, in that case, is not wholly contained within the present activity of thought. It is therefore no wilful paradox but a necessary consequence of fundamental principles that all being of the past, as past, is denied.

Naturally Croce has said much on the writing of history and has impressively maintained that the true historian is one for whom the past becomes the living present and in whose soul the thoughts and emotions of another age " vibrate again ". But even one who accepts whole-heartedly the idealist position and holds with full conviction that there is no existence apart from mind may feel grave difficulties about this historical idealism. Perhaps most of them come to a head when we ask, What do we mean by historical truth ? I cannot see how on the theory of Croce we can avoid complete historical scepticism. We should agree, probably, that some histories are better than others, and that " better " in this connexion has some relation with " truer ". The events which are recounted are more accurately determined, more wisely selected, and more adequately interpreted. But, in Croce's view, what can these words mean ? If every attempt to write history is a revival of the past in the present consciousness of the historian, and the past has no existence outside the present consciousness, what basis is left for discriminating the relative values of rival histories of the same period ? One man's re-living of the past is as good as another's. Of course this problem of truth and error in the writing of history is only one aspect of the general problem of error, which receives very scanty attention in this theory of immanent idealism. And plainly it must be difficult to give any account of error if there is, by hypothesis, no objective reality to be known. Croce has, it is true, some remarks on error. He holds that it is due to the intrusion of practical motives into theoretical work, and consequently, we may suppose, the errors of historians are the result of preoccupation with personal or social hopes and fears. But we may ask whether this partly true remark throws any light on our real difficulty. We want to know not so much how error arises but what error is. If we are told that every opinion and every object of thought is " within the Spirit " which is always present Spirit, we are puzzled to know how there can be any difference between the true and the false.

We are led to the conclusion that this attempt to develop an idealistic philosophy of pure immanence fails in its object. Even if we allow that history is the sole concrete reality and abandon the conception of an order of nature independent of history, we find that we cannot have even history without the tacit presupposition of something which transcends history. I should agree that it is most true that we cannot have facts which are " mere facts ", and there are no events which have any existence for us in which interpretation of some kind is not inextricably mingled. A fact or an event which is entirely independent of some mind or experience is to me unintelligible. But it follows that we needs must retain some universal Mind or Experience in order to have any meaning for historical truth. Without it we are abandoned to subjectivism and caprice. It would, of course, be too hasty to infer directly from this transcendent implication of history the truth of Theism, and doubtless some views of Reality which are not Theistic can avoid the dilemma to which " historical idealism " leads ; but at least the Theistic hypothesis, simple-minded and mytho-

logical as it appears to Signor Croce to be, seems to
support our conviction that there is a real history of
the past and some meaning in describing an historical
narrative as true. Historical idealism, because it is a
doctrine of pure immanence, really destroys history :
Theism, because it is a doctrine of transcendence as well
as immanence, secures it. For the theist holds that true
history is the history which God knows, and the truest
historical narrative is that which approximates most
closely to the knowledge of the eternal Mind.

We have thus found that the proposal to treat history
as the sole existence and to eliminate from it all trans-
scendent relations is no less untenable than the similar
proposal to regard " nature " as a self-subsistent and
self-explanatory whole. We have space here only to refer
to some other lines of reflection which tend to the same
conclusion. The place and function of great personalities in the development of history is a matter of
controversy, but it would be contrary to the most obvious
facts of experience to hold that history has, in the last
resort, nothing to do with persons. Yet this is the
conclusion to which a purely immanent conception of
history is led. The historical process itself is the reality
of the world and the persons who appear within it are no
more than bubbles in the stream. " This historical web ",
writes Croce, " which is and is not the work of individuals,
constitutes the work of the universal Spirit, of which
individuals are manifestations and instruments."[1] But
it may be questioned whether even the word " instruments " is really in harmony with the doctrine of pure
immanence, for it implies a relation of transcendence
between the Spirit and the instrument. There is no point
in speaking of an instrument unless there is some distinc-

[1] *Phil. of the Practical.* Pt. I, sect. 2, chap. 5.

tion between it and the user. But in any case, a serious consideration of the place of persons in history is bound to expose the hollowness of the doctrine of immanence as held by " historical idealism ". There can be little question that an essential element of " experience as history " is that it is the experience by persons of the consequences of personal activities. A philosophy which has no ultimately significant place for persons may be very respectable on other grounds, but it is certainly not a " historical " philosophy. But when once we have admitted the reality of persons and personal activity we have broken the chain of immanence. Something transcendent to the process has been found, for if the historical process is itself, in some degree at least, the creation of persons, we cannot dissolve those persons into the historical process without remainder. However much we may allow the influence of circumstance and environment to have contributed to the content of the personal experience and to determining the nature of its action, the person is not the process by which it is influenced and on which it acts. The person transcends the history of which, in one aspect, it is a part.[1]

If the reader is not weary of the subject he may be invited to consider one further matter which throws light on the transcendent implications of history. It is not quite clear what kind of study the writing of history really is. Plainly the simple-minded belief that it is the narrative of events as they actually occurred will not take us very far. Even if there are such things as " brute facts," which may be questioned, historical writing is obviously not a description of all the facts but a selection and an interpretation. We may agree with Croce that history is not a science in the sense of a natural science.

---

[1] Cf. *The Philosophy of Personality*, by H. D. Oakeley, pp. 62 ff.

It does not discover casual laws which may be made the basis of prediction of the future. But, at the same time, history is a kind of *Wissenschaft*, not concerned therefore solely with particular events but with " universals." The writings of Professors H. Rickert and E. Troeltsch have drawn attention to the importance of values in the work of the genuine historian.[1] And this is surely true. In history we are concerned not only with the external events and their chronological order, but far more with the " spirit of the time," with that complex of value-judgments which, half-consciously, the men of the time strove to express in action and institution. The historian may indeed stop there, and when he has disclosed the ideas of value which actually prevailed leave to others the estimation of their comparative worth. But it would seem that the full task of history has not been accomplished, and it certainly has not answered the question which is in our mind, unless it goes beyond this. History is an interpretation of the past through the ideas of value which dominated its various phases. But it is always also, explicitly or implicitly, a judgment of the past, and for this reason has a practical function in the present. He who judges the past proclaims himself in that act as being in possession of some absolute standard or at least as holding that an absolute standard exists—one, that is, which transcends the passing periods.

If this view of the purpose of history is true, the thought is not far off that the writing of history involves the appeal to a Truth and Reality which are not historical. The historical process may be conceived as a many-coloured appearance in time of the Absolute Value which never in time can be perfectly expressed. Some such

[1] See Troeltsch's essay : *Moderne Geschichtsphilosophie* in *Gesammelte Schriften*. Vol. II.

conception was in the mind of one of the greatest of modern English thinkers when he wrote : " Our world and every other possible world are from one side worthless equally. As regions of mere fact and event, the bringing into being and the maintenance of temporal existence, they all alike have no value. It counts for nothing where or when such existence is taken to have its place. The difference of past and future, of dreaming and waking, of " on earth " or elsewhere, are one and all immaterial. Our life has value only because and in so far as it realizes in fact that which transcends time and existence."[1]

[1] F. H. Bradley : *Essays on Truth and Reality*, p. 468.

CHAPTER VIII

THE LIVING AND PERSONAL GOD

WE are concerned with the God who is known in the experience of religion, and primarily with the interpretation of Christian experience. The question what kind of Deity or Absolute, if any, the intellect may be led to conceive when exercised without reference to the religious life of man is not therefore our main interest. We shall not then pursue the path of the pure metaphysician, who is accustomed to approach the problem of religion and the idea of God at the end of his inquiry. We are committed to the view that the religious consciousness is of supreme significance and that the ideas of religion cannot profitably be considered except from within religion. Our first task is consequently to interrogate religion itself and make, if we can, its answer coherent and intelligible. Naturally we cannot be indifferent to the considerations and criticisms which are suggested by philosophy and science, even though we assert that the final word does not lie with them. Several results of a critical examination of religious ideas are possible. We might conceivably find that the conclusions to which we seemed to be forced by philosophical reflection were in complete opposition to those which seem to follow from a study of religious experience. Even if that were the position in which we were compelled to remain, it would not be reasonable to dismiss the religious life as based upon mere illusion. To do this would be to place a surely unwarranted confidence in the completeness of our philosophical insight and its finality. But we should be reduced to the uncomfortable expedient of admitting that there was a contradiction between two forms or aspects of our spiritual life which we could not resolve ; and we should have to abandon for the time being all attempts to present belief in the God of religion as capable of rational defence. We should be forced back upon the experience itself as the sole ground of faith in, and knowledge of, its Object.

No one would really be satisfied with such a situation, and we should still appeal to a science and philosophy " better informed ", even though we might be able to see no means of acquiring that better information. We cannot believe that, in the end, the life of the spirit is thus divided against itself. More probably we might find that our philosophical conclusions and our religious experience were not in sheer contradiction, but that the ideas of religion needed some clarification and criticism to bring them into harmony with the deliverances of the pure intelligence. In that case it would be the obvious course to enquire how far the images and symbols in which the religious mind has summed up its experience can be interpreted and modified by the reason without injury to their content of spiritual value. The one expedient which is unwarranted is to dismiss the religious consciousness as having no relation with reality and its evidence as wholly nugatory. To do that would not be, in principle, different from the procedure of a thinker who, because he could find no satisfactory proof of the reality of nature, should write down his direct experience of an objective world as no better than a dream.

I

We have then first to enquire whether religious experience, taken as a whole, bears witness to a personal God.

The ordinary man, when asked if he believed that God was personal, would probably reply that he could not see why anyone should trouble themselves about an impersonal Deity, but would immediately go on to qualify his answer by saying that, of course, God cannot be personal in precisely the same sense as we are personal. The opinions of " ordinary men " in religion and morals are worthy of more attention than they commonly receive from philosophers, for, though they may lack logical consistency, they are formed in that commerce of the life of humanity from which our data in theology and ethics must be drawn. We shall find reason to believe that the plain man is right in this question of the divine personality. His conviction that God must be personal is based upon his own religious life and what he has gathered of the religious experience of others ; but his suspicion that God must be personal in a mode different from that of human personality is also based partly on some moments of religious feeling as well as on the vague reflection that the divine Nature must be very different from ours.

Indeed the testimony of religious experience to the personality of God is not so unequivocal as our plain man might suppose. Had we chosen our witness from the Eastern races and framed our question in the form, Is the Divine personal ? We should have had perhaps a different answer. *Neti, neti,* " it is not that ", has been on the whole the reply of Indian religion to all attempts to determine the divine Nature. But apart from the influence of divergent theological traditions, there are moments of genuinely spiritual insight, which everyone would call religious but which neither suggest nor imply the presence of a personal God. States of the soul in which it comes to an overwhelming consciousness of its own nothingness in the face of the immensity of Being, the mere feeling of dependence on the infinite, are elements in any religious consciousness which has passed beyond the barbarous stage, but they do not, as such, contain the immediate suggestion of a personal response. A contemplation of the " starry heavens " may induce a religious emotion which has no tendency to evoke the thought of a Creator, nor does the religiousness of the contemplation depend necessarily on hearing the voice in "reason's ear " proclaiming, "the hand that made us is Divine ".[1]

When due allowance has been made, however, for this apparent gap in the testimony and for the fact that great religions have produced impersonal theologies, we must still maintain that the verdict of our ordinary man is justified. Clearly the conception of the nature of the religious experience which we have adopted commits us to some agreement with him. If that is in the main true, the essence of the religious situation is the intuition of a response to the human spirit which goes beyond every other type of responsiveness by reason of the fact that it is active and living. Now the highest and completest forms of living activity and the most varied powers of responsiveness are manifestly those which we call personal. If we are convinced that any God with whom we are concerned must be a living God, we shall be led of necessity

---

[1] " In reason's ear they all rejoice,
     And utter forth a glorious voice ;
     For ever singing as they shine,
     The hand that made us is Divine."

                                        J. Addison.

to think of Him as personal, for to be a person is the most adequate way of being alive.

We must recall here also that element in the religious attitude which we have ventured to indicate by the phrase "the substantiation of values." Whether the phrase be a good one or not, the fact which it is intended to describe is undeniable. Religion seeks in God the assurance that the permanent judgments of good and evil which the human mind is impelled to make have their ground in Reality. But so far as we know, no value of any kind can exist or have meaning apart from personal life and experience. Take away from the world every personal consciousness and, at a stroke, you destroy every value. At the most we could perhaps argue that the conditions would remain which would give rise to values when personal consciousness once more appeared. Moreover, the creation of values, æsthetic and moral, is in our experience the work of personal imaginations and wills. There is an abstract way of talking, much in favour at the present time, which speaks of the Eternal Values as if they had some independent existence or subsistence. This manner of speech may be useful enough for particular purposes, just as we are not wrong in forming a conception of "nature" as existing apart from mind; but the one abstraction may be as misleading as the other if it is forgotten that they are abstractions made for convenience. In fact we know neither nature apart from mind nor value apart from personality.

We must hold, therefore, that those religious states of the soul, and those expressions of devotion which do not explicitly envisage the Divine Personality, are imperfect and one-sided when taken by themselves. And this is confirmed by a study of those religions which have a non-theistic theology or philosophy as their ostensible basis.

M

The actual religion of the majority of the members of the Church or community is generally polytheistic, and even the higher types of devotion are saturated with personal imagery. Buddhism is the crux of all theories of religion, and, if we take it as it was when conceived in the mind of its Founder, it furnishes us with the example of a missionary creed which can find no place for a personal God. The religion of Gotama is founded on a nihilistic, even an atheistic, view of the world. But we must distinguish between Buddha and Buddhism. Doubtless the later developments of Buddhism, particularly in its Mahayana form, are, in many respects, a decline from the teaching of the Founder; but the transition, though ethically and philosophically perhaps a degeneration, is also a passage to religion from an ethical doctrine based upon a pessimistic psychology. The significant fact about Buddhism is that it could not remain at the standpoint of Buddha. To be a religion it was compelled by an inner necessity to have personal deities, and the veneration of the Path has been absorbed in the more personal veneration of the Redeemer who discovered it.

But here again we must be on our guard against accepting the language of devotion at its face value as evidence of the attitude of the soul and of the dominant ideas of the religion which it expresses. All prayer and adoration is full of half-conscious symbol and image. The worshipper is inevitably a poet who indicates his object rather than defines it. And the literature of devotion is, of course, full of acknowledgments of the inadequacy of all the words and pictures which it employs. Every utterance and thought of ours falls short of the Reality: this is not a conclusion of philosophy but a central conviction of the religious consciousness itself. It would not, therefore, be safe to affirm that religious experience bears witness to Divine Personality without reserve. If the idea of the " supra-personal " has any meaning, it could certainly be claimed that the religious consciousness would be, on the whole, in favour of ascribing this to God. But it is definitely opposed to the idea that supra-personal is equivalent to " impersonal ". God is at least personal ; and if the assertion of the divine Personality is an inadequate statement containing some element of illusion, it is not mere illusion but an imperfect account of that which transcends all our categories.

The Christian doctrine of God is concerned to maintain this position—that He is not less than personal, and that when we think of Him under personal terms we are not utterly misrepresenting His nature : moreover, that this personal conception is far more true and adequate than any impersonal or abstract thought. Further than this we need not go. It would be an error to suppose that the Christian faith has ever been committed to the belief that God is a person, though that belief may be quite compatible with orthodoxy. But the doctrine of the Trinity as generally interpreted is not easily reconciled with the view that the Godhead is a Person ; rather it implies that the Godhead is a unity of Persons. Nevertheless the Christian faith and the Christian experience are alike involved in the assertion that in the divine Life is the perfection of personality so that it is manifested in the Incarnation through the life of a perfect human Person.

II

So far we have been using the words " person " and " personal " as if their meaning were clear and well-known ; but we must now approach the problem of the nature of personality in order that we may consider the implications of Divine Personality and any reasons which, apart from the testimony of religious experience, may be urged in defence of this belief. Discussions of this kind usually begin with an attempt to define the word " person " and to distinguish the characteristic qualities which mark " persons " off from all other kinds of being. I will say at once that I propose to offer no definition, for the very good reason that I believe personality to be indefinable. As we shall see in the sequel, personality is that which for us is ultimately real, that from which we derive all our conceptions of reality and being, and at the same time is incapable of being an object of knowledge in the ordinary sense. It is not surprising, therefore, that all proposed definitions of personality have so far been failures. But though we cannot hope to frame a logical definition, we are not on that account precluded from all knowledge about personality. Even if we can never gain a clear concept of " person " we may have, as Berkeley phrased it, a "notion " or describe an intuition so that it may be recognized by others.

An enquirer into the nature of personality may occupy either of two points of view. He may treat the problem " objectively " and consider persons as one species of objects among the many which make up the world ; or he may adopt the " subjective " standpoint and strive to enter into the meaning of personality by reflection upon himself. The two methods are not mutually exclusive, indeed the one implies the other ; but it is obvious that we may expect to gain a deeper apprehension of personal life through consideration of our own experience than by the observation of other persons.

When we take persons as part of the world of objects, we notice at once that they belong to the class of living beings and occupy the highest segment of the scale which ranges down from man to the simplest cell. The difference between the higher and the lower members of the series of living beings may be defined in various ways, but one of the simplest and most illuminating is to follow the clue of individuality. The living being of whatever grade is an individual in a sense which is not true of any non-living material object. It may indeed be a question whether the word individual should be applied below the level of life except in a derived or metaphorical sense. But we need not enter into this discussion : it is sufficient for our purpose that the living being is distinctively an individual ; it constitutes a whole and acts as a whole through a period of time. Further, every rise in the scale of life is an increase of individuality. The dog is plainly more individual than the oyster.

But this accretion of individuality is attended by, and intimately connected with, an increase of complexity both in structure and function. From the beginning, the individual is a unity of multiplicity, a systematic whole of parts and activities. In the more completely individual beings both the complexity and the unity have grown greater. This attribute of living things, unity with complexity, is known to us first of all through their behaviour ; and even if we confine ourselves to this, we can observe a consistency of behaviour through changing circumstances, an adaptability in the pursuit of remote ends, which marks off the types at the higher end of the scale from those at the lower. But even in an objective approach to the problem, we need not confine ourselves to noting external behaviour. Though the mode of consciousness or sentience of the simpler forms of individuality may be inconceivable to us, we are aware that there is a rise in the scale of consciousness corresponding to the rise in the scale of structure and function. An inner complexity answers to the outward. And here too the same general characteristics present themselves : the higher types of individuality are unities of very complex mental elements. But when we take into account the inner aspect of individuals, we notice a quality of the more advanced types which might have escaped our attention while we confined ourselves to external behaviour. That spontaneity, that living and acting from a centre, which is present in some measure in every living being, comes to a full development in those individuals which we should call persons. They are self-conscious and self-directing, capable of modifying behaviour in accordance with general principles or judgments of value.

It is of great importance to dwell on this aspect of personal individuality, for, from the objective point of view, herein lies its primary distinction from other forms of individuality. The spontaneity of the lower forms of life is exercised within narrow limits, and the individuals who belong to these grades of being run in grooves from which they cannot escape. Their spontaneity is, to borrow Bergson's favourite word, " canalized ". Of man alone can it be said that his potentialities are without known limit. In him spontaneity has become creativity ; and, with the emergence of this new quality, we are confronted with a new type of being. Creativeness is the mark of personality. If we would see what personality is we may look at its achievements. Culture, art, civilization have been made by persons : and these creations of personal mind, which transcend the realm of nature, are sustained by persons. They live by a continual act of creative power which proceeds from innumerable persons. Take away personal life and they vanish as though they had never been.

Though we may gain indispensable insight into the

nature of personality from an objective consideration of its phenomena, we may expect that a subjective approach will offer us profounder acquaintance and more perplexing problems. The analytical type of psychology which starts from the data of introspection has much to say on this question, but has too often been misleading on account of an imperfection in its method. It has dealt with the problem of the self as if it was a mere question of analysis. It has tacitly assumed that the self is a composite existence which can be understood by discriminating the elements which compose it and exhibiting their relation with one another. In the process of this analysis the idea of a substantial " soul " or " self " which " has " its states, or is the bearer of its experiences, has disappeared, and the self has been reduced to a sum or series of states or experiences. Nor has philosophy been, on the whole, inclined to accept the real substantive being of self or soul. In the Absolute Idealism which has been, until recently, the prevailing academic philosophy in England and America, selfhood has been represented as but a passing appearance of the Absolute.[1] In spite of this converging attack, however, the plain man has found it difficult to believe that his self is a mere mental construction, and has obstinately continued to believe that he is, in some way, more real than his states of consciousness and experiences—that he has them rather than that they are he.

Recent movements of psychological enquiry seem to promise some support to this obstinate conviction. Dr. Tennant has pointed out the fallacious method involved in giving exclusive attention to the " rational aspects of personality ", such as " its capacity for fellowship " or " membership of a system of real beings ",

---

[1] Cf. Bradley, *Appearence and Reality*, second edition, p. 173.

for in this way a fundamental element of personality is overlooked. Dr. Tennant calls this neglected factor " the impervious individuality " and the " alogical core ".[1] The former phrase is perhaps sufficiently explicit, and the truth which it expresses is evident when we reflect that my experience, though it may be almost identical in content with yours, remains mine and is not in fact identical with yours. However greatly I may sympathize with your pain I do not feel it, nor can you feel mine. Persons are not, as Dr. Tennant remarks, " entirely fluid " : they have or are centres of experience. By the " alogical element " Dr. Tennant means to indicate that, at the centre of the self, there is a factor which defies intellectual analysis. But we may venture to take a further step and ask ourselves what this " core " is and why it evades our understanding. The answer which we may suggest is that the central and essential self is activity, and that movement and activity are, by their nature, beyond the grasp of the analytical intellect.

In following up this suggestion we must distinguish between the concept of self or personality and the intuition of selfhood. Psychologists have not always kept this distinction in mind, and have consequently been satisfied with an account of how the idea of self has originated, which is only part of the whole problem. James Ward in his *Principles of Psychology* insisted on the impossibility of constructing a psychology of the self without admitting a subject of experience as the essential datum.[2] Subsequent developments of psychology have confirmed Ward's view. There are signs that the reaction against the merely analytical view will go much further. An important contribution has been made to

[1] F. R. Tennant, *Philosophical Theology*, Vol. I. pp. 126, 127.
[2] *Principles of Psychology*, pp. 34–41.

the discussion by Dr. Francis Aveling in his *Psychological Approach to Reality*, which is based upon empirical and experimental investigations on the experience of the self, and has attempted to relate them to the problems of philosophy.   Dr. Aveling contends that the lived and cognized experience, from which we must set out in any philosophical construction, is always an experience of a self or " ego ".   " The primordial fact of knowing consists in the cognized experience which may be stated and only may be stated in the form of such a judgment as ' I know something '."[1] It may be expressed fully only by the formula, " I conscious of myself as feeling, willing, or knowing, know myself feeling, willing, or knowing something ".   There is always " given " in experience the central, organizing and active ego.

The importance of this view is obvious, and we must confess that it has no consensus of psychologists in its favour.   That the existence of this central, active, and organizing self is an immediate datum of conscious experience would certainly be denied by many authorities. But in this matter the decision lies with the test of introspection.   No amount of reasoning or analysis can settle the question at issue.   At the most it can show the unsatisfactory nature of theories of the self which ignore the central ego and may suggest, as Dr. Aveling has done, an explanation of the failure of many investigators to discover this fundamental intuition of the self.   It is interesting to notice that here too the psychological theory can claim the support of a philosophical school.   The denial of the " real " self on the grounds of analytical psychology finds confirmation in the philosophy of Absolute Idealism ; the affirmation of the reality of the self as given in conscious activity is in harmony with the

[1] *Op. cit.*, pp. 192–3.

" activist " Idealism of Gentile. There is indeed a remarkable and evidently independent agreement between Dr. Aveling and the Italian philosopher.

We must emphasize again the sharp distinction between the " activist " view of the self which we are defending and that conception which is current in most modern psychology. According to that theory the self grows out of prior elements, being built up: in our view from the first the central and essential element in selfhood is the real and active ego, which is continually creative. We must not, however, fall into the error of supposing that we have an intuition of the self as " substance " in the common meaning of the word. We do not have immediate acquaintance with the self as an entity which has the potentiality of knowing, feeling, and willing ; the self is known in experience always and only as activity. The self revealed in intuition must not, again, be identified with the " pure subject " which has played a great part in theories of knowledge. The real and central ego is never intuited as the mere knower, the characterless logical subject, but always as the feeling, willing, and knowing activity. Our deepest self-consciousness, then, is an immediate awareness of " the profound self which is the subject of knowledge, the bearer of feeling and the agent in willing ".[1]   It is in this self-experience that we touch the one indubitable reality from which all our conceptions of the meaning of " reality " are ultimately derived. Descartes was not wrong when he found in " cogito ergo sum " the unassailable foundation of knowledge ; but he mistook the significance of this discovery when he interpreted the knowing self as " thinking substance ". The one fundamental reality is the activity of thinking, which includes within it feeling and will.

This activist conception of the self is not put forward

[1] Aveling, *op. cit.*, p. 205.

as a substitute for the doctrines of scientific psychology. They have truth in them and can be harmonized with the conception of the organizing and moulding activity to which, as we maintain, we are led by introspection. Among the psychological conclusions concerning personality we may dwell on that which is of the highest importance. The progress of a self towards full personality is undoubtedly a process of integration, the achievement of greater coherence and unity. In other words, that activity which is the life of the self may reach a higher degree of significance and assume, as it were, the shape of an intelligible curve rather than that of an aimless zig-zag. Further, this coherence is conditioned by and dependent on the adoption of ideal ends, so that it is true to say that the personal life is pre-eminently one which has a meaning beyond that of the mere self, it stands for something in the world in a sense which would not be true of lower centres of consciousness and activity. This characteristic of personality is closely connected with another which it is no less important to keep in mind— personality is essentially social : fellowship with other persons, response to them and reaction to their activities, are, so far as we know, permanent conditions of personal life.

Analytical psychology has much to teach us on the subject of self-consciousness. Though the " deep " consciousness of the self is an immediate intuition of a constitutive activity, we have a more intellectual acquaintance with ourselves in which the self is taken as an object for knowledge and reflection. We form an idea of our self, of our character and disposition and powers. It is clear that, like all reflective knowledge, this is liable to error. The phenomenon of mistaken estimates of character and capacity formed by their possessor is sufficiently common. It is also obvious that, for discursive thought, the self is unknowable in its completeness. The " I " which is the knower, the subject, must always be distinct from the " me " which is known, the object. We are forced to admit that our idea of ourselves must always be imperfect and we cannot fully know what we are. But it does not follow from this that our self-knowledge is utterly false and valueless. The conception of ourselves which we form and reflect upon is a construction based upon the tendencies to action, the impulses, ideas, and ideals which have actually been manifested in our activity as persons ; and though it is impossible that we should know ourselves with such accuracy that we could predict certainly our mode of action in any future situation, we can at least form probable opinions concerning both ourselves and others.

There is, however, a further defect in this knowledge of self which is ineradicable from the human consciousness. The intuition of the actuality of the self as activity can never be translated into an adequate intellectual knowledge of its nature, because the " me ", which is the object of our reflection and criticism, can never be the product of the active Ego alone, and hence it can never be the representation of the real self and of nothing else. For the acts and impulses, which, retained in memory, form the data of our conception of the self are, to a large extent, to an indefinite extent, modified by circumstances which are beyond our power to influence or radically alter. In so far as our activity is determined by the environment we are debarred from a complete knowledge of ourselves. The " me " which I contemplate is not simply the creation of the Ego but the resultant of the central activity of the self modified by the circumstances in which that activity has been exercised. Personality, as we know it, is defective in this respect, that though self-knowledge is present and indeed an indispensable character of personal existence, it cannot be complete and adequate. Precisely the same line of thought will convince us that a like remark must be made about freedom. Though the creative activity of the ego is the essence of personality, that without which it could not exist, the freedom cannot in human persons be absolute, for the activity is partly determined and limited by the conditions and the environment. We are thus in a position to see that personality in its human form is imperfect, and to note the obvious suggestions which it contains of a Personality in which its limitations are removed.

III

We may now approach the personality of God with a somewhat more definite conception of the nature of the problems involved, and perhaps with a deeper appreciation of the kind of justification which may be found for the religious conviction that God is personal. The idea of God is, first, the idea of the Most Real Being. But, as we have seen, the intuition of the self is that element and moment in our experience in which we come upon that which is most unquestionably real, and that moreover from which all our concepts of reality are, in the last resort, derived. On this ground then the personality of God suggests itself as the most acceptable hypothesis. The idea of God, again, is the idea of the Source of all other beings : the Creator. But we have seen that creation is, in our experience, a distinctive mark of personal life. The conception of a Source of being suggests the hypothesis of a Personal God. The idea of God is the idea of the Ground of unity, of the Being in whom all things cohere. But personal life is the most definite form of multiplicity in unity with which we are acquainted, and on this ground it is most reasonable to think of God as personal. Moreover, personality as we know it, is a type of existence which bears on its face the promise of a greater perfection and a higher degree of individuality. From the very imperfect unities which our own selves present we are led to form the conception of a personal Life in which these imperfections have vanished. The perfect Person would be the solution of the problem of the one and the many which has haunted philosophy. This does not mean, however, that the problem is solved by the hypothesis of a personal God from the standpoint of philosophy, because, as we have seen, the concept of personality cannot be made " clear and distinct ".

Such metaphysical considerations as these powerfully support the evidence drawn from the religious and moral consciousness. We may cheerfully admit that, taken by themselves, they would not take us further than the conclusion that the hypothesis of a personal God is one for which something can be said. It is at least a tenable theory among others, and if it presents difficulties they are not more serious than those which arise in connexion with rival hypotheses. The only kind of philosopher who has no difficulties to face is the one who makes no positive statement about Reality at all. But he who sets out in the quest for Reality without any reference to the apparent testimonies of religion and morals can scarcely be supposed to be in earnest, for he is inviting gratuitous error by omitting the most significant data. If, however, we are convinced that the religious and moral experience of man is of real value, the considerations to which we have just referred will give us additional reason for adhering to that belief in a personal God which is the outcome of religion taken as a whole.

We must not dismiss the subject without some brief reference to the special objections which have been alleged against the conception of a personal Creator. Some of these are connected with the problem of evil and must be considered in a later chapter ; but there are others which arise from the nature of personality rather than from the nature of the creation. The most famous and most fundamental of the latter class is that with which Lotze grappled in a well-known passage of the *Microcosmos*. It is said that personality implies the existence of a contrast between self and not-self, the distinction between the ego and an " other ", but that it is impossible to admit any " other " or not-self when we are trying to conceive divine Personality or infinite self-hood. The view of personality to which we have been led in this discussion will allow us to reply in general to this difficulty as Lotze replied. Though the contrast between ego and non-ego is an invariable accompaniment of personality as known to us, the essential nature of personality does not and cannot consist in the contrast taken by itself. Its being is a positive activity. That this activity should find itself opposed and limited by forces or conditions which are not created by itself may therefore be, not a necessary element in personality as such, but a characteristic of human personality.

The same difficulty has been stated more recently by writers on psychology, who have pointed out that personal life seems to be possible only within an environment. Thus Dr. William Brown holds that God must be conceived as supra-personal. He cannot be properly thought of as a person in the same sense as we are persons, because He can have no environment and we cannot maintain that there is anything " outside " Him.[1]

[1] W. Brown, *Science and Personality*, pp. 224 ff.

We might perhaps add to this that the responsiveness which is characteristic of personal existence, and the capacity for fellowship, seem to imply that there must be an environment not only of impersonal reality other than the person but of other persons as well. We need the social environment as well as that of nature for our personal existence.

We must say at once that we are not concerned to defend any doctrine of the solitary personality of God, nor are we committed to the opinion that God is an infinite Person in such a sense that there can be nothing which is not, in every possible meaning of the words, " included " within Him. We are concerned to maintain the validity of creative Personality, the God on whom all things depend, not the idea of an Absolute in whom all things are. The Divine Unity, moreover, must be, in our view, a concrete unity, which means a unity of multiplicity and not a bare unitary self. In the next chapter we shall have to consider the doctrine of the Trinity ; but we must here anticipate some of the conclusions which will there be drawn. We have argued in this chapter that the quality of self-knowledge, which is, in some measure, a necessary attribute of personality, cannot be present in full measure in human persons, and that the perfect Personality of God alone can possess this quality in its completeness. In the Divine experience, and in no other experience, can the " me ", the self known, be the " express image," the adequate representation, of the " I ", the knower. But a moment's reflection will show us that we must go further. We cannot stop with the idea of the " me " (the Son) as the merely passive construction of the " I " (the Father), because such a passive object of contemplation would not be in the most complete manner the " express image " of the Contemplator. It would leave out precisely that element which constitutes the essence of self-hood and personality—that of being a centre of knowing and activity. The Son, therefore, must Himself be a centre of knowing and activity. He cannot be a passive object, but rather a living Other in whose activity the Father knows Himself. Thus we have no need to refuse the test of reciprocal activity and of responsiveness and fellowship when we are considering the Personality of God. On the contrary, our conception of God naturally leads us to think of the Divine Nature as a unity of Persons in mutual responsiveness and fellowship.

But when this has been granted we still have not entirely disposed of the difficulty that, if God is personal, there must be something " outside " Him. Let us come to grips with the general problem. Obviously, the use of images such as " outside " and " inside ", which are derived from space, are likely to be misleading unless we continually remind ourselves that they are symbols, and insist on translating the symbol into its equivalent at every turn of the discussion. There is plainly a meaning of " outside " in which no intelligent Theist could admit that there is anything " outside " God—the literal meaning. If we agreed that there could be anything " outside " God without qualification, we should find ourselves committed to the proposition that God is in space and that He is in some place and not in other places. If, however, by " outside " is meant " distinct from ", we may reasonably agree that there is something " outside God." There can be no occasion to dissent from the statement, " there are beings from which God distinguishes Himself ". This is, in fact, a necessary tenet of Theism and specially of Christian Theism, though this truth has not always been understood by Theistic philosophers. Any disguise of this distinction between God and His creatures in

N

imagined loyalty to the "infinity" of God leads straight in the direction of Pantheism. We shall maintain at length hereafter that the creation, though dependent upon God, is distinct from Him.

The contention that the creatures are distinct from God can be shown to be necessary from another point of view, when we take into account an important aspect of personality on which perhaps we have so far laid insufficient stress. The personal individual is the ethical individual. As we have seen, the unity of those active centres of consciousness which have attained the dignity of personality is conditioned by the recognition of values and the pursuit of ideals. Now the attempt to realize an ideal implies that there is some sphere of being where the ideal waits to be realized. The mind for which an ideal end has any meaning is one for which there is a contrast between the content of its own thought and some actual state of things. No doctrine of God could, of course, allow that the imperfection, the contrast with the ideal, is in the Godhead itself. It would be no less absurd than blasphemous to imagine that God is trying to become better, or that one Person within the Godhead is striving for the amelioration of another. If therefore we hold that God is personal, we are forced to the conclusion that He finds in the created world, or in the creatures, the sphere, distinct from Himself, in which His ideal ends are to be attained. Apart from that created order with its imperfection and its capacity for progress He could not be personal. Here we are concerned simply with the problem of divine Personality; but the idea which we have here tried to make clear has obviously further implications which must be reserved for our discussion of creation.

Let us try to get the difficult investigations of this

chapter into some kind of perspective. The reader may justly complain that a great deal of what has here been presented for his acceptance is highly speculative, and that the psychological portion has not behind it even a consensus of psychologists. He may be inclined to reject the whole because some parts are not clearly made out. I would at least implore him not to wait for a consensus of psychologists before making up his mind on this question : he might more hopefully look for a *consensus patrum*. The main thesis which has been defended here does not stand or fall with the more speculative arguments. It is that the Divine Being is not wrongly thought of when conceived in terms of personal life. Possibly the Godhead is best described as " supra-personal ", but impersonal categories are not admissible. They give us a false conception of the Divine, not a higher one. Though the nature of personality is not strictly definable, we have gained some notion of what personal existence implies ; and our reflections upon it have led us to a view which enables us to ascribe personality to God in a sense which is not different in kind from that in which we use the term of human persons. Only we must suppose the Divine Experience to be the sole example of personality in its completeness. Doubtless at some points in our argument there is much matter for controversy, but the main line of thought does not, I believe, rest upon assumptions which are really doubtful. Our chief business, after all, is not to arrive at a final definition of " person " but to justify and clarify the Christian experience of personal relationship with God. At the same time, I would most stoutly maintain the general accuracy of the " activist " account of the self which has been adopted in this chapter. Its importance may be more obvious as we proceed.

CHAPTER IX

THE HOLY TRINITY

THE doctrine of the Trinity is variously regarded both by opponents and defenders of Christianity. We are well acquainted with the man who dismisses the whole conception as baseless and useless speculation having no connexion with genuine religion. He is supported in his view by those theologians who urge us to return to the simple gospel of Jesus freed from the accretions of human philosophy and word spinning. But it is also frequently asserted that the idea of the Trinity is the distinctive characteristic of the Christian thought of God, and that here we find that which marks the superiority of the Christian belief in God over all others. An element of truth can be allowed to each of these opinions. It must be admitted by everyone who has the rudiments of an historical sense that the doctrine of the Trinity, as a doctrine, formed no part of the original message. St. Paul knew it not, and would have been unable to understand the meaning of the terms used in the theological formula on which the Church ultimately agreed. Judged by the strict standard of theological orthodoxy, some of his own statements would only escape the imputation of heresy on the ground that they were metaphorical or devotional utterances, or perhaps on that of " invincible ignorance ". The gospel gained its first and most decisive triumph without any formulated Trinitarian doctrine. But it is none the less true that a doctrine of the Trinity is an essential part of Christian theology now, not only in the sense that the doctrine has become historically an integral part of that complex of ideas which we call the Christian Faith, but also in the sense that it sums up and guards the specifically Christian experience of God. Though the doctrine itself cannot be found explicitly stated in the New Testament, the basis on which it was erected is there, and the thoughts which have been formulated in abstract terms in the dogma of the Trinity are implicit in the earliest Christian devotion.

We shall not here review, even in the most summary way, the Biblical evidence or the history of the development of the doctrine in the Church. Dr. Wheeler Robinson, in another book of this series, has stated the salient facts with admirable clearness and precision.[1] The older theologians delighted in finding hints and adumbrations of the Trinity in the Old Testament, many of which were without any foundation. But there were developments both in Hebrew and Greek religious thought which tended in the direction of the recognition of distinctions within the Being of God. Hebrew religion made great use of the idea of the Spirit of God. At first the idea of a Divine afflatus which was the source of remarkable human activities and powers, whether of craftsmanship or of mantic frenzy, became in the course of religious development moralized and refined ; but never within the Old Testament can the Spirit of God be said to be explicitly distinct from Jahveh. The Spirit is always the power or influence of Jahveh. The Word of God, again, has, particularly in the Wisdom literature, almost the attributes of a distinct though subordinate deity. In the

---

[1] See his *Christian Experience of the Holy Spirit*, Part III ; also Dr. K. E. Kirk's essay on " The Evolution of the Doctrine of the Trinity " in *Essays on the Trinity and the Incarnation*, edited by A. E. J. Raw inson.

same way, to the Wisdom of God is ascribed activity which, if taken literally, would be equivalent to the assertion of a second divine personality. But these and other hypostatizations of the divine attributes appear to be rather poetical and metaphorical than statements of explicit belief. The motive of reverence has had its influence on these modes of expression. Effects in the world of change and evil may be ascribed to the Word or Wisdom of God in order to avoid the suggestion of a direct contact between God in His supreme holiness and this lower sphere. But though such habits of thought and speech were a kind of preparation for trinitarian dogma and provided patristic writers with many " proof texts " from the Old Testament, it is certainly true that Christianity did not inherit a trinitarian conception of God from Judaism. In fact Christianity arrived at a trinitarian doctrine of God almost in spite of the Jewish monotheism out of which it came.

Much more plausible is the suggestion that the idea of the Trinity may have been adopted into the Christian religion from the pagan environment in which the Church grew up. The fact may be admitted that the conception of differentiation within the divine Being was familiar in the philosophical speculations of Hellenism. The theology of Plato himself is an obscure subject, into which it is not necessary to enter here, but it may be stated that his most mature reflection certainly seems to have led to the thought of a distinction within the Divine. The Creative God is not identical with the Idea of the Good, though we must remember that the latter cannot be described as in any sense personal.[1] Later Platonism came nearer to a definitely trinitarian doctrine, and in Plotinus we have something which resembles the Christian concep-

[1] See A. E. Taylor, *Plato : the Man and his Work*, pp. 489 ff.

tion in the three Principles—the One, the Reason and the World Soul. But we must observe that there are very important differences even here, which distinguish the neo-Platonic trinity from that of Christian theology. The Trinity of neo-Platonism is not an absolute one, for the principle of Nature is sometimes regarded as a fourth member of the divine hierarchy. It is, further, a Trinity which depends on the principle of emanation, so that the other Principles proceed by necessity from the One, and are inferior and dependent. The One alone is the Supreme Being ; and though the members of the neo-Platonic trinity are " coeternal " they are not " coequal." Though the speculations of later Platonism had a great influence on the statements of the Christian doctrine of the Trinity and provided some of the categories in which it was expressed, it would be far from the truth to find in philosophy the cause of its formulation or its significance. In a learned criticism of recent theories of Pagan influence on Christian dogma Dr. Kirk has shown that the prevailing tendency of thought in the early centuries of Christianity was towards the idea of two differentiations within the Divine Nature rather than three.[1]

The suggestion that the Christian doctrine of the Trinity has been borrowed from or seriously influenced by pagan religion hardly seems worthy of serious consideration. Students of the history of religion are, of course, familiar with many divine triads as well as with dyads and other numerical groupings, but there is no evidence to support the inherently improbable hypothesis that the Christian faith borrowed from the cults which it condemned. It need scarcely be added that these mythological triads are really quite different in character from

---

[1] In his essay, already referred to, in *The Trinity and the Incarnation*.

the trinitarian conception of the being of God, and have nothing more in common with it than the number three.

We may assume then that the Christian doctrine of the Trinity springs from the Christian experience of God. That is its only root, though the form in which it has been expressed has doubtless been modified by the intellectual habits of the first three centuries of our era. We have, therefore, to describe this experience and then to consider its rationalization in the terms of present-day thought. How may we interpret to ourselves the significance of this experience, and to what extent can we show that it is in harmony with reason ?

We have already briefly indicated the chief element in the religious attitude which the doctrine of the Trinity formulates and protects. It is the experience of God in Christ. As we have seen, beyond all question a Christ-centred devotion is the keynote of Apostolic Christianity.[1] Jesus, crucified and risen, is for it not only Messiah and Redeemer but the living object of adoration. Though St. Paul probably never explicitly calls Christ God, there can be no doubt that for him Christ has " the value " of God. The presence of the Living Christ as a divine and saving power is the basis of the apostolic religion. The theoretical question of the relation of Christ to God receives various answers in the New Testament, or rather many different images and ideas are employed to express the truth, which for the writers is a fact of living experience rather than an intellectual proposition. Son, Image, Logos, the Perfect Priest, these and others are " flung out " at the inexpressible reality. The doctrine of the Trinity is historically the outcome of an attempt to preserve the two essential features of Christian experience

[1] See Chap. vi.

—that God is one and that Jesus Christ is of right the object of worship, and hence neither merely human nor a demi-god.

So far the situation might have been met by a dyadic conception of God; and in fact, as has been pointed out by Dr. Wheeler Robinson, the theology of the Spirit was not thought out with anything like the consistency of the theology of the Incarnation.[1] The idea of Holy Spirit was, as we have seen, a legacy from the Jewish religion; but at the same time there were aspects of the Christian experience which led to a modification and renewed emphasis on the work of the Holy Spirit. The Spirit in the New Testament is indissolubly connected with the Church. It was the new life of fellowship in the Brotherhood, with its heightened power of ethical achievement and confidence, which ensured that the Spirit should form a part of Christian doctrine. It is well known that the New Testament doctrine of the Holy Spirit is not easy to define. St. Paul, though he certainly at times means to distinguish between the Lord and the Spirit, does not differentiate between them in any decisive manner. It is impossible, for example, to hold that there is any real difference between the significance of the two phrases " in the Lord " and " in the Spirit ". It is also doubtful whether St. Paul conceives of the Spirit as being more than an impersonal influence or power, though he uses phrases, such as " grieve not the Holy Spirit," which suggest personality.[2] Only in the Johannine writings do we find a clear distinction between the Son and the Spirit, who is presented as " another Comforter ; " but even here we must observe that the distinction seems to be bound up with time, the coming

[1] *The Christian Experience of the Holy Spirit*, pp. 1 and 2.
[2] Eph. iv. 30.

of the Spirit depending upon the going away of the Son.[1]

What elements in the Christian experience of God necessitated a trinitarian formulation of the doctrine of God's nature ? That there were such elements is beyond question in face of the historical development, and the fact that baptism at least from very early times, if not from the earliest, was in the name of the Father, Son, and Holy Spirit. Various answers have been given to this question which are not necessarily inconsistent with one another. Schleiermacher sees in the doctrine a summing up of the affirmations about Christ and His redemptive work which are implicit in the Christian consciousness : " The union of the Divine Essence with human nature, both in the personality of Christ and in the common fellowship of the Church. . . . For unless the being of God in Christ is assumed, the idea of redemption could not be thus concentrated in His Person. And unless there were such a union also in the common Spirit of the Church, the Church could not thus be the Bearer and Perpetuation of the redemption through Christ."[2] Dr. Wheeler Robinson is content to say simply that " the values of the New Testament experience are primarily those of Fatherhood, Saviourhood, and Spirithood, and the central ideas attaching to each are respectively those of creation, redemption and sanctification."[3] Dr. K. Kirk has an interesting suggestion which, in my opinion, takes us further. The Christian Gospel, he argues, emphasizes three distinct types of relation between God and Man. First, the Κύριος-δοῦλος relation : God as Creator and Lawgiver has " visited and redeemed His people ", showing Himself to be full of compassion and mercy.

[1] St. John xvi. 16 ; xvi: 7:
[2] *Christliche Glaube*, 170. 1. E.T., p. 738.
[3] *Christian Experience of the Holy Spirit*, p. 236.

Secondly, the relation of communion through Christ, in which the personal freedom and conscious choice of the individual are active. Thirdly, there remains in Christian experience something which corresponds to the Old Testament idea of possession—" a relationship in which the human spirit is wholly controlled, if not superseded, by the divine ". In the New Testament the fruits of the Spirit are moral and spiritual, though " speaking with tongues " is a spiritual gift ; but it seems clear that the experience of being lifted beyond the sphere of the conscious personal activity and carried forward by a power which was " irresistible " is well attested by the Apostolic writings.[1] If we add to this the aspect to which Schleiermacher draws attention, we shall probably do greater justice to the third " moment " in the Christian attitude towards God. The partaking of the Spirit is associated with the fellowship in the community of which the Spirit is the life.

The long debate on the doctrine of the Trinity had then as its motive the preservation and defence of the Christian gospel as it was accepted and lived from the beginning. The salient points on which the controversy turned were the unity of God, the true divinity of the Incarnate Son, the reality of grace within the fellowship of the Church. It is well known that the formula which ultimately prevailed μία οὐσία ἐν τρίσιν ὑποστάσεσιν,—One substance in three persons—was only reached at the end of much verbal confusion, and in fact the terms employed had to be given a slightly different meaning from that which they had borne before their use for this theological purpose, since both οὐσία and ὑπόστασις signified " being " or " substance ".[2] The word " person " again is one which

---

[1] Kirk, *op. cit.*, pp. 227 ff.
[2] Cf. *The Doctrine of the Incarnation*, by R. L. Ottley, pp. 572 ff.

has a somewhat indefinite meaning in the use of theologians. It is often said that the " persons " of the doctrine of the Trinity are not persons in our modern sense of the term. We have seen that the modern conception of " personality " is not perhaps easy to make definite ; and it is, of course, true that the idea of personality has been greatly developed since the fourth century, largely, as Professor C. C. J. Webb has shown,[1] under the influence of Christian theology ; but we must not exaggerate this difference between the concept " person " in ancient and in modern times. The doctrine of the Trinity does mean to assert at least that there are three distinct Beings within the unity of the Godhead, with each of whom personal relations on the part of man are possible. There is, however, a difference in approach to the conception of divine Personality which is of great importance. To us it is not natural to employ the category of "substance ", though it can be used with proper explanations. To the modern thinker the ideas of " subject " and " activity " are those which suggest themselves as the most important when we are considering personality, and therefore when we are thinking of the personality of God. Our doctrine of the Trinity will be expressed in different language and must attach itself to the conclusions of the previous chapter ; but it will be an attempt to justify the same experience of God and will be, in essence, the same doctrine.

It may, however, be objected that any speculative doctrine of the Trinity is unnecessary, and in fact precluded by the point of view which we have adopted in this book. We have based our whole discussion upon the concrete facts of religious experience as a whole and of Christian experience in particular. Must we not then be content to say that the idea of the Trinity sums up

[1] *God and Personality.*

certain important and probably permanent elements or tendencies in the Christian consciousness of God, that God is known to us as Threefold in function and yet as Unity, but that beyond this we cannot go ? To turn this doctrine from a summary of experience into an " onto-logical " dogma, to put it forward as a piece of insight into " ultimate reality ", is equivalent to presuming that we can make true statements about God in Himself apart from experience. It is passing from the firm ground of experience, and theology based on experience, into the shadow-land of metaphysics. The idea of an " economic " Trinity, which is that God appears to us as Triune but that we have no right to say more than this or to make statements about His essential being, has been held in diverse forms, some of which would be repudiated by any Christian theologian at the present time. Among these outworn thoughts we may reckon surely the so-called Sabellian heresy, that the distinctions made between Father, Son, and Holy Spirit refer to temporal phases of the activity of God in the world and thus are connected with succession in time. We have referred already to Schleiermacher's attitude towards the doctrine of the Trinity, and we must add that his view is definitely economic. The ecclesiastical formulations and explana-tions of the Trinity have for him no interest. They have no bearing upon religion. The doctrine has value simply as a concise statement of moments in the Christian experience of God.[1]

We may readily admit that the practical interests of religion depend to a very small degree on whether a man holds an " economic " or " ontological " Trinity; and it

[1] Cf. A. E. Garvie: *Christian Doctrine of the Godhead*, pp. 462 ff. I do not mean to imply that Dr. Garvie's doctrine of the Trinity is an economic one.

is certain that the overwhelming majority of Christians could not be made to understand the issue involved in the discussion. Yet it is not unimportant, for it raises the question of the nature of religious knowledge in general.

The view that the doctrine of the Trinity is *merely* economic seems to me untenable chiefly because it presupposes a distinction which most of the modern upholders of the " economic " view would reject. It takes for granted that there is a God in Himself and a God as revealed in human experience, and asserts that the former is unknowable. The position is therefore an ultimate agnosticism. It is assumed that the full knowledge of God would be that of God apart from creation, absolutely unrevealed, the solitary Absolute, and that this knowledge is, by its nature, beyond our ken for ever. But the conception of God in Himself in this sense is probably unmeaning. At least we shall argue later that creation and revelation—the going forth into " otherness " —is no accidental or arbitrary characteristic of Deity, but, of the essence of the Divine Being, so that the idea of " God in Himself " is as useless a thought as " thing in itself " or " self in itself ".

In our view, therefore, the Christian experience of God is an experience of Reality, and we are impelled to give some speculative account of it in order to show that the deliverances of the Christian consciousness are at least not contrary to reason.

The reader will perhaps remember that, in the previous chapter, we arrived at some conclusions with regard to the Divine Personality which seemed to throw light upon the conception of distinctions within the Divine Unity. To some of these we must now recur. We concluded that the Divine Self-Consciousness, or better, self-knowledge, which must be predicated if we hold the personality of

God, necessarily implied a distinction within the Divine Being. The "I" and the "me", which we are compelled to distinguish from one another in considering human self-knowledge, must have their archetype in the divine Experience. But further, we saw reason to hold that the self-knowledge of the human being must always be imperfect, since the "me" which is the object of knowledge, the passive, constructed concept of the self, derived from the memory of past thoughts, impulses, and acts, can never be the concept of that which the I has produced and of that alone. To an indefinite degree the "image" of the "I" is a distorted image. In the perfectly personal life of God this imperfection will be absent. But we need not confine ourselves to the mere statement that it must be absent ; we can see why and how this disability of human self-consciousness is transcended. The source of the disability does not exist in the case of the Divine Being. Nothing in the activity of Him who is the Creator is forced from without. God's thought of Himself, therefore, must be a completely adequate thought. We have no difficulty then in approving the proposition " In the beginning was the Thought ". God's thought of Himself is coæval with God's existence. In thinking Himself he " begets " the Son.

But we must carry this train of reflection a little further. There is another obstacle to self-knowledge in our human case. We have seen that at the centre of this self is an activity, which is not in any ordinary sense a substance or the potentiality of a substance, but just creative, formative act. This inmost reality of the self is precisely that which can never be to us an object of knowledge. We know of it by the intuition which we may have of the self in its activity. The " me " then, for us, must always lack that which is the essential condition of there being any self at all. Though in words we may state that the self is activity, as we are doing now, the actual intellectual apprehension of that activity in its concrete reality is not possible. But a perfectly self-conscious personal experience would be free from this limitation. The knowledge of self in us falls, so to speak, into two kinds of knowing, the intuitive knowing of the activity which constitutes the ego and the discursive knowing of the settled ways of acting which the ego has acquired. In God these two acts of knowing are not separate : He knows Himself fully and in one immediate act of apprehension. It follows then that the " me ", the thought of God, is not passive object but active correlated subject—the perfect Image of the Father.

It is well known that Theology has made use of two classes of analogy in order to thrown light upon the doctrine of the Trinity—that of the individual person and that of a society. The first of these has been the most common in the West and is employed by Augustine, the Father of most western Theology ; the second was used by the Cappadocian Fathers and has been revived by Dr. Tennant and others in modern times.[1] Obviously any direct application of either analogy is out of the question. The one would issue in the crudest Unitarian anthropomorphism, the other in a kind of polytheism. It is admitted that the analogies are suggestive, indicative of the line along which an understanding of the doctrine of the Trinity might lie, rather than a clear reply to our questions. If the human personality shows a multiplicity in unity, if further there are three fundamental aspects or functions included within it, then it is not absurd to hold that there is a triune nature of God ; and if again the most perfect

[1] Cf., however, F. R. Tennant, *Philosophical Theology*, Vol. II, p. 267, or Dr. Tennant's latest view.

societies known to us exhibit a multiplicity in unity, and if this unity becomes the more complete as the society becomes more perfect, there is nothing contrary to reason in supposing the divine Nature to exhibit these character-istics in the most complete manner. In a former work I noted these two possible approaches to the understanding of the Trinity as valuable but not, so far as our thought is able to go, meeting. It then appeared to me that we must hold that the two analogies are not ultimately divergent, though we could not see how they converged.[1] It now seems to me that we can go further and see that the two analogies really converge. If our argument about the nature of the divine self-knowledge is not mistaken, the thorough working out of the personal analogy leads us to the social analogy and shows itself to be coherent with it. Perhaps in the same way if we pursued the social analogy to its conclusion and thought out the implications of a perfect social whole, we should be brought to the same conclusion of the convergence of the two analogies. But of this I do not feel so sure.

That the thought of God as personal involves us in the conclusion that there are distinctions within the Godhead is arguable also from another and more general point of view. One of the most popular and most frequently used arguments for the reasonableness of the doctrine of the Trinity is derived from the love of God. If God is love, there must have been always an object of His love. In this precise form the argument does not appear conclusive, for it assumes that there was a time when there was no created object, and it involves once again the concept of God in Himself. To the present writer neither of these ideas seems satisfactory. There is surely no logical contradic-tion in the belief of the Unitarian that God is love, so

[1] Cf. *Studies in Christian Philosophy*, 2nd Ed. pp. 170 ff.

o

long as he holds that there is always some created object
of the divine love.   We may agree that the bare and solitary Absolute cannot be love ; but that would take us
only a short distance towards the Trinity.   The same
thought is perhaps better stated if we use the idea of
" responsiveness ".   Personal life, so far as we can see,
always implies the responsiveness of the person to the
environment and the response of the social environment
to the person.   Personal life grows and exists in intercourse with other persons.   The quality of that personal
life depends upon the degree of responsiveness of the individual and the quality of the social environment, chiefly
of the other persons, to which it responds.   Thus it is
conceivable that a person who had the potentialities of a
very high degree of development might remain at a
relatively low stage because there was no adequate
stimulus or response in the social environment.   A " mute
inglorious Milton " is not a Milton but, so to speak, one
half of the potentiality of a Milton.   The completely
personal being, the being in whom personal existence
achieves the highest quality, must be a being for whom
there exists a responsive object adequate to himself.   Once
again we are led to the thought of a plurality within the
unity of the Godhead, we come back again to the conception
of a reciprocal relatedness of active and conscious centres.

It has been said that no philosophical or theological
argument has ever succeeded in showing why there should
be three Persons in one God.   The reality of distinctions
within the Divine Experience may be shown to be a
tenable proposition, but no ground can be discovered
for the conclusion that these distinctions are not two or
more than three.   We must admit that the social analogy
by itself is open to this criticism and suffers from this
limitation, we must confess also that so far we have not,

in our present discussion, gone beyond the "Binitarian" idea—the real being of Father and Son. Many philosophical interpretations of the doctrine of the Trinity have professed, at any rate, to show the inevitability of the number three, though it may be, as Dr. Gore and Dr. Kirk allege, their confidence is misplaced. The relation between the Father and Son has been held to constitute a third term, and the formula " in the unity of the Spirit " suggests that the Holy Spirit proceeds from the Father and the Son in an analogous manner to that in which the spirit of a Society proceeds from the relation of the individuals who compose it. The abstract statement that the Third Person in the Holy Trinity is the relation between the other two is, on the face of it, unsatisfactory, since the religious value of the belief in the Holy Spirit is not in any way preserved by such a conception, and moreover the statement itself is not even logically respectable. It depends upon the unacceptable notion that the relation between two terms is itself a third term. This does not necessarily imply that the general idea of the Spirit, which has been put in this unfortunately abstract manner, is valueless. The Holy Spirit, we may say, is not a relation ; but the relation between Father and Son gives rise (not, of course, temporally) to the being of the Holy Spirit.

It is well to confess that the personality of the Holy Spirit offers a real difficulty both theologically and philosophically ; and any speculative suggestion which is advanced on the subject here is made in a tentative manner. The New Testament evidence for the personal conception of the Holy Spirit is mixed, and I cannot resist the conclusion that, in many cases, the Holy Spirit is thought of as the power, influence, or presence of God through Christ. I am sure that the normal attitude of most Christians towards the Holy Spirit is of this character, and the idea of personal relations with the Spirit is very little prominent in the life of devotion. Perhaps this state of things is the mark of imperfection. It is undoubtedly true that the faith in the power and presence of the Holy Spirit is grievously weak in most Christians at the present time, and it is possible that, if we had a clearer conception of the real and distinct being of the Spirit within the unity of the Godhead, the practical defects of our religion would be remedied. At least there is some support in the New Testament and in the Christian consciousness for the belief that the Spirit is a divine Person, and the Catholic Church has decided that the doctrine is a part of the Christian faith. To the present writer this last fact, though not finally decisive, is of very great moment. I should be very slow to recognize that, in a matter of this fundamental importance, the mind of the Church has been mistaken, and should prefer to hold, even if there were less to be said in support of the dogma than there is, that the inability to make the belief real to myself was due to defect of spiritual insight or understanding.

The analogy of society does suggest an approach to the conception of the personality of the Spirit which is worthy of consideration. The idea of the mind or will of a society has been used in modern thought by social philosophers, some of whom would regard a highly organized society on its spiritual side as an individual in a completer degree than the members who constitute it. So far has this been carried that it is even held that the individual man is a kind of abstraction from the concrete reality of the social whole.[1] In Bolshevist Russia, according to Fülöp Miller,

---

[1] Mr. Albion W. Small, we are told, advocates " the abolition of the word individual ", finding in it the suggestion of a " discredited hypothesis " ! (*Technique of Controversy* by Rozoslovsky, p. 6.)

we are confronted with the practical attempt to create the "collective man" who abolishes all individuality but his own.[1] But these extreme views are not the only possible version of the theory of a social mind. A more reasonable opinion is that the individuality of the members of the society is not abolished by the collective consciousness, nor are they mere abstractions, but that their individuality depends upon and is nourished by the "social mind" within which they live. Thus Dr. Bosanquet, commenting on Plato's *Republic* and the rule of the philosopher Guardians remarks : "Those who have to deliberate on behalf of society as a unit must bring to bear on every problem a complete or concrete idea of the social whole, in which idea society becomes, as it were, self-conscious through the minds of its members. . . . We do not now rely as Plato proposed to do, mainly on the completeness of the statesman's knowledge, but rather on a logic of fact and community of sentiment by which the ideas of all classes work out their joint results."[2] There is much virtue in "as it were", and we must recognize the note of hesitation, but the suggestion is clearly that the social mind is, in some sense, a reality which transcends the individuals, though having no existence apart from them. On the other hand, it is argued that the social mind or will is nothing more than a misleading metaphor, the sole basis of which is the obvious truth that individuals in social relations with one another are affected intellectually, emotionally and volitionally by that relation.[3]

The debate between social philosophers on this subject seems likely to continue indefinitely. We must not enter

---

[1] Cf. *The Mind and Face of Bolshevism.*
[2] *Companion to the Republic*, p. 135.
[3] See, e.g., R. M. Maciver in *Community*, pp. 74 ff.

upon it here ; but we shall do well to keep it in mind in order that we may not attribute too much certainty to statements about the " social mind " when they are used with theological intention. With this caution, however, we may note that even if the " social mind " is a mere metaphor, it is a metaphor for some real group of phenomena. There is a true meaning of the phrase " the mind of the nation " or " the mind of the Church ", and to speak of a " general will " is not to use words without any significance. The association of human beings in any kind of group, whether family, club, or state, or even crowd, engenders some impulse to common action and hence some common thought and feeling. Nor can the common action, thought, or feeling be identified with that of any single person or class of persons within the group. The leaders may have the greatest influence, or may be really " representative men ", but they do not sum up in themselves completely what we describe, perhaps wrongly, as the mind of the society. If then there is, in the very imperfect societies which are known to us, something which, transcending all individuals taken singly, can be called even metaphorically a social mind, we might expect that this characteristic would be perfectly developed in a perfect Society. Perhaps that would mean that, in this instance alone, the " social mind " would have passed beyond all metaphor and be " real mind "—fully personal will and intelligence. This speculation may be accepted for what it is worth. I do not claim more for it than that it indicates the possibility that, in the case of the Godhead, the relation between the First and Second Persons may itself be Personal.

We must avert our eyes from the heights towards which they have been straining and, admitting the inevitable failure of the human reason to catch more than a glimpse of the nature of God, seek to discern the activity of the Trinity in the created order. That in general will be the subject of the following chapter, but here, for the sake of completeness, something must be said on the distinct operations of the one divine Life and Thought.

Christian Theology has always associated the Son with the creative process, though of course both Biblical and dogmatic authority would be against any belief that the Father and Holy Spirit were not concerned in creation. It is the Son, " through whom the worlds were made." We may interpret this in full accordance with the Platonic thought of orthodoxy. The ground of Creation, the motive of the process, is the ideal perfection which each level and aspect of the created order contains within it, half revealed and half concealed. In every thing which has its place in finite existence there is, revealed to thought or to imaginative insight, a state of being, which is not in fact actually achieved, but which if achieved would be the perfection, the realization of the full value, of that object. For the sake of that perfection, which is as yet suggested and not attained, the objects have been or are being created. The full justification of creation would be the complete realization of that order, inclusive of every aspect of the finite world, which now and for our experience is but partially manifested.

On this ground, again, we can see the fundamental reasonableness of the dogma that the Son is the Person of the Trinity who becomes Incarnate. The doctrine of the Incarnation is the assertion that the divine Person, who is the Agent of creation, is Himself manifested within the creation. Here, in this historical Person, the Perfection which is the source of all being takes flesh and dwells

among us. Nothing can minimize the paradoxical
character of this belief. But the Christian doctrine of
God has been based upon it ; and though it can never be
" demonstrated ", it does at least harmonize with a
conception of the universe which has rational ground.
Malebranche, among other Christian thinkers, has put
forward the view that God creates the world for the sake
of Jesus Christ, or for the sake of His Glory in Jesus
Christ.[1] We may adopt this opinion, if we are allowed
to give it a scope which probably Malebranche himself
would have admitted. The justification of creation is in
those ideal elements, or suggested tendencies, which we
may discern, in the perfection at which the world hints.
This perfection, in the sphere of human life, lives in the
person of the Incarnate Son. In the light of this conception we may interpret those sayings of the Fourth Gospel
in which Jesus seems to claim an exclusive right to
introduce men to the Father. " No man cometh unto
the Father but by me."[2] Here the eternal Son is speaking.
The divine Logos proclaims His universal mediatorship.
As the words of the Son they are true, and so far from
being exclusive, are universal in their implication. No
man has come or can come to the Father except through
the apprehension and contemplation of that within
himself and the environment which speaks of a higher
than self and a beyond nature. Through the image of
God, which is obscured but still present in the creature,
all approach to the Reality of God must take place.

The activity of the Spirit may perhaps best be expressed,
in the most general terms, as that *nisus* in things and in
persons which seems to drive them forward towards a
higher degree of perfection. As we have seen, the idea of
a *nisus* of this character is not foreign to modern philo-

---

[1] *Dialogues on Metaphysics*, IX.   [2] St. John xiv. 6.

sophies of evolution. Alexander and Bergson, in their different manners, and the New Idealists have recognized a tendency in the natural world towards higher types and states of existence. It has been widely admitted that here the philosophy of evolution seems to hold out a hand to the Christian belief in the Holy Spirit. But it is not always seen that the Christian doctrine of the Trinity has one great advantage over the pure doctrine of the immanent life-force or the *nisus* in things. It has a basis for the idea of value, for the conception of "higher" and "more perfect." In the words of the prayer, " all things are returning to perfection through Him from whom they took their origin "—they are moving towards the Creator. In the higher reaches of creation this movement or impulse of transcendence takes a specific form. What in the lower types of being appears as a tendency or striving, becomes in persons a conscious act of will which is guided by the idea of value. The movement of " return " is no longer one in which the objects appear to be acted upon, or to be the passive participants in a general trend ; the individuals are now moved from within by the spontaneous response of the self to ideal ends. Thus it is said of the Spirit both that " He shall take of mine and show it unto you," and that " He shall guide you into all truth."[1] These two activities of the Spirit are identical. The Spirit moves the will of personal beings by presenting to them the Son in whom they see the truth of their nature, its ideal perfection. And when they perceive Him, they desire to move towards Him.

[1] St. John xvi. 14.   St. John xvi. 13.

CHAPTER X

CREATOR OF HEAVEN AND EARTH

WE have been led by the course of our argument to attach great importance to the idea of creation. We have concluded that religion is deeply concerned to maintain that there is a response of a personal kind to the aspirations and longings of the human spirit, and hence to hold fast to a belief in the personality of God. But our reflection upon the nature of personality in ourselves and in God brought us to the thought of creation in two ways. First, we found that creative power was a salient quality of those persons who are open to our direct observation, of beings like ourselves, and consequently we were compelled to attribute a supreme degree of creativeness to the Most High. Secondly, we saw reason to hold that personal life was indissolubly connected with the pursuit of ideal ends, and hence that this condition must, in some way, be present in the experience of the personal God. But this in turn implied that there must exist a sphere of being within which those ends could be realized. Thus on these two grounds, we must conclude that the personality of God implies that there is a created order, and further, it would seem, that this order, taken at any moment, must be imperfect.

Apart from these considerations, which may perhaps be thought to arise from our method of approach to the question and from some special presuppositions which are open to dispute, it is obvious enough that the Christian doctrine of God must contain a doctrine of God as Creator. On the conception of creation rests the characteristic Christian view of the relation of the human soul with God. That relation is one admittedly of dependence, but one also which includes the possibility of free communion and fellowship with God. Through its continual emphasis on the fact of creation Christian theology has kept itself clear of the abyss of pantheism, and has maintained that moral distinctions are not mere seeming and the moral struggle is a real conflict. We are not parts of God, but His creatures ; not phases or aspects of the Absolute, but spirits with some limited but genuine freedom to seek God or to turn away from Him. The belief in creation then safeguards the truth that all beings depend upon God as their Source and Sustainer, but, at the same time, preserves the dignity of personal spirits as self-determining agents, who are capable of receiving, in their development, the power of a " new creation " which proceeds from the same God who called them into existence.

Though the importance of the idea of creation will be readily admitted, its precise meaning is not without obscurity. Probably much of the difficulty which is felt by reflective men on the subject is due to the presence in the traditional doctrine of creation of images which are really mythological survivals ; and it is important, there-fore, to free the essential idea from unessential accretions. Two notions in particular which have been associated with the belief in creation give rise to quite irrelevant perplexities. It has been supposed that the creation means a beginning of " the world " in time, and that it must be one temporal act, done once for all. Both these ideas occur almost inevitably in poetical descriptions of creation such as those in Genesis. The imagination must represent to itself the truth under dramatic forms. " He spake the word and they were made, He commanded and they were created." " He saw that it was very good and rested on the seventh day."[1]   That the pictorial element is present in such utterances will be generally agreed, but we do not always realize how far the merely symbolical extends in them.

That creation is a continuous process has become almost a commonplace with enlightened theologians since the coming of evolutionary theories ; and we need not dwell upon the obvious fact that there is no special difficulty in holding that the creative act of God is, so to speak, spread out through time. Not only is this view more in harmony with evolutionary presuppositions, it is the conception which would flow most naturally from the idea of the divine Personality which we have adopted. If creation is an essential work of personal life, we should expect that the personal God would be creative, not at one moment only, but always. There is perhaps a danger that the doctrine of continuous creation may give some support to the belief that God Himself develops. But this is by no means a necessary consequence, as we shall try to show when we consider the relation of God with time.

The closely related idea that creation implies a beginning in time or, to adopt St. Augustine's emendation, a beginning " with time " is of greater importance, because it has seemed to guard a really essential element in the doctrine of creation. The theology of Christianity has developed its doctrine of creation in opposition to every kind of dualism. It explicitly taught that God created the world *ex nihilo* in order to avoid the suggestion of any existence, such as matter, which did not depend upon the

[1] Psalm cxlviii. 5 ; Genesis i. 31, ii. 2.

Creator. In what is probably the earliest explicit statement of the doctrine of creation out of nothing, Irenæus,
writing against the Gnostics, remarks that they do not
understand how much a spiritual and divine Being can
accomplish. "To attribute the substance of created
things to the power and will of Him who is God of all, is
worthy of both credit and acceptance. It is also agreeable
to reason, and there may well be said, regarding such a
belief, that 'the things which are impossible with men
are possible with God.' While men indeed cannot make
anything out of nothing, but only out of matter already
existing, yet God is in this point pre-eminently superior
to men, that He Himself called into being the substance
of His creation, when previously it had no existence."[1]
St. Augustine again, in whose theology the idea of
creation out of nothing plays an important part in
connection with the problem of evil, thought out the
conception with reference to the dualistic theories of the
Manichæans.[2] It might seem then that, if we gave up
the idea of a definite beginning of creation, we should be
committed to a belief in the eternity of the universe, and
thus return to a dualism of God and universe which the
doctrine of creation is intended to deny.

The reluctance of Christian theologians to part with
the conception of a beginning of creation is thus due to an
intelligible and respectable motive, and the danger which
they have discerned would really exist on certain interpretations of the word "universe". If we took the
universe to be a completed whole of being apart from
God, we should have on our hands a dualism of God and
universe which would be not only a stumbling-block to

---

[1] *Haer.* II, x. 3 and 4.
[2] On this subject see further my *Studies in Christian Philosophy*,
2nd edition, pp. 206 ff.

Christian faith, but a singularly unstable intellectual position. The mind would be driven to resolve this dualism either by denying the existence of the universe or, more probably, by denying the existence of God. But this conception of the universe is not ours. We refuse to admit that any " whole " can be more than a relative one : considered apart from God it is necessarily incomplete. The sum of created things existing at any moment is neither identical with God nor is it complete, self-explanatory and consistent in itself. When we assert, therefore, that it is of the nature of God to be creative and infer that every moment of time must be filled with the exercise of His creative power, we do not equate the product of creative activity with the Creator.

It may be objected further, that we seem to be suggesting the dependence of God on creation, and hence to be denying His supreme and unapproachable sovereignty. There is, of course, some truth in this. It certainly is implied in our argument that the being of God as personal is dependent upon the existence of a created order, and that we see no way of holding the personality of a Deity " prior to creation ". But we must make two remarks upon this which will remove the real weight of the objection. Our argument most emphatically does not imply the eternity of this physical universe in which we are, nor of any universe ; it will be satisfied by the admission that, in any possible time, there must be created being of some kind. And further, we do not suggest, nor can it be inferred from our position, that God depends on creation in the same manner as the creation depends upon Him. Created being depends upon God in an absolute sense. It derives its existence wholly from Him. God depends on creation only in the sense that, being what He is, it is a necessity of His nature to create.

When we have eliminated unessential and mythological elements which have clothed the conception of creation in the historical religions, it appears to consist of a few ideas which are simple enough in themselves but difficult to combine into one thought. The primary intention of the doctrine of creation is to affirm the dependence of all things upon God. But this dependence is quite different from that which is exemplified in the case of the relation of parts to a whole, so that, according to the doctrine of creation, God is not to be regarded as the sum of existing things nor as the system which they compose. Creation represents God, not as the Absolute, but as the Ground of the world. Nor again, according to the doctrine of creation, is the relation of Creator and creature to be understood as implying the ultimate unreality of creatures, or that they have a merely illusory existence. Creation excludes every form of the theory of " Maya ". And here, in the assertion of the genuine reality of created things, the real difficulty of the conception of creation comes to light. At first sight, it may appear to bring together two contradictory beliefs—the belief that God is all, and the belief that created beings have some relatively independent reality, some being for self. The idea of creation may be dismissed as a muddle-headed compromise between a clear-sighted monism and a definite pluralism. Before, however, we take the easy line of summary rejection, we may reasonably reflect that neither monism nor pluralism has ever been thought out to the end without destroying some permanent and valuable aspect of our experience ; a fact which is at the root of the strange see-saw of the history of philosophy. Monism is always the parent, by reaction, of pluralism, and pluralism prepares the way for monism. We should consider the possibility that some doctrine of creation may be the synthesis which would reconcile our need for unification with our obstinate prepossession that finite existence is real and freedom true.

One further remark must be made on the meaning of creation. The assertion that God is the " ground " of the " world " may be taken in a logical sense, as in the philosophy of Spinoza. It may be held that temporal things and events follow from the nature of God by mere necessity, much as the conclusion of a syllogism follows from the premises. This is not a doctrine of creation : it is indeed almost its antithesis. The creation of God is the act of a personal Being and analogous, therefore, to our own acts of will and choice. Though it may be a necessity of God's nature that He should create something, what He creates is the result of a free act.

The difficulty of harmonizing the ideas which are included within the conception of creation is illustrated by the history of thought on the subject. Within Christianity itself the Platonic account of creation has been of almost equal importance with the Biblical narratives. That the Divine is creative is a prominent thought in the *Timaeus* : the absence of " envy " in God leads Him to bring into existence as much good as possible.[1] But from the Christian standpoint, the Platonic idea of creation suffered from two defects. It fell short of the assertion of an absolutely creative God. The agent in creation is not, it would appear, for Platonism the Supreme Being ; for the Demiurge, contemplating the Ideas and their harmonious unity in relation with the Idea of the Good, reproduces this heavenly pattern, as far as is possible, in time and space. The highest value is not the Creator. There is also doubt in the Platonic teaching concerning the dependence of all the elements of the created world upon the Creator, for in

[1] *Timaeus*, 29 D.

the *Republic* we are told that God cannot be the cause of all things or indeed of many things, since He is the cause only of good.[1] It seems to be an essential part of the Platonic view of creation that the creative act is limited by " necessity " or by matter.

The Christian philosophy of creation has sought to remedy these defects in the Platonic theory by two amendments. First, it has abolished the distinction between the Divine Mind and the Eternal Forms or patterns and has conceived the latter as thoughts of God, thus giving a subjective turn to Platonism. In this departure, we may observe, Christian thought was anticipated by the Jewish Platonist, Philo. Secondly, it has striven to abolish altogether the idea of any limiting necessity or matter which may appear to be independent of God. This denial is embodied in the epigram that God creates the world " out of nothing."

Here as in other respects the philosophy of Leibniz states the essentials of the traditional Christian view in the most plausible manner. There are, according to Leibniz, " eternal verities " or principles in accordance with which this world, or indeed any possible world, must be created. But these " eternal verities " are not " outside " or independent of the mind of God ; on the contrary, they are the content of that mind, and in respecting them the Creator is being true to His own nature. Nor again in the philosophy of Leibniz is there any independent " stuff " or matter, out of which the world is fashioned and which externally limits the creative act. Even the material world is not in its nature different from life and spirit, for the " monads " of which it is composed are " spirit ", though at the lowest level of development.

[1] *Republic*, 379 C.

P

If we are in search of a complete philosophy of the universe which is in general agreement with Christian doctrine, probably we shall not easily find one which can compete with Leibniz. That in its main principles it can still be defended is shown by the writings of Dr. Wildon Carr.[1] But there are, of course, grave difficulties into which we need not enter here. Historically the philosophy of Leibniz gave birth to the Deistic conception of God, that is of a Deity who is wholly transcendent, standing outside the world. But on the other hand, if we attempt to remove this danger and give up the idea of created " monads " which are distinct from God, it may be that we are upon an inclined plane which will not permit us to stop short of monism. Mr. Bertrand Russell has laid down that pluralism must end in atheism and monism in pantheism, with the implication that, since we must be either pluralists or monists, we cannot logically be Theists.[2] We may confess at least that the doctrine of creation, which would save us from this dilemma has not been worked out so clearly as to provide a genuine *via media*, and we shall often find that speculative conceptions of creation are either pantheism or deism in disguise.

II

Dr. Inge has told us that, " as to the motive and manner of creation we cannot be expected to know much."[3] We may agree that the demand to have all our difficulties resolved is unreasonable, and perhaps the ambition to have a completely articulated ground-plan of the universe is an ambition which we ought not to indulge. It is precisely in connexion with this problem of the

[1] Cf. his *Cogitans Cogitata*.   [2] *Phil. of Leibniz*, p. 172.
[3] *Plotinus*, Vol. II, p. 119.

relation of the creatures to the Creator that we should expect the inadequacy of the human reason to be most evident. To know fully how and why creation takes place we should have to be the Creator. The inability to harmonize two truths, which we are led to believe by adequate reasons, is not sufficient justification for rejecting either, though it is an indication that our apprehension of the truths is imperfect. We must admit that the complete understanding of creation is beyond our power, but we may hope to find some hints in our human experience of the possibility of an ultimate answer to our questions, and of the direction in which it may be sought.

We have said that to understand creation it would be necessary to be the Creator; and it may follow from this that our nearest approach to the comprehension of how creation is possible will be through a consideration of the human mind in its creative aspect. All the higher functions of mind are, in some degree, creative, and we ought not to deny the word to the achievements of scientific and mathematical discovery; but the word "creative" has been reserved primarily for works of the imagination, and justifiably, since the labour of the poet or musician brings into existence products which were not in any sense there already. The law of nature which the scientific researcher formulates may have been, for his mind, the result of a leap of creative imagination, but the law itself was already in existence. Someone else would have found it out if he had not. But the poems of Shelley and the sonatas of Mozart would never have been at all but for the creative genius of two individual minds.

The doctrine of creation has suffered because it has generally been approached with two mistaken presuppositions. Philosophers and theologians have assumed that the simplest analogy is the best, and have tended to think of God under the image of a celestial Artisan ; or they have given way to the intellectualist illusion and supposed that they were bound to conceive of God as " pure thought ". But the world is at least a highly complex system, and the most complex activity of the human mind is more likely to be a clue to its ground than the more elementary ; nor will those who have adopted the " personalist " standpoint, from which this book is written, be willing to allow an exclusive right in the term " mind " to the intellect in the narrower sense. Perhaps the conception of creation as a work of imagination, and God the Creator as the Poet whose works are universes, may take us further into the mystery than any other guide.

The imagination is the Cinderella of psychology, as it was in the past the bogy of philosophers. The psychological text-books are lamentably meagre in their accounts of this function of mind, on which so much that is valuable depends. They show embarrassment even in dealing with the problem of its distinction from recollection. We ought not to be surprised that analytical psychology should be unable to deal with that aspect of mind in which it manifests most clearly its originality and spontaneity. If we are right, however, the imagination is of the essence of mind and unanalysable, in the last resort, into anything else. The mind is no *tabula rasa* waiting to be impressed from outside ; but from the earliest moment of its existence, leaps out to meet the " sense impressions ", and from the first is a collaborator in the making of its world.

We must, of course, admit that all imagination, as we know it, depends upon remembered previous experience. The possibilities of any given human imagination are limited by the experiences which the person has enjoyed. The imagination is a power by which we are able to combine remembered experiences into new wholes; but if this were all, there would be nothing mysterious or significant about the faculty. It would be a kind of mental kaleidoscope in which, if we knew the pieces, we could predict all the possible combinations. But the highest works of the creative imagination are far more than this. Though they are rooted in previous experience, they are not mere rearrangements of it : they are genuinely new. The reason for this appears to be that the elements drawn from experience form, in the creative imagination, organic wholes, such that each element is modified by its position within the whole. If we take such a creation as Hamlet we can see the meaning of this. To the building up of the character of Hamlet there contributed, doubtless, observations of other men and inner experiences of Shakespeare's own, but Hamlet is not any of those men, nor is he Shakespeare, nor is he a collection of qualities put together. He is a living unity; and the materials out of which he is composed have become fused together, so that no one of them is the same as it was in its original condition as a mere observation or experience. Here is the creative force of the imagination : from the matter of experience it brings forth objects of contemplation and enjoyment which have never been in experience before.

Nothing could be more misleading than to oppose imagination to reason, even though the opposition may seem to have the authority of Plato. We must be careful to avoid the suggestion that to think of the creation as the product of something analogous to imagination is to preclude ourselves from holding that it is rational. The imagination and the reason cannot, in fact, be separated one from the other without reducing both to impotent abstractions. The higher the quality of the imagination the more " fundamental brainwork " may be discerned in it. Bosanquet has spoken of the " logic " which may be said to be implicit in a poem ;[1] but equally we may speak of the imaginative power which is exhibited in the most complex mathematical demonstrations. Indeed, it may be suggested that the most rigidly rational systems, such as those of geometry and the game of chess, depend upon certain conditions which are " posited " by the imagination. Given the postulates which the imagination has invented, the whole closely determined structure follows.[2] No one probably would be prepared to deny that the greatest works of the poetical genius are monuments of intellect. But we must not pursue the subject of the relation of intellect and imagination into its remote implications ; our purpose here is simply to maintain that the creative imagination is not irrational.

If then we may think of the world as the product of the imagination of God, we have some faint indication of an ultimate reconciliation of those ideas, at first sight hopelessly discordant, which the doctrine of creation holds together. The work of art, the poem or the musical composition, while it exists only in the mind of the artist, is wholly dependent upon him. If he were suddenly annihilated, the work of art would be annihilated too. But the work of art has also a relative independence. Once it has begun to take shape the creator has not absolute power over it : it has a character of its own, and that inherent character must limit the possible continuations which the mind of the creator may conceive. Could

[1] B. Bosanquet, *The Principle of Individuality and Value*, pp. 331, ff.
[2] Cf. D. Fawcett, *Divine Imagining*, Chap. III, and cf. also *The World as Imagination*, by the same author.

Shakespeare have turned *Macbeth* after the second act into a farce or transformed its central figures into the characters of an harlequinade ? Only by destroying the play and creating an entirely different one.

This relative independence of the products of the creative imagination is perhaps most plainly seen in the works of great novelists and dramatists. The interest of the novel or play consists largely in the introduction of characters and the results which they produce. But the interest fails if the *personæ dramatis* are merely types and their relations determined by the lines of a well-contrived plot. It is in proportion as they are really individuals that the true effect of drama is produced ; and we do not gain the full æsthetic satisfaction if we feel that the plot comes from the dramatist and not from the characters. Indeed it is a commonplace that the characters have often, during the process of composition, taken on so much independence that they have refused to conform to the plan which the author had devised. I suppose, for instance, it is one of the defects of Dickens that his characters are often too large and too vital for the somewhat conventional plots of his stories.

The line of thought which we are pursuing is easily open to misinterpretation and even to ridicule. It may be misrepresented as being the thesis that we are all characters in a cosmic novel. But this would be a gratuitous error. We are not arguing that God's creation of the world is precisely like a poetical creation of the human mind. We are applying, in a somewhat unusual sphere, the old method of the *via eminentiæ*. If the creative imagination is a power of human mind, and, as we hold, fundamental in the activity of mind, then we must conceive this power to be represented, though perfectly and not in a partial form, in the divine Mind. We shall expect, therefore, that the tendencies which can be but imperfectly discerned in human imagination will be completely realized in God. But we discover some indication, even in the very limited achievements of human art, that dependence and distinctive being are on the way to reconciliation.

Perhaps we may without presumption pursue our analogy still further. The thought of the divine Artist will lead us to a somewhat different conception of the continuity of creation than that which would naturally follow from the thought of God as the supreme Thinker or the Artificer. The two latter analogies suggest the conception of a completed whole. The mere maker hastens to the end in order that the finished work, which is the sole purpose of his labours, may be possessed. The ideal of mere thought is the coherent and perfect system. Creative work, however, is its own end, and there is a value in its exercise as well as in its products. The artist, *qua* artist, would wish always to be creating. And we may suppose that the creative activity of God likewise is without limit or desire of cessation. The tireless fertility of the Divine can know no bounds.

It may be suggested, however, that we have allowed no place for the order of nature, and that to think of creation as analogous to a poem is to ignore the scientific assumption, justified by results, that nature exhibits a system of orderly sequences. The objection is mistaken. Obviously the whole of reality, as we experience it, cannot be summed up in " laws " or expressed in equations. No array of laws of nature can include the aspects of reality which constitute its value for us, its beauty, and its individuality. The scientific statements of the regularity of nature's operations are an abstraction from its concrete being. Nor can we " explain " the world, as we experience it, by such formulas. What then is the relation of the " laws " to the individual existences, to the full and varied individualities which are the stuff of living experience ? Are we to suppose that these regularities are the mould into which concrete being is poured, and that they exist somehow apart from the instances from which they are known ?

The suggestion lies near at hand which would fuse the regularities and the diversities, the laws and the " brute facts ", the equations and the qualities, together. Imaginative creation is not lawless or incoherent. The most inspired imagination expresses itself through rhythm ; and falls, by an impulse which is part of its nature, into the most complex harmonies. But the poet does not construct his metrical outline and proceed to fill it with concrete material ; though literary competitions may set this task as an exercise. The poet inevitably finds his rhythmical structure. It is not something imposed upon the poem, but the poem itself. The greatest poets have often been ignorant of the laws of prosody. The literary critic and analyst finds the regularity and describes it. He may draw up elaborate systems of the rhythmic structure of the verse ; but the structure is not the poem. I have seen a doctor's thesis which consisted in a complete metrical analysis of the poems of Keats ; a book which contained scarcely anything but the conventional marks for stressed and unstressed syllables and "longs and shorts ". Perhaps the student knew more at the end of his labour about Keats's poetry, but the skeleton was not the living body of the poetry. Much the same may be said of the laws of nature. They are the abstract and largely conventional statements of uniformities and rhythms which the creation displays ; they are not the foundation of the quality, value, and meaning of that creation. The creation is not rational because it is a system of natural

law : natural law may be discovered within it because
it has the higher rationality of a work of art.

While keeping steadily before us the necessary inadequacy of our analogy, we may pursue it a little further
and apply it to the problem of divine immanence. The
Christian doctrine of God has always asserted in terms
the complete immanence of the Divine in creation, at
least since the doctrine became formulated in philosophical
order and the attribute of " omnipresence " became recognized as one of the fundamental qualities of God. But in
practice and in detail, the conception of immanence has
been treated with little consistency, and modern theistic
philosophies have been embarrassed by the difficulty of
preventing a genuine doctrine of immanence from degene-
rating into a pantheism. We have already seen that the
analogy of human creation goes some way to reconcile the
dependence of all things upon God with a real being-for-
self of the creation. In the same way, the illustration
will hint at a reconciliation of immanence and transcendence. If we think of a poem or a dramatic composition while it is, though completely fashioned, still in the
mind of the author, it is plain that the relation is one of
complete immanence, while at the same time, the author
transcends his poem, distinguishing himself from it, and
indeed is only immanent in it through the act of distinguishing it from himself. The immanence of God in the
world cannot be thought of as partial or restricted to certain parts or aspects of creation. We must affirm an
immanence complete and definite, such that no element or
portion of the creation is not upheld and permeated by the
divine Thought ; but this need not mean, and indeed
cannot mean, that the divine Mind is identical with, or
exhaustively contained in, that in which it is immanent any
more than the mind of the poet is identical with the poem.

There is no doubt a true thought behind the statement which is sometimes made, that there are degrees of divine immanence, but the expression is misleading. We are certainly constrained to hold that some aspects of creation, human personality, for example, are in some way nearer to the Divine than others; but we could not without absurdity say that only a small part of God was present in the stone and a much larger part in the human persons. As Augustine pointed out, the introduction of quantitative conceptions into the interpretation of God's omnipresence might lead us to the conclusion that there was more of God in the elephant than in the other animals.[1] The orthodox doctrine of the Divine omnipresence is the only one which can stand criticism—the doctrine that God is present in the fullness of His being at every point of space and in every moment of time. The truth which the conception of degrees of immanence attempts to guard is better stated in the form, " there are degrees of significance ". Some elements in the dramas of Shakespeare are more fully indicative of the intention and mind of the author than others. It would be a strange criticism which found as much matter for reflection on the poet's intellect in Feste as in Hamlet. So the personalities of human beings are indefinitely more indicative of the purpose and nature of the Creator than the dead world of matter, even though He be present in the latter no less than in the former.

III

Can we attain to an adequate conception of the general purpose and end of creation ? Does the Christian doctrine of God furnish us with any answer to the question which most philosophers have given up as insoluble—why there

[1] *Confessions*, VII, 1.

should be any finite being at all ?   We have already answered this question in part when we argued that the
nature of God is such that it must, being supreme personality, manifest itself in creation.   But we may go further ;
the created order exists that it may be the sphere in which
free moral personalities arise and develop, attaining,
through struggle and aspiration, the Kingdom of God,
of which the essential character is the communion in
unrestricted intercourse of the created persons with the
supreme Father of Spirits.   From the standpoint of this
purpose, the creation in general has a meaning and a
justification.   It exists for an end which we can regard
as good, one which would realize the highest aspirations
of which we are capable and crown the partial goods
for which we strive when we labour for social justice and
brotherhood in the present order.   In so far as the creation
is the necessary condition of the fulfilment of the Kingdom
of God, it has a *raison d'être*.

This consideration will take us further than might at
first sight appear.   We are often disturbed by the
apparent contrast between the spiritual ideals, in the
light of which we could give some account of
the purpose of creation, and the actual conditions of
the world.   On the one hand, we are compelled to
regard the world as a sphere in which freedom is
achieved ; but, on the other hand, nature seems to
be the sphere of necessity and determinism.   The recent
developments of physics appear to have brought with
them a weakening of the hold of the idea of the " reign
of law " on the scientific mind.   It is at least no longer
regarded as axiomatic that rigid necessity pervades the
whole realm of nature.   Mr. Bertrand Russell has told us
that the principle of the uniformity of nature is not only
incapable of proof but probably untrue, and Professor

Eddington has adopted the hypothesis that most, if not all, the " laws " of nature are " statistical averages, which maintain a uniformity for practical purposes on account of the vast number of individual events to which they refer—a suggestion which had been made already by Emile Boutroux.[1] There is no ground, therefore, for asserting that the uniformities which science finds are to be interpreted as meaning that there is a necessity pervading the universe in such a manner as to rule out *a priori* every possibility of freedom. We are confronted, so far as science is concerned, with regular sequences, but not with anything more. Necessity is the inference which some philosophers have drawn, illegitimately, from the more modest postulates and observations of science.

Such uniformity as science properly requires is no contradiction of the insight that the creation is, beyond all else, the sphere in which spiritual beings exercise freedom and may aspire to the higher freedom of the service of God. On the contrary, the presence of uniform and regular working in the environment is a requisite condition for the activity of beings capable of moral and intellectual progress. A merely random world, if such could be conceived, would offer no possibilities to the mind and will. The education of man, which comes from the struggle for mastery over the environment, depends upon the fact that the environment can be, in some degree, understood. And this regularity, which is not the same as necessity, must needs extend to the mental life of man himself. That there are psychological laws is no more a proof of necessity than is the fact that there are physical laws, and it is equally a requisite condition for the reality and development of spiritual freedom. To master his environment is not the

[1] *Analysis of Matter* by B. Russell ; *Nature of the Physical World* by Eddington ; *Natural Law* by E. Boutroux.

whole duty of man nor the sole means of his progress ;
even more important is his mastery over himself. It is
only because there are uniformities within the psychical
sphere that self-control becomes possible. Because habits
can be formed and thoughts have their consequences and
acts of will tend to repeat themselves, man may begin
the more arduous task of mastering and even understanding himself.

But at the conclusion of this chapter, we will remember
our ignorance. Though the purpose and even the mode
of creation are not wholly dark to us, there is much which
we cannot know. Those spiritual values which we sum
up under the term the Kingdom of God, are part at
least of the purpose of creation ; but we have no sufficient
ground for believing that they are the whole purpose.
Some Christian theology has been open to the charge of
laying exclusive emphasis on human values and ethical
ends. It is difficult, when we contemplate the far-stretching
distances of the physical universe, to convince ourselves
that none of it has any meaning apart from beings like
ourselves, or that the whole is the condition of our development, and exists for no other purpose. The frame seems
too large for the picture. The purpose of creation, we
may believe, is spiritual, and that the world has no meaning
apart from personal spirit we must needs hold ; but there
are doubtless purposes which are in no immediate relation
to us, and the stone and the star must have value for God
which we cannot understand. In ways beyond our
fathoming the Lord rejoices in all His works.

CHAPTER XI

LOVE AND EVIL

THE Christian belief about God, as we have seen, is not primarily belief in the personal Creator, but the conviction that this creative God is love. In this affirmation we may rightly discern both its distinctive character and the source of its greatest theoretical difficulty. Though other religions have conceived the Divine as including within its nature qualities of compassion, no other faith has carried out the thought of the loving-kindness of God with such consistency or held so definitely that love is the fundamental quality of the divine Being. A dispassionate and objective consideration of the universe, apart from the spiritual consciousness of man, would give little ground for the conclusion that it was the production of a benevolent Creator. The case is indeed altered when we allow its proper weight to the moral experience of the human race; and a philosophy which bases itself upon the inner life of the spirit and the judgments of value which proceed from that life, might entertain the hypothesis of divine love as a probable conjecture. At any rate, it is clear that the Christian belief in the love of God did not originate in philosophical reflection or an estimate of probabilities. For the New Testament writers the love of God is revealed in Jesus Christ. Because we find God in Christ, we discover that God is love. " One of the surprising results yielded by any close study of Christianity as revealed in the New Testament ", says Dr. Moffat, " is that apart from the redeeming action of the Lord Jesus Christ the early Church evidently saw no ground whatever for believing in a God of love."[1]

The revelation of the Father in the experience, Person, and saving work of Jesus does not, however, remain an isolated word without context. It obtains increasing corroboration through the experience of those who have found that trust in the love of God is the way to successful dealing with life. But though we may hold that this faith is abundantly justified by its works, it remains faith. We cannot hope to demonstrate that God is love according to the methods of the scientific or deductive reason, nor can we remove completely the objection which life no less than philosophy suggests. In this chapter, then, we are not attempting to prove the love of God as a proposition which can be defended on abstract principles. Basing ourselves on the Christian experience, we are to grapple with a smaller problem, but one sufficiently formidable. We must try to reach some understanding of the meaning of love in God, and deal, so far as may be, with that standing contradiction, as it seems, to our faith—the fact of evil.

The central insight in which the Gospel is founded is that the Holy One who laid down His life for His friends is not only the supreme example of heroic human goodness, but the most complete revelation of the character of God. But the precise meaning of love as it exists in God is nowhere defined in the New Testament. One conception of supreme importance has been touched upon in an earlier chapter. From the words of Jesus we may collect that love in God is to be understood by analogy with human affection and good will. The divine love is, so to speak,

---

[1] J. Moffat, *Love in the New Testament*, p. 5.

continuous with human love in such a way that from the one we may begin to apprehend the other. Indeed the Johannine writer makes the love of the brethren a requisite condition of the knowledge of God.[1] God, in the teaching of Jesus, is like a patient and forgiving father who longs for the return of his ungrateful children, and (a touch which transcends all other faiths) goes forth to seek them. His generosity must far exceed the effects of the natural human impulse which leads even evil men to give good gifts to their children. The Apostolic church found its analogue of the divine love in the sacrifice of Jesus, which was indeed, for its thought, not separable from the love of the Father.

It need scarcely be said that the divine Love is not conceived after the pattern of a natural emotion or a passing sentiment. Nor is the love which Christians are expected to bear one to another of this nature. Love is a settled and permanent disposition of the will, so that only he that " dwelleth in love " dwelleth in God.[2] Nor again is the love of God to be equated with a readiness to remit penalties, for the New Testament proclamation of the love of God is consistent with a steady conviction of the sternness of the divine righteousness ; it is not incompatible with the wrath of God against sin—and against sinners. The conception of the love of God must be combined with that of an awful and mysterious Holiness. The love of God is holy. And finally, we must not take the saying, " God is love," as if it were, in the language of logicians, a simply convertible proposition. It is not equivalent to the statement that " love is God ". This remark is of some importance, for the Johannine text has sometimes been used as the support of a vague sentimentalism which loses hold of the truth that God is

---

[1] 1 St. John iv. 20.   [2] 1 St. John iv. 16.

Q

holy and creative Personality. God is a personal life whose fundamental quality is love, whose acts and purposes are to be interpreted in the light of this conviction. Love is not God but " *of* God."[1]

The attempts of theologians to explain the doctrine of the love of God and to draw out its consequences, have not been among the most successful achievements of their science. The systems of an Augustine or a Calvin impel us to reflect that, if God be love, His love must be quite different from what we call by that name in human beings. The terrible doctrine of predestination to endless torment lies like a scar over the face of much traditional Christian theology, which has too often succeeded in interpreting the Christian message in such a way as to explain away the original creative intention of the Father in Heaven. No small part of this failure of theology has been due to the disaster that, from the first, it was dominated by the dogma of the infallible book. When every part of the Bible was supposed to be equally the utterance of the Holy Spirit, inevitably the proportion of the faith was lost, and the imperfect conceptions of the Old Testament and the figurative expressions of the New had to find their place in the system of Christian doctrine. But there has been another cause at work. The abstractive and rationalist method has here produced its greatest havoc. Love has been made a matter of logical definition, and the concrete apprehension of the pristine experience of God in Christ has been dissolved in Aristotelian intellectualism.

In the Aristotelian system, the love, which in some measure animates all finite beings, is a tendency towards God. But Aristotle did not leave any room for the belief that God himself loves. God does not move towards

[1] 1 St. John iv. 7.

anything, but being in His nature self-sufficient, cannot
love any object other than Himself. When Aristotle
was enlisted in the service of Christian theology, the
recruit became the general and the philosopher prevailed
over the evangelist. The Scholastic theology could
not, of course, deny that God is love ; but it succeeded
in representing the love of God as so different from the love
of human beings that the terms " love of God " and
" love of man " have very little in common.

The main object of the Scholastic thinkers was to dis-
engage the conception of love in God from the taint of
" passio ", from the suggestion, that is, that God needs
anything or can be affected by anything outside Himself.
To follow the admirably clear exposition of a modern
Scholastic writer : human love is " an instinctive tendency
or impulse which impels us towards a good which we
know ". Love in man, however, is subject to imperfections ; chief among them that blindness or lack of insight
into the nature of good, which causes him to love things
which are unworthy of love and not to love things which
are truly deserving of love. In God these imperfections
are absent. God loves the supreme Good—i.e. Himself.
" Being the infinite good and knowing Himself as such,
He loves Himself necessarily with a love adequate to the
object, that is, with an infinite love." It follows from
this that God loves other beings only in so far as His
own perfections are found in them, each in proportion
to its value ; and, since the different degrees of perfection
in finite beings are gifts of God and imitations of His
essence, everything in them which God finds worthy
of His love is a reflection of His own infinite
perfection.[1]

This is surely very near to a rejection of the belief

[1] G. Sortais, *Traité de Philosophie* II, pp. 595–6.

that God loves the world or human persons at all.   On this
view, in the proper sense the divine Love is self-love.
God loves me only in so far as He finds me good, that is,
only in so far as He finds Himself in me.   The world is,
as it were, a mirror in which God perceives dimly reflected
His own perfection.   We must admit that there is an element of truth in the contention that the highest love is
necessarily concerned with good ; but it can hardly be
questioned that this view runs counter to both the New
Testament revelation and the noblest expressions of
human love.   There is awe and wonder in the Apostolic
faith in God because of His boundless generosity.   It is
precisely because God loved us when we did not deserve
it, because while we were yet sinners Christ died for us,
that there is any good news of God to proclaim.[1]   And the
love of God, if we interpret it after the Scholastic fashion,
falls short of the best human devotion.   It lacks the heroic
note.   A love nicely proportioned to the merit of the object
seems too coldly reasonable to engage our admiration.
That is given to a love which is not daunted by the imperfections of its object, but rather stirred by the defect
and need to more unlimited giving.   We should not feel
any great respect for a son who, when his mother became
a drunkard, carefully reduced his affection in proportion
to the degeneration of her character.

The truth is, perhaps, that a strictly logical account
of love is impossible.   It is not " reasonable " in any
intellectualist sense, and can be justified only by that
Reason which is larger than the logical understanding.
Accounts of it such as that which we have been criticizing
fall short in at least two respects.   They ignore what is
manifestly the primary and essential characteristic of
love—that it is a relation between persons.   Only by a

[1] Romans v. 8.

species of metaphorical transference can we speak of
loving that which is impersonal, whether that object of
metaphorical love be chocolates or the idea of the good.
Any account of love which puts down the proper object
of love as a general term has gone wrong from the beginning. A second source of error is that the relation of love
is thought of in too static a manner. Love fixed upon an
immutable abstract idea becomes itself frozen into
immutability. But when we realize that love is in
essence a personal relation, we can see that it must be
a relation constantly changing, preserving its identity
through change.

We shall be on safer ground if we cease to argue what
love must be, whether in man or God, and confine ourselves to asking what, in our experience, it is. There is
no need to dwell here on the very various meanings of the
word " love " and the different levels of personal activity
to which they belong. We may take for granted that our
best guide to a not unworthy conception of the love of
God will be that human love which is most " spiritual "
and least dependent directly upon physical impulse and
instinct. This is not to deny that in human life the most
exalted states of consciousness have some instinctive
basis, nor to reject altogether the persuasion that in
passionate love some touch is felt with a super-individual
Reality, which must in the end be divine. But clearly
we have to take our examples from those experiences
where the connexion with, and dominance by, the body is
most effectually transcended. Now it is evident that the
most refined and effectual love is much more than a mere
emotion. Nor can we find the greatest type of human
love if we pass to the opposite extreme and consider it
to be a principle of benevolence. We are in search of
something warmer than a " maxim ".

Mr. P. Elmer More has indicated one of the two primary ingredients of the best type of human love in a striking phrase : love is " that outreaching power of the imagination by which we grasp and make real to ourselves the being of others ".[1] This emphasis on the imaginative quality of love seems to me of great importance. The imagination is the link between intellect, emotion, and will. The will is set in motion through the imagination, and through the same means an emotional state is translated into action. The power of the imagination to " make real " to the self what is already real in the outer world is one of its functions which is overlooked by those who agree with Bishop Butler that it is a " delusive faculty ". The man without imagination lives in an illusory world, for he apprehends no part of his environment as it truly is, but only through the symbolical abstractions of the intellect. The loving spirit is the true realist. He alone sees his fellows, not as shadows, but as concrete persons, since for him they are not simply factors of the conditions in which he lives or units of a crowd ; they are persons with an inner life not less vivid than his own.

The quality of imaginative insight is not, however, alone sufficient for the existence of love. In some degree it is possessed by the " good haters," and it seems that we cannot greatly love or hate without this " outreaching power ". We must add to our description that, in love at its best, there is a settled will for the good of the beloved. And it is plain that here too the sympathetic imagination plays an indispensable part. For it is not enough to have a theoretical grasp of the general meaning of good or a rational conception of the logic of values ; in order effectively to love anyone we must apply our

[1] *Christ of the New Testament*, p. 123.

ideas of value to the concrete case and condition of the
individual. Is not this the cause of the ineffectiveness of
much preaching ? In so far as it is concerned with the
moral life it is perforce largely a general statement of the
principles of goodness, and is in danger of becoming a
wearisome elaboration of the truism, " it is good to be
good ". Rarely perhaps can words spoken at large come
home to the special need of the individual and throw a
gleam of light on the path which he is treading alone.
Thus it is that the love of a friend is the great instrument
of progress, and the grace of God is normally mediated
through the fellowship of the brethren. But this creative
love is itself the exercise of the creative imagination. Only
through insight into the present nature of our friend
can we perceive the good which is potentially his ; and,
we may add, only in the same way can we perceive the
good which is potentially ours, and attain a self-love
which is not deadly, but the means of advance. Here,
surely, we have come upon the element of truth in the
doctrine that the good is the sole proper object of love.
As it stands it is false, for persons are the objects of love ;
but it is true that the purest love sees, in some measure,
the good which may be for the person loved, and wills
that it should become actual.

In a previous chapter we were led to apply the analogy
of the imaginative work of poetry and art to the divine
activity of creation. If what was there said may be
accepted, we have reached a position in which we can
conceive the divine Love as the perfection of that highest
love which human beings may exhibit. In all human
loving, the imaginative insight into the nature and
possibilities of the object must always be restricted.
There is an impervious core which resists our penetration.
Being fallible and sinful as we are, we should scarcely

wish that it were not so ; but the gulf which still separates
the reality of the person from the keenest loving imagination implies the necessary limitation of human love.
We may almost say that we cannot love another perfectly
because we have not created him. But the creative
imagination by which God upholds the world is not so
baffled and His insight is perfect.

The second element in love again, the will for the
highest good of the object, in the divine Experience
must be conceived as free from the limitations which
make us sometimes spoil or hinder our dearest friend.
God "searches all hearts", not with the hostile or
censorious intent of the judge, but with the love
which consists of a perfect knowledge of our being
and of our possibilities. We misunderstand the love of
God if we think of it as a general desire for the welfare
of the human race or of the world. The love of God is
individualized. It is a relation with persons. The good
which God wills for me is one prepared for me and not
identical with the good of any other, though the good
for me is not wholly separate from the good for others.
Each must form a part of that Kingdom of God, which is
God's general will, but within the Kingdom there is a
special place for each individual and a special activity.
" He calleth his sheep by name."

In this last respect the Christian faith in a living and
holy God differs from idealistic views of the world which
dispense with the idea of a personal Deity. Many philosophies have put forward a spiritual view of the world,
based upon the deliverances of man's conscience, and have
been able to reach the conception of a common good
towards which we aspire, in which, when attained, each
separate soul will find satisfaction ; but so long as they
leave out the central Person and think of a Kingdom of

Good rather than a Kingdom of God, they must lack the joy and consoling power which arise from the conviction that there is a unique series of " good works prepared for me to walk in ",[1] that there is a unique good for me to attain, and that there is a loving thought and sympathy which knows and enters into every detail of my outward lot and inner experience.

Since the time of Aristotle, philosophers have debated whether moral goodness can be ascribed to God in any sense which is really analogous to human ideas of virtue. It must be admitted that the problem is a formidable one, for it is not easy to see how such cardinal virtues as courage and temperance can be ascribed, in any intelligible way, to the Creator. But the difficulty disappears if we can hold that all the cardinal virtues are different facets of one principle of goodness, and if this can without absurdity be attributed to God. The Christian ethic finds the root of virtue in the quality of love. St. Paul asserts that love is the fulfilling of the law, and, in the same way, love is the source of every virtue.[2] We have found reason to hold that love can be predicated of God in a sense which is quite intelligible, and can be seen to be the same quality as that which we know in human persons, without its imperfections. There is, therefore, no difficulty in principle in asserting the goodness of God with a meaning not essentially different from that which the term has in human life. A further consequence waits to be observed. It would follow that there can be no ultimate distinction between the divine Holiness and the divine Love, for the holiness of God is His love, viewed from the angle of the good which He wills for His creatures.

One great omission still remains in our discussion of divine Love. We began by insisting that the faith of the

[1] Ephesians ii. 10.   [2] Romans xiii. 10.

primitive Church in the love of God was founded on the sacrifice of Christ, and we have proceeded to try to understand what the love of God may mean by considering the best human love. Evidently, in our experience, the most decisive expression of love is sacrifice. " Greater love hath no man than this, that a man lay down his life for his friends." The question presents itself, can this be predicated of God and, if so, in what sense ? Is sacrifice, involving perhaps suffering, an element in the divine Experience ? To this question we must return when we have said something on that which makes sacrifice necessary—evil.

II

The problem of evil is the salient difficulty in the mind of the ordinary man when he asks himself whether he believes in God ; and we can scarcely dispute the reasonableness of his feeling that evil is a kind of crux, which may determine our belief about the world. Unless something can be said on the subject which goes some way to abolish the surface impression of the discrepancy between our faith in a loving Creator and the world of cruelty and sin, we could hardly resist the impulse to seek an alternative belief about the world. For the facts of suffering and sin are not a difficulty for every kind of religious or philosophical creed. They are no theoretical stumbling block to a whole-hearted dualism. For the Christian doctrine of God, however, the problem is acute, because it has held that God is love, and that He is " omnipotent ". Even some types of Theism escape the full pressure of this difficulty. If we could be satisfied, for example, to hold that God existed but was not loving, there would be no special mystery about evil, and we might readily conjecture ways in which the errors and

misfortunes of men would harmonize with the purposes of
a world created by a Deity who was not benevolent. They
might even afford him amusement. Those theistic theories
again which have frankly abandoned belief in omnipotence
in any possible meaning have outflanked the problem, for
we might still hope that God was doing His best to overcome evils for which He had no responsibility. Both these
types of Theism, however, escape the problem of evil at a
cost ruinous to the interests of religion. In the first case,
we should have a God who was not the Most High, in the
sense of the best we can conceive ; in the second case
we should have a God on whom all things did not
depend.

But though many theologies and philosophies evade the
problem of evil, they have to meet the obverse of the same
problem—that of good. In all our judgments of value, and
in all our striving to realize values in life, there seem to
be two postulates implied ; that the good is " objective ",
not depending on any finite mind's thought or preference,
and that our practical effort to attain good and to order
our lives in accordance with objective values is an activity
which brings us nearer to Reality and is in harmony with
the meaning of the world. Obviously, Christian Theism
can justify both these postulates ; but it may be doubted
whether any other theory of existence can ; and at least
it must be required of them that they should show, either
that the postulates can be maintained on other grounds
than Theism, or that they are not in fact necessary for the
life of moral goodness. Theistic philosophers are accustomed to conclude their treatises with a chapter,
admittedly unsatisfactory, on the problem of evil ; it is
surely greatly to be desired that non-theistic philosophers
should be equally candid and provide us with a chapter
on the problem of good. Too easily do they assume that

it is possible to put forward a theory of the nature of the universe and leave the assumptions on which the life of goodness rests unaffected.

The attribute of omnipotence, like the other attributes of God, has too often been discussed as if it were merely a question of the logical definition of a term. Schleiermacher's abiding contribution to theology is to have translated the so-called " metaphysical attributes " back into the universe of discourse of religion. Our first preoccupation as Christian thinkers is to maintain the reasonableness of what Christian experience has found God to be. Religion, as such, is concerned with maintaining the ultimate dependence of all things upon God, so that faith in the trustworthiness of Reality, and its full responsiveness to our deepest aspirations and values, may be sustained. It is obvious that a belief which fell short of the strictly logical definition of the literal meaning of the word " omnipotence " might satisfy the requirements of religion. We may perhaps excuse ourselves, therefore, from entering in detail into the various interpretations which omnipotence has received. Plainly, we cannot mean that God can do anything whatever that we can imagine, for we can imagine His doing irrational and evil things. But in doing such things He would be contradicting His nature. God's action must be limited by His character as Rational and Love. Moreover it follows from this, that the created order cannot attain two contradictory ends at the same time. It cannot, for example, be both a sphere in which free spirits are at liberty to seek good and attain fellowship with God, and also a sphere in which no mistakes are possible and every hardship and disaster is eliminated. It cannot be both a scheme for the production of the greatest possible amount of pleasurable feeling and also a " vale of soul making ".

Leibnitz, in his monumental *Theodicée*, set out to show that this is the "best of all possible worlds", in the sense that all the evils in it are necessary for the production of the greatest possible amount of good. The phrase has been an easy prey for satire by Voltaire and lesser men, who scarcely took the trouble to understand it; but any theistic belief would, it seems, be bound to hold that the creation is adapted to purposes which, if they are understood, must be recognized as good. The general outlines of the world, and the conditions of life which they necessitate, do not support the belief that the world is the "best possible", if we mean by that one adapted to the production of the greatest sum of pleasure and a minimum of pain.

The debate between optimism and pessimism has generally been conducted on this assumption, and we must confess that it has been singularly futile. According to our view, however, value is not identical with pleasure, and the best possible world would be one which fulfilled the purpose of giving scope and opportunity for the development and progress of moral selves. I do not say that this is the sole purpose of creation, but that it is a part of that purpose. In the main, we may hold that a world such as that which we are called upon to live in is adapted to that end. No reflective person who had grasped the conception of the development of free personalities as a good greater than any degree of satisfactory feeling, would desire that existence should be freed from all obstacles, that everything should be given without effort, or that man should be endowed with happiness in such a way as to deprive him of his status as a self-determining and responsible being. As J. S. Mill remarked, no one would really choose to become a cow, even if he could be sure that he would be a perfectly happy cow : still less

would any one really wish to become an automaton,
however contented.

These general considerations, that the best possible
world must include within it the possibility of hardship
and difficulty and the opportunity of moral evil, do not, of
course, in any full measure " solve " the problem of evil.
We may still ask questions to which there can be no conclusive answer. We may wonder, perhaps, whether the
amount of suffering in the world is not more than is needed
for its higher ends, and we may point to instances of pain
which seem to have no possible spiritual purpose. But
beyond these problems, which are in their nature insoluble
by us, there is another which affects profoundly our
thought of God and His relation with His creatures.

Clearly evil, in its various forms of error, sin, and pain,
exists : it has some kind of status in reality, and we
cannot avoid the question of its relation with the Source
of all being. The problem is most acute when we are
considering moral evil and error, for any belief that these
extend as elements into the divine Experience would seem
to be contradictory of our faith in the supreme Wisdom
and Goodness. A view which has had a long and honour-
able history in Christian thought would remove the
difficulty by a denial that evil has any status in reality
in the proper meaning of the term. According to the
principles of the Scholastic theology, evil has no positive
existence ; its nature is to be a defect of being, and as such
can raise no question about its ultimate cause, and give no
ground for the inference that evil may have some place
in the nature or experience of God. We may, without
disrespect, dismiss this view very shortly. Surely it is
the strangest expedient for getting out of a difficulty.
Even if we could plausibly maintain that every evil is
associated with a defect, the absence of some " perfec-

tion ", it is far from true to say that the evil is that
defect. My toothache may be due to a defect in the tooth,
to an absence of a perfection, but the pain itself is positive,
a vivid experience. In the same way, it may possibly be
true that every sin is a failure to realize some good, which
the impulse or instinct which the sinner follows was
adapted to attain, that every transgression is a missing
of the mark ; but the sin itself is an actually occurring act,
flowing from a thought which is just as much a positive
event as the thought of the devout heart when raising
itself to the contemplation of God. The question remains,
What is the relation of these positive events, mental and
physical, to the being and mind of God ?

Perhaps we can present the problem in the most
definite way if we take the case of an evil imagination.
At any moment there are in the world a great number
of nasty, malicious, and degrading thoughts. The vin-
dictive man is rejoicing over the thought of some misfortune which is overtaking his enemy, or his friend.
The lascivious man is gloating over the anticipation of
some deed of darkness. In what way, if any, do these
real facts of the world form part of the divine Experience ?
Can we say that God thinks these thoughts, or that He
is the cause of their being thought ? The Christian
conception of God certainly compels us to assume that
they are not entirely unrelated to Him, since all things,
in the end, depend on Him ; but, on the other hand, we
are not committed to the view that God is all in all at the
present moment—our faith is that He shall be all in all.

The affirmation that God is good and not evil must
preclude us from holding that evil thoughts, as such, form
part of His experience. The attribute of omniscience,
however, is not to be thrown aside without consideration
of its implications. From the standpoint of religion,

omniscience is another aspect of the fundamental faith that all things depend ultimately upon God ; and we cannot, therefore, maintain that even the evil thoughts are unknown to God. To Him " all hearts are open, all desires known." We seem to be led to a position in which we must maintain that God knows the evil of the world without experiencing it as it actually is.

There is no difficulty in finding an analogy in human knowing which would illustrate this distinction. Recently philosophers have distinguished between knowledge of " enjoyment " and " knowledge about," by which they mean to discriminate between that which comes by direct experience and that which is mediated through other experiences. Thus I know my own pain in a way which is open to no other person. I know it by " enjoyment", in the technical meaning of the word. But the doctor may know my pain through my description and by his equipment through training and practice. His knowledge about my pain can never be the actual experience of it, but the " knowledge about " may be more detailed and have more possibility of producing favourable results than my more direct knowledge. In fact, the doctor's efforts to help me would not be furthered but hindered if he were actually to feel the pain which he is attempting to remove. We may conceive then that God's knowledge of sin is knowledge about. It is not part of His experience. He distinguishes Himself from it, and stands in opposition to it.

An important conclusion follows from this concerning our human thinking and willing. Not all our thoughts and determinations of will are the thoughts and will of God ; but some may be. We need not suppose that the shameful thoughts and the trivial ones are shared by God, though He knows them. When we decide to have marmalade for breakfast, God is not willing in us. But we may think and will at a level which is above evil and triviality. When we are thinking sincerely, and when we are pursuing the values which are beyond our small self-interest, and when we are dwelling in love, we may be said to think and will in the Spirit. Doubtless even when we are so thinking and willing, our judgments and our decisions are not wholly good or true. They need to be supplemented before they can be supposed to be identical with the mind and will of God ; but they are imperfect, not inherently false or evil, and they can form a part in that perfect whole which is the divine Thought and Will.[1]

We have not yet, however, finished with our problem of moral evil, even in outline. There still confronts us the primitive difficulty of the divine foreknowledge. We may perhaps agree that the conception of creation carries with it the belief in a real freedom for created selves, and that the omnipotence of God does not mean that He is the direct cause of all events ; but we should gain little help from this in the problem of evil if we were compelled to hold that every event was fore-known, though not predetermined, by God. It has indeed been argued that foreknowledge does not imply determin-ism or fatalism, and that we may in fact foresee an action which is nevertheless free. These reasonings carry little conviction to the plain man. They are beside the point. Though I may predict with some accuracy the action of a friend whom I know very well, I never imagine that my prediction is more than probable, and if I could predict with absolute certainty what my friend would do, it could only be because his actions were completely determined in advance. It seems to me that we cannot escape the same conclusion when we are considering

[1] Cf. Miss May Sinclair's discussion in *The New Idealism*, pp. 305 ff.

R

divine Foreknowledge. If this is absolute, the course of events must be predetermined, either by the will of God or in some other way. I see no escape from the dilemma : either we must hold that all events, including acts of evil will, are determined by the will of God, or we must hold that God's foreknowledge is not absolute.

We have, of course, to recognize that the term " foreknowledge " may be so misleading that we can form no opinion on the relation of the divine Knowledge to temporal events. If it is held that God is " timeless " or " above time ", there is no meaning in foreknowledge ; all knowledge for God must be simultaneous. About the conditions of such experience we can know nothing, and certainly cannot conceive its relation to events which happen in the time series. This very difficult question must be deferred to a later chapter : but we can at least deal with the question of foreknowledge on the assumption that it really has some meaning when applied to God. If there is a real distinction in the divine Experience between " now " and " not yet ", it seems that, if we wish to preserve some self-determination for finite selves and to have some possible solution of the problem of moral evil, we must conclude that the prescience of God is not absolute; for Him the future is not completely determined.

When this statement is made, it is frequently met by the question, Can God be surprised ? as if an affirmative answer were a *reductio ad absurdum* of the whole position. I am not convinced that to hold the possibility of surprise in the divine Experience is absurd. We must distinguish between kinds of surprise. One type of surprise is associated with the feeling of frustration ; it is a revelation of the inconsistency of our purposes with the conditions of the world. A surprise which means a definite baffling of the divine Will cannot be attributed to God : but surprise need not have this association. So long as we hold that there can be no event which God cannot overrule for His purposes, we have committed ourselves to no absurdity or irreverence. To compare the very great with the trivial, we can gain some help from the analogy of the master chess-player. He cannot foretell the moves of his unskilled opponent, and they may often cause him astonishment; but his confidence is unshaken that, whatever they may be, he can meet them and turn them to the advantage of his plan. So we may hold that there can be no thread however dark which God cannot weave into the pattern of His vast tapestry, there can be no note however discordant which cannot be taken up with the divine harmony.

In maintaining that surprise may enter into the divine Experience, we are at least keeping in touch with the utterances of the religious teachers of our faith. We shall be able to attach some real meaning to the word of the Lord through the Prophets speaking of the children who, against expectation, have become a rebellious house, and to the Word of God lamenting over Jerusalem the oft-repeated rejection of divine compassion. Is there not something unreal in the reproaches addressed to the rebellious in the name of God, if the rebellion was foreknown and the surprise a mere figure of speech ? [1]

There is no reason why a line of argument which is used with general approval with respect to other human qualities should not be equally applicable in the case of the capacity for surprise. We must understand the nature of God by analogy with our own nature. Those qualities, it is argued, which are found to constitute man's higher nature must have their counterpart, though in a

---

[1] Isaiah xxx. 1–9 : lxv. 2 ; Jeremiah v. 23 ; Ezekiel v ; St. Matthew xxiii, 37. St. Luke xiii. 34.

more perfect manner, in the nature of God. I can see no ground for applying these principles to the faculties of reason and conscience and refusing to apply them to the sense of humour and the capacity to be surprised. Clearly a human being is imperfect who lacks a sense of humour, and without irreverence it may be supposed that the ground of this good gift is in God.

> " But when they have proved that man is wholly clay
> And God a dream—listen, and far away
> From far beyond the utmost star whose light,
> Dark in the Distance, shines still out of sight,
> You shall hear gentle laughter, soft as tears,
> Such as wells up from human love that hears
> And watches understandingly beguiled,
> The simple, brave complacence of a child."[1]

That we can find fresh interest in the world, and need never feel a prey to the deadly monotony of the given and familiar, is surely no less a good gift than that of humour, and indeed is closely related with it. It would seem, therefore, that we should rightly hold it to be represented *eminenter* in the experience of God.

When we have said all that can be said on the problem of evil, we have done no more than show that, in general, the existence of evil in its various forms is no fatal objection to the faith that God is love. No candid thinker could dismiss the problem as solved and done with. There remain instances of evil which will not fall into our scheme. The pressure of the fact of evil will bear differently on different minds. The suffering of animals has doubtless been exaggerated by sentimentalists, who transfer, in the childish manner, human feelings to sub-human beings ; but when every deduction has been made and rhetoric has been discounted, there remains the

---

[1] St. John Adcock, *Collected Poems*, p. 111, " Knowledge."

sombre truth that the development of species and the process of evolution itself are bound up with the struggle for existence and the preying of creatures one upon another. The pain involved in this is, perhaps, less a problem to the sensitive mind than the impression that " nature " is indifferent to human values and that its business is conducted on principles which are almost the opposite of our conceptions of good. No one, again, can look upon the vacant or terrible face of the idiot or the maniac without being conscious of a mystery in evil which eludes us in the end and covers our " best possible world " with confusion. We are forced to confess that creation is at the best " a scheme imperfectly comprehended ".[1] Though the development of free moral persons and their perfecting is part of the purpose of the world, it is not the whole. We need not abandon our faith that creation is " rational " in the sense that it subserves some end which, if we could know it in full, would appear to us to be supremely good, but the full comprehension of that end is beyond our grasp. We mistake the nature of our cosmic environment when we interpret it exclusively in terms of human good or moral progress. In the overwhelming sense of the sublimity of Reality, in which tragedy and darkness have their part, we catch a glimpse of the end which is beyond human thought or language, and are reminded that the revelation of God must always be the revelation of a Being whom we can know only in a mirror, in a riddle.[2]

III

In the final section of this chapter we must bring together the two topics with which it has been concerned. When we considered love, we noted that it could not be

---

[1] Joseph Butler, *Analogy*, Pt. I, Ch. vii., and *Sermons* xv.
[2] I Cor. xiii. 12.

understood, at least in man's experience, apart from sacrifice; and we left for further reflection the meaning of sacrifice in the divine Experience. When we considered evil, we felt bound to maintain its positive existence and its relative independence of God's thought and will. Evil is real but overruled. But the overruling of evil suggests the problem of divine sacrifice and suffering. In our human world, sin and pain are transmuted into good and become elements in an experience which is no longer simply evil, through heroic love. Love repairs through sacrifice the devastation of selfishness, and the community does not disintegrate because the ravages of the self-assertive persons are in some degree met by the service of the self-devoted. Even evil in the form of error is overruled by an impulse which is akin to love; the ruinous misunderstandings are overcome by those who are stirred by a motive which leads them to "scorn delights and live laborious days."

But the overruling power of love extends beyond the effects of evil will; it is by the appeal of a love which shrinks from no sacrifice that the evil will is most potently prevailed upon to forsake its evil ways. At least it is true that there is no agency which can compare with this in bringing good out of evil. This is beyond question the central thing in the Christian view of life, the ground for its title to be a "new way", that we must lose our immediate selves in order to find our full selves in a loving service which has left behind the self-centred life of claims. The power of the Gospel to transform the characters of evil men and to awaken the careless comes from the cross of Jesus. It does not rest upon any doctrine of the atonement, for the saving grace of the cross has proved its efficacy when interpreted in all the various ways which theologians have devised, and not less when no explicit theory has been held at all. " Jesus died for me " has been the simple statement of the essential creed. This does not imply that we need have no doctrine of the atonement ; but it indicates that the point from which any doctrine must set out is the direct apprehension of the true values of human life which comes through the contemplation of the most heroic sacrifice.

The reasons which have led Christian theologians, on the whole, to reject the idea that suffering can enter into the divine Experience are complex. They have come partly from the tradition, inherited from the Platonic and Aristotelian philosophy, that the essential nature of the Divine is to be immutable and self-sufficient. It has been argued that suffering can only be attributed to beings whose lives are passing and temporal, and, by their finitude, are subject to want. There is, however, a consideration which does not depend upon any philosophical presupposition, but which must present itself to any Christian thinker. Does not suffering imply that there is frustration in the sufferer ? Dare we assert that the divine Experience is not invariably triumphant ? Von Hügel has put the real case against divine suffering when he asks, must we not for the sake of religion itself hold that there is one Being who is beyond the reach of failure ? Shall we not destroy religion if we hold that God, like ourselves, is subject to pain ? [1] Dr. Robert Mackintosh has asserted the dangers of a too facile acceptance of the " passibility " of God with even greater vehemence. "An unhappy God would mean a bankrupt universe, a demonstrated pessimism, a doomed faith." [2] We must take heed of these warnings. The

[1] F. von Hügel, *Essays and Addresses*, 2nd Series, pp. 167 ff.
[2] *Historic Theories of Atonement*, quoted by J. K. Mozley, *Impassibility of God*, p. 171.

attribution of suffering, as such, to God, the assertion
that the divine Experience had pain as its dominant note,
would indeed have the consequences suggested, and
would be an expression of utter pessimism. It is not,
however, necessary to hold that suffering is the predominant note in the life of God, if we assert that God
suffers. Pain may, even in our human life, enter into an
experience which, taken as a whole, is triumphant and
joyous. The faith that God suffers in and with the
creation, and is without ceasing bearing the labour of
redemption, is not a faith in an " unhappy God ". For
the power is adequate to the emergency. There can be no
evil which, in the end, will frustrate the divine redeeming
Will. The suffering of God is transfigured by the vision
of the travail of His soul in which is His satisfaction.

The reasons for holding that suffering enters into the
divine Experience are of greater weight than those against
the belief. The incarnation of the Son and His redeeming
sacrifice are, for the Christian, the supreme revelation of
the divine Nature. Must we not, therefore, conclude that
the cross is no merely historical event, however full of
influence for the future, but a sacrament of the life of God ?
In the sacrifice " once offered " we have, projected into
time, the very heart of the divine Life and Activity. I do
not see how otherwise we can present any doctrine of the
atonement which does justice to the New Testament
experience. Nor can we escape from our conclusion by an
interpretation of the doctrine of the Trinity which would
confine sacrificial love and redemptive suffering to the
Second Person of the Trinity and deny that it entered into
the Godhead. Such a conception would be utterly out of
harmony with the view of the Trinity to which we have
been led, and, I would add, with any conception which
could, in the long run, be compatible with Monotheism.

We must dare to accept the full implications of the Gospel. God is like Christ. "The deepest insight into human life is the open secret of the universe," and the Christian God is "no God or Absolute existing in solitary bliss and perfection, but a God who lives in the perpetual giving of Himself, who shares the life of His finite creatures, bearing in and with them the whole burden of their finitude, their sinful wanderings and sorrows, and the suffering without which they cannot be made perfect."[1]

[1] Pringle Pattison, *Idea of God*, p. 411.

CHAPTER XII

TIME AND PROVIDENCE

REPEATEDLY in the course of our reflections we have come upon the problem of the relation of the temporal and the eternal, and it is now necessary that we should say something explicitly on this subject. From the standpoint of metaphysics it is obviously fundamental, and some excuse may seem to be required for postponing it until the end of our inquiry. Discussions of the Christian doctrine of God on the lines of the traditional philosophical theology begin, quite naturally, with an analysis of the concepts of infinity and eternity ; but we have chosen another method, that of interpreting the Christian experience of God, and hence it is appropriate that the purely metaphysical questions should present themselves at the conclusion rather than at the beginning. Theology, we may suggest, should, like other sciences, get on without metaphysics as long as it can, even though in the end it must try to come to terms with ultimate philosophical concepts. I will say at once that I cannot pretend to have any solution of the difficulties which the subject presents. To make such a claim would indeed be an overweening presumption, since it is admitted that in the problem of time we have one of the central enigmas of philosophy. The problem has become more prominent than ever before in recent discussion, so that Mr. Alexander can say, with only a touch of exaggeration, that we have in current philosophy " discovered time ".

The problem of time is one which haunts every philosophy. This fact is worth dwelling on, because the assumption is sometimes made that time forms a special difficulty for theology. Those who are unversed in the history of thought encounter apparent contradictions in the doctrine of God, which are connected with His relation to the world in time, and they assume that these contradictions arise from the conception of God and would vanish if that conception were given up, whereas the same perplexities break out, in a somewhat different form, whatever view of the universe we may choose to adopt. There could perhaps be no better illustration of this than a consideration of the scientific Realism which is widely held by philosophers at the present day. A system of thought which aims at understanding how nature can be an object of knowledge is obviously far removed from any contamination by mysticism ; but, as we saw when we were discussing the transcendent element in every possible interpretation of experience, the scientific Realist cannot dispense with " universals ". Without universals there can be no knowledge. The modern Realist is compelled to recognize that the universals, as such, do not exist in time, though they are exemplified in temporal events. As we know, Plato drew from this the conclusion that the universals—the Ideas—were real and eternal, while time was simply the " moving image of eternity ". Not all modern Realists would go as far as Whitehead in his agreement with Plato ; but they have all to deal with the same problem—how are we to conceive the relation between that which is not " in time " and that which is passing and changing ? It cannot be said that they have solved this problem. Too often it seems to the outsider that they evade it by the invention of new terms. We are told, for example, that universals

" subsist " and that things and events exist or happen ; but we may wonder whether this is illuminating. We have added a possibly useful word to the vocabulary of philosophy, but the question remains, how that which is independent of time manifests itself in time. Only a philosophy which is willing to give up the idea of truth except in a pragmatist sense can avoid the issue of the temporal and eternal.

We could not, however, admit that even a Pragmatist has nothing to do with the idea of the eternal and the timeless. For even if we hold that true ideas are simply those that " work ", it is obvious that the ideas of eternal truth and of everlasting peace have " worked " in the experience of many human beings, and we must at least try to find a " working " hypothesis which will allow such persons to hold the idea of eternity along with other ideas which also are serviceable for life.

It is a matter of course that the two obvious methods of avoiding the problem of time and eternity should have been tried. On the one hand, it has been denied that the temporal is real, and on the other hand it has been alleged that " duration " is the sole reality. The type of thought which refuses all reality to time and change is represented, in its extreme form, by the pantheistic theology which lies behind much Indian religion. Time and change and all finite existence are, in this system, simply Maya, illusion. Some absolute Idealists in Western philosophy have adopted a view which is not dissimilar. It would not be accurate to say that Mr. Bradley and Mr. Bosanquet regard time and temporal events as merely Maya, but certainly in their philosophy time and events are not ultimately real or true—they are appearances of the timeless Absolute. The philosophy of Bergson stands at the opposite extreme. For him *durée* is the reality, whereas the eternal, changeless, and static are figments of the intellect.

This is not the place to discuss these rival positions; but we are concerned to note the unfortunate consequences which would follow from the acceptance of either. Any denial of the reality of time and change, any doctrine that they are only appearances of an unchanging and timeless Absolute, must have some at least of the results which William James deplored in his criticism of the " block universe ". In such a world there can be no real freedom for the finite selves, and hence no real struggle, defeat, or victory. If everything is an appearance of a perfect Absolute we find ourselves in the somewhat ridiculous position of fighting battles which are already won and striving to improve a world which is already perfect. If the consequences of this view could be realized in the imagination, it would deprive history and personal life of all interest. The view, however, that " duration " is the sole reality and that all is change leads to conclusions even more distasteful. If there are no universals which transcend the time-process, if all is flux and nothing stands, we can have no knowledge of reality—a conclusion which Bergson himself draws when he maintains that we grasp the real not by intellect but by intuition. In the same way, it would be difficult, on this view, to justify absolute moral judgments. There could be no absolute value and no permanent principles of good.

The religious consciousness is vitally interested in holding together the temporal and the eternal; and in the doctrine of God the problem presents itself to us in its starkest form. For religion the problem is more concrete, and perhaps on that account more tractable. The eternity of God which religion must maintain is not identical with the eternity of abstract universals. The

need for the Eternal rises out of the heart of the religious
consciousness. The soul seeks to rest in a God who is not
subject to change : it desires to find One in whom there
can be "no shadow cast by turning".[1] Unless we can be
assured of this, we cannot hold the attitude of trustfulness
towards Reality, or the faith that it is on the side of our
deepest intuitions of value. A Deity who might change in
character and purpose would be no God in whom we could
find rest, nor could we be confident that "underneath
are the everlasting arms"[2] if we entertained the
suspicion that the Creator and Sustainer of the world was
subject to mutability. But we must repeat that the
immutability which the religious mind seeks, and on
which it reposes in trust, is not equivalent to a merely
abstract and logical changelessness, the mere formal
opposite and negation of change. Religion has no knowledge of any God who is not the living God and could find
no satisfaction in the thought of a changeless Reality
which was dead. The needs of the religious consciousness
are met if it can be certified that it has to do with One
whose nature and purposes cannot alter, and who remains
always consistent with Himself.

We can see, therefore, that the religious affirmation of
the immutability of God is not equivalent to an assertion
of His absolute timelessness. It is consistent with a
belief in the reality of change within the divine Experience, and does not require the idea that the ground of the
Universe is a frozen immobility. In our human experience
we have acquaintance with purposes which remain
unaltered through many vicissitudes, and which realize
themselves through many various subordinate acts of
will ; and we know characters on which we confidently
rely, though they may be required to adapt themselves

---

[1] St. James I. 17.   [2] Deuteronomy xxxiii. 27.

to diverse circumstances. The immutability of God, as religion conceives it, is more like the steadfastness of a good man than the unalterable properties of a triangle.

The religious consciousness is no less concerned to hold that events, succession, and " time " are not illusory, and hence to hold that they have meaning and reality for God. Any doctrine of God which implied that He was " beyond time ", in the sense that temporal events had no place in His experience, would be as fatal to religion as the doctrine of the Absolute which we have already rejected. It would mean that our efforts and aspirations, our victories and defeats, our purposes and hopes, had no significance for God and meant, in the last resort, nothing to Him. The Christian conception of God can certainly not be represented as that of a Being who is " timeless " in this meaning of the word. The Christian gospel is irrevocably an historical religion, and finds its supreme revelation of God in events and in a personal life which are part of the history of the world.

II

The problem of the relation of time and eternity seems to be insoluble largely because we do not know the precise meaning of either term. The word " eternal " is used with extraordinary looseness, and frequently has no very definite significance in the minds of those who employ it. Within this vague penumbra of meaning, however, we may distinguish several allied but distinct ideas. As we have seen, the word " eternal " may be used to denote the " timeless " entities or " subsistents " which appear to be non-temporal in their nature. But the same word is not seldom synonymous with " unending ", and is then interchangeable with " everlasting ". Thus the fact that we cannot conceive a conclusion of time is said to suggest the " eternity " of creation.

There is another more positive meaning, which has been of great importance in the discussion of the nature of God—simultaneity. It is frequently held that the divine Experience differs from our experience in that it contains no succession of presentations but, on the contrary, possesses all its wealth in one " eternal now ". Thus the thoughts of God do not succeed one another but constitute a perfect whole, which is apprehended in one act of intellection. Baron von Hügel has made impressive use of this idea in his treatment of the mystical experience, which, in his opinion, has as one of its motives the desire to rise above successiveness to a " simultaneity " which is akin to the divine Thought.[1] The conception of absolute simultaneity is extraordinarily difficult, and, if pressed to its logical conclusion, might lead to the view that the temporal process, as such, has no meaning for God, a view which we have already rejected. On the other hand, we must attribute at least this degree of simultaneity to the divine Experience : it is not in any way at the mercy of succession. In this, on any view, it must differ from the human experience at its fullest. God is always the master of the events which enter into His life ; the resources of His nature are adequate to every change, and there can be no vicissitude through which He cannot realize His will.

It might appear that, since all our thinking and experience is temporally conditioned, we should have a clear idea of the nature of time, even though the meaning of the eternal might remain obscure. But this is far from being true, and we have to recognize that our temporal experience does not disclose to us what time is. It is of

[1] F. von Hügel, *Mystical Element of Religion*, II., pp. 246 ff.

the greatest importance to make clear to ourselves a distinction which it has been one of the achievements of modern philosophy to draw—that between time as experienced and " conceptual time ". We have become accustomed to the idea that the time which is measured by clocks, the time in which we suppose that we are, is something of which we have direct experience, and something which exists quite independent of us. Until comparatively recent days science agreed with common-sense in this prejudice. In the Newtonian physics absolute time and space were taken for granted as the framework within which events happened. In some way this framework was thought of as prior to the events. The characteristic feature of time, its " essence ", was, on this view, that it flowed on at an even pace without cessation and without end. In the spirit of this conception was the strange idea that time not only existed apart from events, but was even capable of exercising some influence upon them. " Time, like an ever-flowing stream, bears all its sons away." But a little reflection shows that time cannot have any existence apart from events, and that it is just as true to say that time is in events as that events are in time. What is it that " flows " if nothing happens ? The conception of an absolutely " empty " time is a contradiction.

A little further reflection shows that this " conceptual time " is not a possible object of experience at all. We arrive at the idea of it by a process of intellectual con-struction, which is based upon real and unquestionable data. What we actually experience is the succession of states or events, primarily within our consciousness, the source of which, in some cases, we think to be outside ourselves. All our experience is characterized by the feeling of " now ", " then ", and " not yet ". This primary

s

datum of our living mental activity is the ground on which
we build our concept of time. We may notice that it is
first of all a " private " affair, lived and known by the
individual consciousness.

But this " time " of our direct experience does not
possess that quality of even flow which is the essence
of conceptual time. Our lives move swiftly or sluggishly,
time creeps or gallops with us. The invention of conceptual time seems to be necessitated by our position
as social beings. If time were purely " private ", and
there were no co-ordination between the duration experience of one individual and that of another, co-operation between the individuals would be impossible. For
social life we need " public " time. The evenly-flowing
time which is measured by clocks is a device to integrate
the activity of a multitude of persons. It does not, of
course, follow from this that conceptual time is a mere
figment which has no relation with reality. Indeed the
fact that we are able to co-operate seems to indicate that
the successions which we experience are not merely
" private ", or at least are not all private. One conclusion, however, does seem to follow from all this—that
the idea of an absolute time is not one which is " given ".
It may be that this construction of the intellect, useful
and necessary as it is, has been extended illegitimately
to include all events. There is nothing self-contradictory
or absurd in the suggestion that some beings or activities
may not be " in time ", if by that we mean the absolute
time of the older physics.

It is well known that recent physics has had great
difficulty with the concept of time. The theory of
relativity has thrown serious doubt on the absoluteness
of both space and time. But perhaps of greater interest
are the problems which are raised by research into the

structure of the atom. The discontinuity, as it appears, of some atomic action has led to the suggestion that it may not take place in what we call space and time.[1] The only sure result of these considerations is that the idea of " absolute time " is necessary for practical purposes and is justified so far as it " works ", whether in ordinary life or in science, but it now appears to be less universally applicable than had formerly been supposed.

On the other hand, there is an undeniable core of reality in time—the successiveness of our experience. For me, at any rate, " now ", " then ", and " not yet " are significant terms. But we may go a step further and observe in what aspect of my experience these terms become significant. The psychology of time is still in a confused state, and it would be absurd to dogmatize on the nature of the most rudimentary perceptions of time ; but it is certain that time comes to be important for us, and assumes a central place in our thought, in so far as we have purposes. In conation and will I encounter time as a necessary factor. For a being entirely devoid of will time would have no importance, and perhaps even no meaning. The past is that which the will cannot alter, the future is the possible realization of purposes, the present is the possession of purposes, which come out of the past and look towards the future. Of course, our perception of time involves memory, but this too probably has a direct dependence on the purposive and conative side of our life, for we remember with a purpose. There is then truth in the dictum that " time is the form of the will " and in the statement that " the innermost meaning of time is the inalienable difference between what is and what ought to be."[2] At least we may say that because I am a purposive

---

[1] N. Bohr, quoted by Gunn, *Problem of Time*, p. 398.
[2] *Introduction to Philosophy*, by W. Windelband, p. 359.

being I recognize the reality of time, and because I am a purposive being I must, in some sense, be " in time ".

But this cannot be the whole truth about me. To say that I am " in time " without qualification may mean one of two things : first it may mean that I am an event or a series of events within absolute time. But we have already criticised the conception of absolute time. Or, secondly, it may mean that I am nothing more than my successive states of consciousness. This idea we rejected when we were discussing personality and need not repeat what was then said. We saw reason for preferring the phrase the self *has* states of consciousness. But it is important to remember another truth about personality, which we tried to bring out in that discussion. The person does not exist, and, as we argued, could not exist, apart from its successive experiences. Though it is not simply identical with its activities and perceptions, it has no being apart from them. It is in them and exists through them. Thus in considering human personality, there seems to be a necessity to think together the " temporal " and the " eternal ", or at any rate the successive and that which is not successive.

A distinction has often been drawn between the " noumenal " or " real " self and the " empirical " or temporal self, and it is sometimes held that the former is somehow complete apart from the empirical self, which is an " appearance ". This, I suppose, is the opinion of Dr. McTaggart.[1] The conclusion which we are advocating differs from that theory. We have not argued that succession is unreal or that it is no essential element in personal experience. For us the self is rather the whole which is formed by the super-temporal subject and its successive experiences. Thus both the statements, " time

---

[1] Cf. his *Nature of Existence* and *Studies in Hegelian Cosmology.*

is in us ", and " we are in time " are true ; but neither is true by itself. The self which may be called " super-temporal " has no existence apart from the temporal succession of its experience, and the temporal succession is unthinkable apart from the " super-temporal " ego.[1]

The conclusion to which we have been led is not simple. The problem of our own nature is beyond our penetration, and we are brought to face the mystery of Being most of all when we attempt to understand ourselves. If we are unable to unravel with precision our own relation with time we need not be astonished that God's relation with time presents insoluble problems. Let us, however, continue to tread resolutely the path of the " higher anthropomorphism " which we have followed hitherto. If we are right, our relation with time will be the best guide that we have to any understanding of God and time.

We may begin by stating that God cannot be " in time ", if we mean by that phrase that His whole Being is subject to succession and change. As we have seen, there is doubt whether this assertion could be made even of human personality. God, we must suppose, in His being unites the eternal and the successive in a manner which is hinted at by our own personal life. We are therefore justified on more than one ground in believing that God is not " timeless ". To argue that succession does not in any way enter into the divine Experience would be equivalent to a denial of the divine Personality. Though

[1] It would be unwise to lay much stress on the provisional conceptions of physics which are rapidly developing, but the quotation from N. Bohr given above suggests an interesting speculation. Atomic action, it seems, cannot be wholly explained as " in time " ; and we find at the centre of personality an activity which is probably " super-temporal ". Atomic action is the ultimate basis of the physical world and personal activity of the spiritual. Perhaps then all activity is ultimately super-temporal.

God does not consist of a succession of states, and it would be impossible to predicate of Him an experience developing towards maturity, succession must be real for Him. And hence it would seem " not yet " must have some meaning for God, though we cannot, of course, understand precisely what meaning. If God were absolutely timeless, the conception of the divine Will would be meaningless. We must hold fast, therefore, to the conviction that succession is real for God, and His immutability must be interpreted in moral and spiritual rather than logical terms : it is that of permanent purpose and unchanging character. Any other view, I am persuaded, must logically end in the conclusion that the sphere of history and human endeavour are illusory—a position which is intolerable for Christian faith.

The experience of change which enters into the divine Life must obviously be that of the changes of the created order, and it is in the sphere of creation that God's purposiveness is exercised. Our discussion of creation attempted to show that the ultimate dependence of all things upon God is not necessarily in contradiction with the real freedom and self-determination of some finite and created beings, and that, though we cannot see in detail how ultimate dependence and relative independence are reconciled, we can see that they are not irreconcilable. Our doctrine of creation insists upon the existence of " free causes ". We must apply the results of that discussion to our present problem. The created order includes some beings with limited spontaneity and others in whom spontaneity has become freedom. If then some part of the purpose of creation is the " creation of creators ", we must conclude that the succession which enters into the experience of God is not, in every detail, directly willed by Him. He wills that there should be a created order and that, within this order, there should be " free causes " ; thus the order and the existence of the free causes depend directly upon the divine Will, but the manner in which that bestowed freedom is exercised may be contrary to the will of God, even though the possibility that it should be so exercised depends constantly upon His will.

The doctrine that there is a super-temporal element in every human person suggests a speculation which we must briefly notice. It seems to be an obvious simplification to go on to argue that there is only one Subject in all created instances of self-hood—that, in theological terms, God is the universal Subject, the super-temporal Ego in every self. The philosophies of Kant and T. H. Green both include a doctrine of the " noumenal " self, which is not " in time " ; but neither of these thinkers has made it clear whether the noumenal self is singular or plural. Fichte and Gentile have cut the knot by maintaining that there is only one transcendent Ego or Subject. We must explicitly and steadfastly refuse to adopt this tempting simplification, both on the ground of the Christian experience of God and on more general grounds of experience. We have more than once insisted that the Christian faith in God implies an ultimate and insurmountable distinction between the Creator and the created. Unless this be held fast the whole structure of Christian life and worship lies in ruins. Hence as Christian theologians, we must maintain that, though there is an element in human personality which is not in time, it is still created and not identical with God. But this conclusion can be supported also on general grounds. The plurality of centres of consciousness and of selves is surely one of the few facts about the world of which we are assured with a surety which cannot be shaken by dialectic ; and perhaps we may add that most of us are reasonably certain that we are not God.

The caution which we have suggested with regard to speculations tending to abolish the distinction between Creator and creature need not, however, stand in the way of our reflection upon the relation of the human ego to God, and particularly upon that relation which is included under the term " grace ". We may justly represent to ourselves that the self in its " noumenal " aspect must, in some way, be more immediately in contact with God than in its empirical and temporal aspect ; and hence it would seem obvious to suppose that the possibility of the influx of supernatural grace is connected with the fact that the human spirit has root in the unseen and eternal. We may go further and find here the theoretical justification for the belief, common to mystics and other persons of first-hand devotional life, that they enjoy immediate knowledge of and communion with God : that His presence is not only a well-founded inference but an experienced fact. But though these beliefs are consistent with our own and seem to follow from it, they do not conflict with the distinction upon which we are here insisting. God dwells in the soul by grace, and not by metaphysical necessity.

III

These reflections, dim and inclusive as they are, may have some value when we consider the nature of Divine Providence. Probably there is no department of Christian doctrine where the inconveniences of an incoherent conception of the nature of God are more plainly demonstrated and have more effect on practical life. Even the plainest Christian man must sometimes have been perplexed when he seems to be bidden to regard all the events of his own life, and all the course of history, as the will of God and providentially ordered, while he is no less urgently exhorted to remember that he has disobeyed the divine will and frustrated the purpose of God, and is moreover a member of a rebellious race. The legitimate anxiety of Christian teachers to maintain the supremacy of God without compromise and the absolute dependence upon Him of all created being has found an ally in the logical conceptions of infinity and eternity ; and on this dual basis has been erected a conception of Providence which seems to conflict with other important elements in the Christian view of God and man.

In our survey of the New Testament experience of God, we briefly noticed that some sayings of Jesus, which have been taken to indicate a belief in an absolute providential order such that every event is directly willed by God, need not, in fact, have this implication ; while there are other words which seem to have a directly opposite intention. It is true that St. Paul's Rabbinical heritage and his polemic against the idea of human " merit " inclined him to a more drastic statement of the doctrine of Providence, and it cannot be denied that belief in an absolute providential ordering of events and thorough-going predestination can find support in the Apostle's writings. But, in spite of phrases which may be so interpreted, it cannot be admitted that the settled view of St. Paul is that of a complete theological determinism. Indeed this theory would make nonsense of his general religious and moral position. He allows the real freedom of the self to accept or refuse the grace of God ; and even his interpretation of the significance of the rejection of Israel is really more in harmony with the conception of an overruling than with that of a completely determining Providence.[1]　Probably St. Paul had not thought out a coherent theory of Providence, but gave expression to both sides of the religious paradox, with characteristic vehemence, as occasion required.　We have constantly to remind ourselves that the Apostles were not professors of theology.　With Augustine the full doctrine of Providence enters into Christian thought ;　and since his day the prevailing teaching of Christian theologians, though not of Christian preachers, has been that all events are, not only foreknown, but predetermined by God.

The question is one of far more than merely theoretical interest.　It is of great practical moment ;　for upon our answer to it will depend our conception of the characteristic quality of the truly Christian life.　If we accept the view that there is an inviolable and inevitable providential order we must surely draw the conclusion that " all is given " ;　though we shall add it is given by the good hand of God.　The most fitting attitude for the devout soul will then be that of resignation and acceptance.　Doubtless, as history abundantly shows, this resignation may be combined with vigorous activity ;　but it is not compatible with the belief that, in the end, anything depends upon my choice or act, or with the spirit of adventure.　On the other hand, if we reject the idea of an absolutely closed providential order, we may hold that the proper attitude of the Christian towards life is that of eagerness to co-operate with the divine Will, the determination that our part shall be fulfilled.　We need not repeat here what has been said in connection with the problem of evil, but we must bear in mind the very intimate relation between that problem and any doctrine of Providence. Such light as we were able to find upon that dark question

[1] Romans ix. and xi.

of sin and suffering would be grievously dimmed, if not extinguished, if we were compelled to hold that every event was completely determined by a pre-established plan.

It need scarcely be said that the conclusion which follows from our discussion of the nature of God and His relation with creation is against any doctrine of absolute Providence. And we may notice that the support which theological determinism has formerly seemed to obtain from natural science is not now forthcoming. Until recently it was taken for granted that science must assume the thorough-going determination of all events, in such a way that, theoretically, given a full knowledge of the relevant conditions, any event could be predicted. Few physicists would now be willing to make this assertion; and it seems that the determinism of science is only a " methodological postulate ", which in fact breaks down when we are concerned with atomic action. Professor S. C. Thompson points out that one of the general results of the study of the constitution of matter has been to swing science away from the determinist assumption.[1] Theological determinism can no longer claim to be more in harmony with the philosophy of nature than an alternative view. According to the thesis which has been presented in this study, the creation has as its object, or as part of its object, the development of self-determining persons ; and the created world, therefore, includes within it " free causes ". We must urge that the Creator has taken the full consequences of this creative act.

Dr. Tennant concludes his valuable work on Philosophical Theology with the phrase, " an adventure of love ".[2] We may adopt this in its full meaning. The creation has involved what may be called risk, and, as

---

[1] *The Atom*, pp. 239 ff.   [2] *Philosophical Theology*, Vol. II, p. 259.

we have argued, redemptive suffering is an element in the divine Experience. The quality of courage is not perhaps, after all, so remote as we thought from any conception of God which we can form. We can see that courage might have a real meaning for God—the sustaining of the " adventure of love " through all the wanderings and rebellions of the creatures.

We must not allow ourselves, however, to be intimidated by the dilemma : either absolute Providence, or no Providence. We may still maintain a providential government which meets all the genuine demands of the religious consciousness. As we saw in the last chapter, the existence of free causes, and even of rebellion within the created world, does not overthrow the belief in an overruling divine Purpose. From no point of view could we maintain that the freedom is unlimited or that the rebellion is able to disrupt the whole structure of the creation. From the standpoint of the belief in God we may interpret this as meaning that the rebellion of " free causes " cannot totally frustrate and bring to naught the counsel of God. The manifold wisdom ($\pi o \lambda v \pi o i \kappa \iota \lambda o s$ $\sigma o \phi i a$) of God is manifested most signally through the turning of rebellion itself into a means of the furtherance of the divine Purpose.[1] Though I think we could not assent to the full implication of the familiar lines, " O felix culpa quae tantum et talem meruit habere Redemptorem ",[2] there is a truth in them which can be understood by anyone who out of weakness has been made strong. He would shrink, and rightly, from saying " felix culpa ", but he would thankfully acknowledge that the sin and weakness, overcome through the grace of God, have become a part of a good which could not have been exactly as it is without them ; and we can

---

[1] Ephesians iii. 10, cf. H. Martensen, *Christian Dogmatics*, p. 114.
[2] Roman Missal, Office for Holy Saturday.

agree with Mr. Shebbeare that " the world would not be the richer, but the poorer, without its Calvarys and Gethsemanes ", if we may understand by " the world " " our world ".[1]

The general Providence of God is to be found most clearly where the Prophets found it—in the course of history. Christian Theism must be unalterably opposed to every theory which " explains " historical development by causes which are less than spiritual. The " economic " interpretation, though legitimate and useful as a statement of one aspect of the whole process, when elevated into a complete account becomes a ludicrous abstraction. The significance of history lies primarily in its being a process in which social, moral and spiritual values are realized. But the providential order will be almost equally misinterpreted if history is regarded as akin to the unrolling of a cinematograph film which has been prepared beforehand and the same criticism will apply to the view that history is a kind of impersonal process, even though that process be described, as by Croce, as the life of immanent Spirit. History is made by persons who are, within limits, " free causes ". The emergence of "homo sapiens" from the brutal condition of the anthropoid ; the beginning of primitive culture ; the passage from savagery to the ordered life of the city ; the slow development of political freedom and ideals of fellowship ; are, for the Theist, revelations of the purpose of God.

It cannot be questioned that the general course of history is perfectly harmonious with a belief in a superintending Providence. The failure of empires and nations to carry the cause of social and moral progress beyond a certain point, and their decay and disappearance, looks like the

---

[1] *Problems of Providence*, p. 20. I gladly refer to this able book, which defends a view of Providence almost the opposite of that which is here presented.

expression of a constant purpose, which is partially frustrated by human failure to respond to opportunity, and begins, unhasting but unceasing, to work towards its goal with other instruments. At the present day the ideal of a concourse of nations to eliminate war from human life, which had made sporadic appearances in the past, has taken shape in concrete form. Hitherto it has been prevented from becoming a reality by the stupidity and narrow interests of the men who might have helped it forward. If the Great War should give birth to an international organization, based on the consent of all civilized peoples, which hereafter may assume positive leadership in the affairs of the human race as a whole, we shall have the most impressive instance of the over-ruling of a great disaster for the ultimate good and progress of the world. But this overruling, we must observe, will take place not, as an inevitable event, but by the provision of opportunities which may be muddled or refused.

The instinctive tendency to find striking examples of providential interference in the great catastrophes of history is not wholly wrong, and it is indeed difficult to resist the impression that even natural convulsions have sometimes had a providential character. The point of view, however, in this matter makes all the difference ; for the storm which dispersed the Armada, which was to English patriots a manifest dispensation of God, to the Romanists of Europe appeared as a part of the problem of evil. We are on safer ground when we consider the catastrophes of history. The great debacles, which bring down venerable systems and mark the end of epochs, are not mere accidents. They have many concurrent immediate causes, economic, social, political, and even geographical ; but it is a true insight, which has seen in them the terrible judgment of God. For the ultimate causes are moral and spiritual, and the great crashes of history are the outcome of failure to rise to new conditions and to maintain the ancient vigour by fresh adaptations. " The things which are shaken " are removed when they have reached an intolerable degree of rottenness.[1]

But here again we should beware of placing too narrowly moralistic an interpretation on the facts. Well-meaning persons have sometimes contributed as much to the tragedies of history as the wicked. The judgment is upon human stupidity hardly less than on human perversity. But we can regard the great downfalls in human history as vindications of the moral Will and Reason which is within human life ; and this truth is not affected by the truth that often the highest individual virtue may be on the side which is defeated. The cynical remark that God is on the side of the big battalions is singularly untrue when judged by the evidence of history. The big battalions have generally been on the side which has gone down, and the turning-points of the human story have rather illustrated the principle that God has chosen the weak things of the earth to confound the strong.[2] In general, then, we may conclude that, though we cannot hold every turn of history to have been preordained in some divine plan of campaign, yet the general trend of human affairs is a revelation of the Providence of God.

The crises of history have produced great individuals, who have profoundly affected its future development. The historical process is not like a stream, which consists of a homogeneous substance determined in its course by external conditions. No research into general causes and factors can eliminate the decisive action of great personalities, who cannot be explained completely by the circumstances of their time. Only an heroic adhesion to a preconceived thesis could seriously maintain that the world has not been radically modified by the personal

[1] Hebrews xii. 27.   [2] 1 Corinthians i. 27.

character of such men as Luther and Napoleon I.   Had they not been born, the whole subsequent condition of civilization would have been different.   The mystery which must always attend the coming of genius has given ground for the belief that great leaders are raised up by the Providence of God.   The men themselves have felt this; and no small part of their power has been derived from the conviction that they were in some way " called " to fulfil a definite and unique function.   The root of this conviction is the perception of their own powers, and of the adaptation of these powers to the needs of the crisis.   When this conviction is well founded, what might seem in others to be overweening self-confidence appears to be a necessary virtue.   The creative genius in human affairs knows himself to be a " man of destiny " or a " man of Providence ".

There is perhaps a difference between the two types of great historical personage which we have indicated by these phrases.   Not every man of destiny is a man of Providence.   The crisis and the individual meet; but the question is still to be decided, how the individual will deal with the crisis.   Nothing probably can prevent him from being a man of destiny.   His actions will be decisive.   But they may be inspired by no really constructive ideal; they may be actuated by some empty impulse for glory, or some irrational motive of a merely personal kind.   In that case, the main effects of the activity of the great man will be destructive.   Like Napoleon, he may sweep over an outworn social and political order as a cleansing wind; and though at his passing " kings creep out again to feel the sun ",[1] they are not the same kings, nor can the world ever return to what it was before.   Yet the constructive consequences of the career of such a man are indirect. They have no relation to what he willed.   The man of

[1] E. B. Browning, *Crowned and Buried*.

Providence, on the contrary, has seen some vision, fragmentary and imperfect though it be, of the divine Purpose. He is seeking no individual good or glory, but the coming of the Kingdom of God. The precise vision, as he has seen it, never comes to pass, and he builds always both better and worse than he knew ; but the truly creative persons of history are those who have served an ideal which was super-individual. The men of Providence are the men of destiny who have risen to the height of their opportunity. The Providence of God works through the understanding and will of those who are raised up for the hour of crisis.

Plainly the distinction which we make between great historical persons and other men, though useful and real from one point of view, is from a more general standpoint only relative. The mass of mankind is composed of in-dividual men, each one with his crises and his oppor-tunities. Each one of us, therefore, is in some manner a man of destiny, and may become a man of Providence. For us, as for the great men, the test is the acceptance or rejection of opportunity, whether we shall discern the values involved in our situation and steadily pursue them. There is, therefore, no final difference between general Providence and particular Providence. The " special providences " which relate to individuals are the warp and woof of the web which is the general Providence of the world.

For the Christian, the central fact of history is the life, death, and resurrection of Christ, which is, moreover, that which gives all other history its true meaning and enables us to see it in its proper proportion. In the Incarnation we have the supreme instance of God's providential guidance and a revelation of His providential Purpose. The advent of the Redeemer is " in the fullness of time "; and here, more than anywhere else, we might imagine

T

that the doctrine of an absolute Providence was suggested.
But this interpretation of the predestined coming of the
Redeemer is, in truth, not the one which most easily
harmonizes with all the conditions. The coming of Christ
as Saviour has meaning because He comes to a human
world which needs redemption, that is, to one which is in
rebellion and alienation, to one in which the Will of God
is not done. That Jesus is the supreme example of the
Man of Providence is not due solely to the fact that He
comes in the fullness of time, as the person prepared for
the opportunity ; it is equally because He responds to
the demands of the crisis with perfect insight into the
divine Will and complete devotion to its realization.
And having become the Man of Providence above all
others, he not only bears the sin of the world and obeys
the Will of God, but reveals the Father's purpose.

The Christian conception of Providence is an extension
and application of the idea of the Kingdom of God.
In this phrase Jesus summed up the values of human life
when in right relation with God. The providential purpose of God in the world is the establishment of the Kingdom ; and the world discloses itself to us as a providential
order when we see it as the sphere in which the Kingdom
can begin and can increase. Other purposes, which do not
fall within the conception of the Kingdom, may be
imagined as being worked out in creation, and we have in
this discussion refused to commit ourselves to the opinion
that there are no goods or values in creation except those
which have some relation to human life ; but so far as
human beings are concerned, we must hold that the
Providence of God seeks, through all the turns of history,
the coming in power of that Kingdom which began in the
spirit of Jesus. The " natural man ", that is, the man
in whom the Kingdom has not begun, even as a grain
of mustard seed, cannot discern the providential order.

Only by faith can we apprehend the work of Providence in the events of history and our lives, for apart from faith we have not any real acquaintance with the values which are the purpose of the world.

Of the nature of that Kingdom we must not here speak at length. The central conception is that of the rule of God in the minds and wills of men, and of a divine Sovereignty which is exercised, not by power, but through the response of human spirits to the Love which is at the heart of creation. The Kingdom grows through the free surrender of the human self to the Personal Good, who is both the beginning and the end of Creation, its first Cause, and its final Goal. But though the Kingdom comes in the minds and wills of human individuals, and lives in the response of human persons, one by one, to the grace of God, it is no merely individual affair, transacted between the soul and God. The grace is mediated through fellowship with other persons and comes to the individual always as a member of a society. It issues in a new social relationship of communion with those who are children of God, in which the latent spiritual powers of all are called forth and exercised.

The Church is, before all others, the Providential Society, just as Christ is, before all others, the Providential Person. It cannot be identified with the Kingdom ; but it is the appointed instrument of the Kingdom, and ideally its life is the preparation and foretaste of the perfected life— the suburb of the *urbs caelestis*. The history of the Church is the standing instance of the providential government of the world and the most impressive example of its nature. That history is chequered with disastrous failures and wonderful victories, with opportunities taken and missed. New truth has been denied and persecuted, the unity of the body has been shattered by self-seeking, ignorance, and worldly motives. But the Church itself has not been destroyed. It seems to be possessed of unlimited powers of renewal, and to be presented always with new opportunities. Even now the course of events makes it possible to repair some of the errors of the past, to advance towards the unity of the Spirit, and the bond of peace, and to achieve a more united witness to the God and Father of the Lord Jesus Christ, for which the world, distracted by partial philosophies and unsatisfying ideals, is deeply in need. The Church, in the Providence of God, will never be allowed to rest until it becomes the joy of the whole earth and the manifest Bride of Christ.

But even a renovated and restored Church will not be the completed Kingdom of God, which is the fellowship of all rational spirits with God through Christ and, in Him, with one another. The full meaning of that perfected life and consummation of the creation we, who are still *in via*, cannot apprehend in any but abstract and general ideas : " eye hath not seen nor ear heard, neither hath it entered into the heart of man ". For the purposes of divine Providence cannot find their full realization within the temporal process, and the end of history cannot be an historical event. However far we advance towards the ideal of brotherhood in human relations, and however deeply in the future we may be penetrated by a consciousness of the divine Presence in us and with us, the limitations of our present state preclude the unrestricted enjoyment of that twofold fellowship, apart from which we cannot be made perfect. The purposes of God run into the unseen. Here and now only an approximation to the ideal can be achieved ; but even here and now the presence of God, which we may know imperfectly and intermittently and the human fellowship in which we may join with others in loving service, are real, and they give to life a value and nobility which have the presage of immortality. They point beyond themselves to a fulfilment.

INDEX

I. INDEX OF SUBJECTS

II. INDEX OF NAMES

III. INDEX OF BIBLICAL REFERENCES